Rehabilitating and R[illegible]s
in the C[illegible]

Rehabilitating and Resettling Offenders in the Community

Anthony H. Goodman

A John Wiley & Sons, Ltd., Publication

This edition first published 2012

Wiley-Blackwell is an imprint of John Wiley & Sons, formed by the merger of Wiley's global Scientific, Technical and Medical business with Blackwell Publishing.

Registered Office
John Wiley & Sons Ltd, The Atrium, Southern Gate, Chichester, West Sussex, PO19 8SQ, UK

Editorial Offices
350 Main Street, Malden, MA 02148-5020, USA
9600 Garsington Road, Oxford, OX4 2DQ, UK
The Atrium, Southern Gate, Chichester, West Sussex, PO19 8SQ, UK

For details of our global editorial offices, for customer services, and for information about how to apply for permission to reuse the copyright material in this book please see our website at www.wiley.com/wiley-blackwell.

Library of Congress Cataloging-in-Publication Data

Goodman, Anthony (Anthony Harvey)
Rehabilitating and resettling offenders in the community / Anthony H. Goodman.
p. cm.
Includes bibliographical references and index.
ISBN 978-0-470-99099-5 (cloth) – ISBN 978-0-470-99170-1 (pbk.)
1. Criminals–Rehabilitation–Great Britain. 2. Ex-convicts–Services for–Great Britain.
3. Prisoners—Deinstitutionalization–Great Britain. I. Title.
HV9345.A5G66 2012
365′.66–dc23

2012009203

A catalogue record for this book is available from the British Library.

Set in 10.5/13pt Minion by SPi Publisher Services, Pondicherry, India
Printed in Singapore by Ho Printing Singapore Pte Ltd

1 2012

For my grandchildren – Mia, Oliver and Caleb

Contents

About the Author

Anthony Goodman is Professor of Criminal and Community Justice Studies at Middlesex University in the UK. He was a probation officer for 15 years prior to entering the university, during which time he was based in a number of settings, including field teams, training, Holloway women's prison and a specialist unit for the homeless and rootless in London.

Acknowledgements

Too many people over the years have had an influence on my thinking, and it would be impossible to name them all. My academic career began when, in the late 1970s, I attended the then Middlesex Polytechnic to undertake a Master's degree in the Sociology of Deviance, having been intrigued by the radical perspectives of Jock Young and John Lea, who were at the cutting edge of new thinking. They were instrumental in encouraging me to question what was going on in society, in particular those issues that affected disadvantaged and minority groups, as well as those who were deemed to be vulnerable.

As my academic career progressed I was delighted to be offered a 'chair' within the Department of Criminology and Sociology at the newly named Middlesex University, which has enabled me to continue with the tradition of critical thinking. Our Crime and Conflict Research Centre, led by Professor Vincenzo Ruggiero, is a thriving area within the university, encouraging staff to research and publish in such diverse areas as penal abolitionism, drugs, policing and community safety. My thinking continues to be shaped by colleagues, new and old, who themselves are challenging established thinking.

I would also like to thank the *British Journal of Community Justice* for permission to draw on an article that I wrote and was first published in the special centenary edition in 2007 entitled '289 Borough High Street, The After-Care and Resettlement Unit, in the Inner London Probation Service 1965–1990'.

This book could not have been written without the stimulation and openness of many probation professionals who, for confidentiality reasons, I will not name. You know who you are! I have also benefited over the years from conversations with many academic colleagues, some of whom I would like to thank personally, namely Professor David Denney, Dr Wendy Fitzgibbon, Dr Simon Green and colleagues at Hull University, Dr Peter Kennison, Dr Bronwen Martin, who introduced me to semiotic analysis, Professor Mike Nellis, Professor Paul Senior and colleagues at Sheffield Hallam University, and many others.

1

Introduction

How Should We Treat Offenders and What Can We Learn from the Past?

Rehabilitation work with offenders is a challenging task and responsibility, for this has moved from its roots in philanthropy to an offender management system, supervised by the probation service, often working in collaboration with the voluntary and private sector. This development has taken place over the past century and it is important not to lose this history and indeed to understand why it has evolved into the current structure. This means that the history, pressures and politics within the criminal justice system need to be conceptualized and analysed. In particular, change has not been steady but rather the last twenty years in particular have been a 'rollercoaster ride' as politicians have become interested in micro-managing this area to an extent not generally understood by the general public.

In organizational terms the probation service has moved from locally managed services to a national service (in 2001). Even as this was being implemented, there was a further major change proposed in a review of community justice undertaken by Patrick Carter in 2003 (Carter, 2003). His report, which recommended end-to-end management of offenders, was to have a profound effect on the probation service when the government agreed to implement his proposals without further debate. He introduced the notion of 'contestability' with the intention of forcing probation to compete for the work that it undertook. However, there was never an evidence base for this (Nellis and Goodman, 2009). Probation became in effect a junior partner (in terms of size and influence) with the prison service in a single managed organization, the National Offender Management Service (NOMS; see Home Office, 2005a). The move to making probation part of a market-driven model was formalized in the Offender Management Act 2007 (it received Royal Assent on 26 July 2007). This Act transferred to the Secretary of State the statutory duty to provide probation services, which can be commissioned by providers in the public, private and voluntary sectors.

Rehabilitating and Resettling Offenders in the Community, First Edition. Anthony H. Goodman.

The actual commissioning process is somewhat opaque as it will not only fall to the Secretary of State to undertake this. Probation Services were to become (public sector) Trusts who might compete for the work as well as commissioning work themselves. The implications of this will be considered in this book.

Probation has been at more crossroads in its long history than many other areas within the criminal justice system. This book is being written at a time of some uncertainty about its future. A professional organization needs a trained workforce and the present training arrangements represent more uncertainty, which is unfair on a service with a proud history of resettling offenders. In particular the growth of semi (or lesser) trained probation service officers at the expense of fully trained probation officers (POs) could lead to the public being put at more risk from offenders under supervision. It is also unfair on the offenders. As Senior comments about the new (2010) Probation Qualifications Framework: 'a Rolls Royce award is being superseded by a more building block approach…it remains to be seen whether routes to full probation officer status remain possible in this tightening fiscal climate' (Senior, 2010, p. 1). If probation officers become the minority element in comparison to the number of probation service officers then the training will have a minimum impact on practice and on how 'the probation service as an organization understands its job and its relationship with offenders and with wider society' (Dominey and Hill, 2010, p. 11).

A training manager was very concerned when speaking to me, at the end of 2010, that the probation service, being much smaller than the prison service component of the NOMS, was in danger of being squeezed when resources were 'needed' to produce yet more prison places. NOMS joins the prison and probation services together at the top level, but is it too large an organization to deal effectively with both arms? This will be discussed further in Chapter 9.

Responsibility for resettling offenders has been an activity that has oscillated between the voluntary and statutory sectors. Resettlement has had a number of contradictory and complementary philosophical underpinnings and contexts. These range from the religious and the saving of souls, to punishment, including banishment overseas. As well as the roles of religion and philanthropic endeavours needs to be added the development of the treatment ideal and the concept of the scientific management of offenders. The early police court missionaries, while having religious beliefs, were also eugenicists and were comfortable with the notion of locking up morally defective juveniles to prevent them from breeding the next generation like themselves (Vanstone, 2004).

Probation has a fascinating history, starting with a Boston cobbler, John Augustus, operating in Massachusetts between 1841 until his death in 1859, who stood bail and then supervised offenders until they received their sentence at court. This notion of working with offenders prior to them receiving a sentence was central to the early history of work with offenders. Augustus wrote reports for courts, but was *not* an official of the court. The Howard Association brought his work to the attention of the Home Secretary (in Gladstone's new government) towards the end of the nineteenth century when there was a mood in government for a more enlightened approach to dealing with young offenders (Bochel, 1976).

Thus the notion of reclaiming offenders was located in the tradition of voluntary service, for the good of the public.

The rationale for supervision has changed greatly over time as the probation service has embarked on a quest for professionalism and an attempt to first find a role, and then maintain one, in its work with offenders. From its early work of reclaiming drunks and taking pledges to remain free of alcohol came the notion of befriending, and offering counselling support to offenders. When there was pessimism that this did not change offending behaviour, a further change occurred which represented a major break with past tradition, when the notion of the offender as a person with problems moved to one of a free-thinking individual, who made rational choices. Therefore the choice to offend represents a faulty conditioning of the person's thought processes. To change this, no longer was it appropriate to offer counselling; rather, the person needs to be taught cognitive skills and pro-social modelling. The latter aimed to enhance positive views of looking 'legitimately' at the world. The jargon has changed from 'counselling' to 'promoting behavioural change'. The question to be answered is whether by focusing on the choices made by the offender, the background experiences, deprivations and inequalities are at least downplayed, but more likely ignored, when explanations for offending are now sought. There are major implications for ethnic minorities and gender difference in terms of economic disadvantage and lack of opportunity.

The individual redemption of the offender is less important than the protection of the public, in whose name all actions are taken. National Standards for supervising offenders lays down regularity of contact and changes the ethos of the agency to one of offering 'punishment'. For the sake of 'programme integrity' offenders are put through identical programmes throughout England and Wales. These programmes are to be taught to probation officers: will this make them operatives or reflective professionals? Indeed, will probation officers or unqualified officers deliver these programmes, and is this a spurious distinction, if the tasks are so preset that discretion is a vacuous term? I asked probation staff how they experienced the changes in their practice: was it still appropriate to see the task of probation officers as to 'advise, assist and befriend' offenders, or has the notion of befriending been overtaken by the requirement to maintain a surveillance role, filling in forms to feed into computers to check whether the offender has become more or less dangerous? If this is the case, then actuarial computation has taken precedence over the clinical judgement of front-line staff, as far as decisions of risk are concerned, and the emphasis on working with offenders has shifted to considerations of risk to the public, away from individualized concerns for and about the offender, as if these concepts are mutually exclusive (Feeley and Simon 1992, 1994).

Personal Experience

My interest in working with offenders is difficult to explain, and was not from any sense of philanthropy. I used to go on a soup run with the homeless and rootless before I had thought about a career, and it was distinctly preferable to the maths degree I was studying. It was nearly always middle-aged single men who appreciated a hot drink and food, and they enjoyed the opportunity to have a talk with a person who did not judge them. After graduating, a conversation with a probation officer was enough to get me 'hooked' on the idea of working with offenders, and after a two-year training course I started as a probation officer in 1975 in the London borough of Hackney, the area that I was born and brought up in. The training for the job was completely focused on psycho-dynamic counselling, human growth and development, and discussion of 'change agents' and systems. The sociology of deviance or criminology was not on the agenda.

Probation officers were all white, working with a predominantly young black client group, disaffected and with suspicious relationships with the police. Relations between the black community and the police were poor and the overuse of the 'sus' law (the police at this time used Section 4 of the Vagrancy Act 1824, which referred to 'being a suspected person loitering with intent to commit a felonious offence', or 'sus' for short) ensured that it was getting worse, culminating in the riots of 1981 in areas of several cities including London (Brixton, Hackney), Liverpool (Toxteth) and Birmingham (Handsworth). Individual probation officers adopted a community work approach but this was frowned upon by management (discussed in Chapter 6).

The staff group was very committed to practicing in a way that did not discriminate, which meant knowing and working with community agencies and resources. However, practice was individualistic and idiosyncratic and often idealistic. I left the service in 1990 to train probation officers in a university social work department, having had a varied experience of field posts, prison probation (HMP Holloway), the After-Care (resettlement) Unit for the homeless and rootless, and various training responsibilities.

When I left the probation service, the emphasis was still on casework skills, although the Home Office had begun to set priorities for the service and probation management had acknowledged these, even if most probation officers had not changed their traditional ways of working. My training for the job had been a two-year postgraduate course and was at the transition point from the time when it had been an 'in-house' venture, run by the Home Office. Further training within the probation service included 'trust games' and person-centred therapy, rather than considerations of the seriousness of the offence and the degree of dangerousness of the offender. Offenders could be 'treated' for their personal difficulties and the frequency of probationers reporting to their probation officers was variable, although parolees were supervised conscientiously. Parole had started in 1967 and was the first experience of the power of the Legal Executive as opposed to judicial power (Carlisle Committee, 1988). Probation officers from the 1960s had seen themselves as caseworkers, rather than evangelical saviours or missionaries (McWilliams, 1983, 1985, 1986, 1987) and this continued into the 1980s and beyond (Fielding, 1984).

Over the years I have conducted a number of interviews with probation staff and other relevant professionals, and I have drawn on this archive for the book. I carried out a piece of research for the Inner London Probation Service (ILPS) in 1986 that investigated the consistency of contact by different probation staff with prisoners. I discovered great variation in practice and very little control by management. I revisited some of the informants in 1994, which revealed the need to gain a wider picture of the profound changes occurring within the probation service. By this stage staff had virtually stopped visiting prisoners, the concept of through-care support had stalled, and was linked to statutory responsibility when parole reports were needed.

This book will draw on the case study of the After-Care Unit (ACU) to demonstrate that probation work with the homeless was sacrificed at the end of the 1980s, as the priority was changed to working with offenders in the community, rather than the resettlement of ex-prisoners. Offenders sentenced to one year or less in prison might be seen either by volunteers or (more likely) not at all. They were no longer allocated to probation officers, as contact with them would be voluntary on discharge, as they would not be subject to a period of statutory supervision on licence on discharge from prison. It was claimed that as probation moved to working only with statutory offenders this would mean they had committed more serious crimes. Ironically, the ACU did have a high-risk 'heavy end' caseload as, typically, they were offenders wanting a fresh start in the London area. The work of the ACU could lay claim to being the precursor to 'joined-up thinking' in relation to working with offenders as it included close working relationships with psychiatrists from the Institute of Psychiatry and a number of institutions, including hostels, throughout London. Perhaps the homeless and rootless offender, like aggressive car window cleaners at traffic lights, much cited by politicians, are perceived as a visible threat to the public as they represent the 'underachieving' element who have yet to find a stake in society.

Thus if a focus specifically on work with prisoners and ex-prisoners could not give a full picture of the changing nature of probation practice, it became necessary to investigate, with probation staff, the full range of their work, and this became my principal research interest. Personnel interviewed were open and honest about their practice and how the probation task and role was changing. These changes were on a number of different levels: frequency of contact, the expectation that failed appointments would not be ignored but would lead to action being taken, including the offender being returned to court for resentencing for the original offence. Offenders were likely to be placed on group work programmes to deal with their perceived 'faulty thinking', rather than being seen individually for practical and emotional support.

The book examines, from both a practice and theoretical context, the changing nature of probation practice with offenders, from its evangelical roots to 'treatment' and most recently actuarial justice and risk management. It draws on 27 interviews with relevant professionals conducted between 1996 and 1999. In addition, probation archival material was drawn on, as well as interviews with the founder of the London Probation Service (1935), a Borstal After-Care Association worker from the 1950s, a probation manager from the 1960s and a voluntary hostel manager running houses for ex-offenders, which were managed and organized by staff from a specialist probation office working with homeless and rootless offenders.

In 1987 I was given a sabbatical from the probation service I was working for to carry out a study of probation practice with prisoners and ex-prisoners. I interviewed 19 probation and senior probation officers and I have drawn on the conclusions from this study. Five interviews were undertaken in July 1994 with probation staff working with prisoners and ex-prisoners. These interviewees had been part of the group interviewed in 1987.

The interviews with retired staff were useful in placing probation practice in an historical context, as did the case study of the After-Care and Resettlement Unit. This was an exemplar of practice with the homeless and in describing how innovation in service delivery stemmed from meeting needs unmet by the other agencies, voluntary and statutory, in the state system, not necessarily in criminal justice. The rise and demise of the unit served as an example of how the changing tensions and priorities within the probation service impacted on practice and priorities. This was particularly apposite in December 1999 as the Labour government rediscovered that ex-prisoners and offenders were over-represented among the homeless, a fact well known to officers who had worked in the ACU decades earlier.

The use of the interviews from 1987 showed the then nature of probation practice with prisoners and ex-prisoners and the ad hoc nature of what might be offered to them. The interviews undertaken in 1994 demonstrated the changing nature of the service, the drive to use partnership organizations to deliver work with offenders, and a resistance among some probation officers to take on board National Standards. This was after the first version of National Standards 1992 (Home Office, 1992b), which still acknowledged the social work skills of practitioners.

I spent time in probation offices, especially Newham in London, observing interviews and socializing with staff. As a former probation officer I was accepted and trusted by them and they took me into their confidence. I was conscious of the dangers of 'going native'. I have sympathy for the difficulty of working in an environment where the process of working with offenders has been seen as more important than the outcome of the intervention. The views of these staff did not differ significantly from those of other probation staff I interviewed. I would not describe my role as that of 'poacher turned gamekeeper'; however, my previous profession meant that I was familiar with their jargon, culture and work tasks.

Most recently, in the aftermath of some high-profile supervision failures, I set up a Master's programme in public protection, in close collaboration with a large probation area. I have continued to interview staff both formally and informally, with agreement for their comments to be used in this book. Working with staff who have a strong commitment to work with high-risk offenders has been a stimulating and exciting experience that has reinforced my belief that the time has come for probation to be left to develop and strengthen its knowledge and skills in order to rehabilitate offenders and protect the public. The frenetic pace of change needs to be slowed, and a moratorium on 'common sense' innovation stalled. The views of these staff and others are drawn upon in Chapter 6 when current practice and ideas are discussed.

From Professional to Technical Skills

The concept of personal discretion is intimately bound up with the question of whether the probation task is still a *professional* activity. As probation evolved from its philanthropic origins, it changed to an activity whereby individual staff worked with offenders using their skill and judgement. We shall see that practice is changing to probation staff carrying out set programmes with offenders, drawing on a well defined script. Schön usefully outlined the difference between activity of a mechanical nature and one where personal decision-making was called for, involving professional judgement:

> 'When a practitioner reflects in and on his practice, the possible objects of his reflection are as varied as the kinds of phenomena before him and the systems of knowing-in-practice which he brings to them. He may reflect on the tacit norms and appreciations which underlie a judgement, or on the strategies and theories implicit in a pattern of behaviour. He may reflect on the feeling for a situation which has led him to adopt a particular course of action, on the way in which he has framed the problem he is trying to solve, or on the role he has constructed for himself within a larger institutional context. Reflection-in-action, in these several modes, is central to the art through which practitioners sometimes cope with the troublesome "divergent" situations of practice.' (Schön, 1991, p. 62)

The process of change from unadulterated individual discretion began in 1984 when the Home Office produced its Statement of National Objectives and Priorities (SNOP). The process, which is still continuing, consists of a tightening of authority on probation priorities backed up by the threat of financial sanction. Local areas, after SNOP, were required to produce their local statements of priorities, and the failure to follow the Home Office lead was revealed by a Cambridge Institute study (Lloyd, 1986). In 1989 the future direction of the criminal justice system was flagged in two government papers: the White Paper *Crime, Justice and Protecting the Public* (Cm 965) (Home Office, 1990a) and the Green Paper *Supervision and Punishment in the Community* (Cm 966) (Home Office, 1990b). The proposals were enacted in the 1991 Criminal Justice Act which made community orders sentences of the court in their own right, and promoted a new managerialist approach to practice, which had to recognize that the Court was the 'client' of the probation service, not the offender. Furthermore, the probation role had to change from being the exclusive provider of services to more of a case management role, with closer cooperation with the other agencies in the criminal justice system and community. The Green Paper made it clear that probation training, located within social work, did not provide sufficient detail on probation matters (paras 9.16–9.24, Home Office, 1990b, 33–35).

Probation officers were given National Standards (NS) to work in community service in 1989 which outlined minimum expectations of compliance. In 1992 National Standards for all probation practice was published, which were also to be used for young offenders. The Standards could be described as good practice initiatives: they drew on, and acknowledged, the skills of the professionals as *social work* practitioners. In 1995 a second edition of the Standards was published, which had a very different emphasis. Supervision was now about punishment and the role of the probation officer was more akin to that of a 'technician' who had to adhere to the imperative to see the offender more often. NS 1992 mentioned the offering of 12 *appointments* in the first three months, NS 1995 changed this to *interviews*. In the second Standards the probation officer, while retaining the possibility not to take an offender back to court after two missed appointments, had to discuss this with their senior after the first missed appointment, and could not take this decision themselves. This coincided with a new Home Secretary, Michael Howard, who made it clear that, in his opinion, prison worked and probation didn't. Probation was to receive a major shock in terms of how its ethos was to change from professional social work to the administration of punishment in the name of the public. This theme will be considered at length in Chapter 4.

In 1995, after a public debate and what was described as a review (very few individuals or organizations agreed with the outcome), the link with social work training was severed. There was an unprecedented alliance of ACOP (Association of Chief Officers of Probation), NAPO (National Association of Probation Officers), Standing Conference of Probation Tutors (SCOPT), Central Probation Council (employers), Association of Black Probation Officers (ABPO), Joint University Council Social Work Education Committee (JUC/SWEC), Committee of Vice-Chancellors and Principals (CVCP) who met regularly to try to thwart plans to bring in 'on the job' training or even (as was rumoured at one stage), ex-armed services personnel as direct recruits. I was a regular attendee of the meetings in my role as a committee member of SCOPT and, as will be detailed in the research, it was successful in delaying any decisions on the future of training until after the general election of 1997 (Wood, 1999).

Fast-Track Punishment

In terms of legislation there were further Criminal Justice Acts in 1993 and 1994 which had major implications for probation practice. Law and order was high on the political agenda in the run-up to the general election and in their pre-election material 'New Labour' made it clear that they would be adopting a hard-line attitude to offenders, especially young offenders. The mantra on billboards said, 'tough on crime, tough on the causes of crime' and also 'fast-track punishment for young offenders'. What this was going to mean in practice was not spelled out, but it was clear that the Conservatives had had their traditional hard line on law and order matched by New Labour (Brownlee, 1998; Dunbar and Langdon, 1998; James and Raine, 1998; Nash, 1999). The final act of the Conservative government was to publish a Green Paper which advocated a raft of tough policies. After the election the incoming Labour government implemented a number of these policies in their first Criminal

Justice Act in 1997. This was followed up with the Crime and Disorder Act 1998 and the Youth Justice and Criminal Evidence Act 1999 which targeted first-time offenders. The Queen's Speech in November 1999 contained a number of Home Office Bills.

In terms of the probation service, the Home Secretary, Jack Straw, and the Minister of State for Prisons and Probation, Paul Boateng, have been aggressively disparaging about the probation service's inability to enforce National Standards: in particular, the rate of returning offenders to court was seen as far too infrequent. This was echoed by the Home Affairs Committee's Third Report (Home Affairs Committee, 1998), which was vociferous in its condemnation of the failure of probation officers to take offenders who did not keep their appointments back to court (this is known as breaching the offender). Simultaneous to this drive to toughen probation practice was a commitment to 'what works' and the 'effective practice' initiative. This has one weapon in the armoury of stopping offenders from reoffending, namely the teaching of cognitive skills. National pathfinder schemes are being set up in England and Wales with a view to evaluating and selecting the ones seen as most effective. These schemes will then be replicated and will become the *only* way that offenders will be worked with. In mid-November 1999 Paul Boateng gave a speech to Chief Probation Officers and Chairs of Probation Committees. He took the opportunity to state where the probation service was going under the heading of '*modernization as a coherent whole*' (Boateng, 1999, italics in original).

What Works?

The theme of modernization, according to Boateng, comprised three elements. First, 'what works': to ensure that probation practice 'on the basis of sound evidence' really did reduce offending. Second, probation was to be judged on compliance to (revised) National Standards. Third, the infrastructure had to be right, meaning that 'structures and powers' were in place for these 'improvements'. Given that the audience was made up of probation personnel, it was a little surprising that when Boateng spelled out his vision of 'what works' he started by outlining joint work with the prison service on 'core curriculum' changing offending behaviour programmes. Services were told that they would have to give up 'long-cherished programmes' which could not be shown to work and, by implication, this ruled out earlier ways of working. Underpinning all of this was offender assessment using a new assessment tool, OASys, an acronym for 'Offender Assessment SYStem', jointly with the prison service, from August 2000. Thus there was a continuing notion of change into the new millennium.

Boateng flagged up the need to contain the 'relatively small number' of people presenting a risk to the public due to severe personality disorder. His first priority was protection of the public. The next priority was 'punishment and the enforcement of sentences'. This included the notion of the 'seamless sentence'. Drug Treatment and Testing Orders had been brought in under the 1998 Crime and Disorder Act, and £20 million had been allocated to 'arrest referral' schemes (that is, intervention at the pre-establishing of guilt stage). Electronic monitoring was seen as a useful tool, not just to ensure home detention as a punishment but 'as an effective means of easing the transition from custody back into the community'. The explanation Boateng gave was that this 'provide[d] an element of stability, which can help to disrupt offending patterns'. He was excited at this extension to supervision, and commented that the new technology could be used in the future in new ways – such as for reverse tagging and to keep people out of certain areas: 'Our work is at an early stage but this is an exciting and *growing* area' (my emphasis).

The probation service could not fail to see where the Labour government saw probation: 'Let us be clear: *the probation service is a law enforcement agency*' (italics in original). This was linked to strong criticism of the lack of order enforcement, and responsibility for this was placed firmly with Chief Officers and Probation Committees. From 1 April 2000 the revised National Standards would cut the 'tolerance' of unacceptable failures of probationers to meet with their probation officers from two to one. Finally he mentioned two further 'issues' which will be dealt with at length in this book. First, 'ethnic minority representation'. Boateng mentioned that this minority representation was present at basic probation officer grade level but not beyond this. He did not mention ethnic minority representation among offenders. The issue of anti-discriminatory practice, which was a major consideration under the old training and in professional practice, was not commented upon. Second, he raised the issue of homelessness. This is very interesting as the major theme in probation practice, clearly identified above, is protection of the public. However, he commented that the Social Exclusion Unit report (2002) on rough sleepers noted that many had been through the prison system as well as other institutions. Prisons and probation were to 'have a new focus on homelessness'. How the probation service continued to be altered and 'modernized' under New Labour is described and analysed in Chapter 4, and can be described as a process of continuous change. It has served to demoralize and destabilize many of the staff. Despite this, the probation service remains highly committed to its professional task but uncertain whether it has a future in its current structure and training.

The Future of Professional Practice

The evidence base of what works is complex and does not provide an easy blueprint on how to engage with offenders (Goodman, 2008). Craissati and Sindall (2009) examined the cases of 94 serious further offences (SFOs) committed by offenders who had been under supervision by the London Probation Trust in a 14-month period between 2004–2006, collecting data on background and 'criminogenic' variables. Of interest is the observation, 'in terms of a description of the SFO offenders, the most striking impression is the absence of any remarkable features to their presentation as captured by the variables researched' (Craissati and Sindall, 2009, p. 21). The conclusion was that the social circumstances that the offender finds himself in might trigger a serious further offence, so preventing this means dealing with his everyday problems rather than concentrating on issues such as his anger management skills.

Merely being competent to record the characteristics of the individual offender, to produce an accurate offender risk analysis, would not lead to an accurate prophecy of further harm. In this respect therefore I would contend that professional skills and judgement (and confidence) are needed. Indeed, the conclusion that it is the *situational context* that might trigger a criminal event is underestimated in the way that the work of probation staff is managed: 'the emphasis on structured assessments and risk prediction – although important – exacerbates this difficulty' (p. 26). This is at the core of professional practice. The contact between offender and probation officer or offender manager or whatever new descriptor is dreamed up is essential to the job. Irrespective of whether this person operates in the public, voluntary or for profit sector, they needs to be competent and effective. Whether they work with the offender or put them on to a programme, this must not be completed according to a predetermined script based on a risk scale. As Pawson and Tilley (1997) comment: 'Our baseline argument throughout has not been that programmes are things that may (or may not) work; rather they contain certain ideas which work for certain subjects in certain situations' (p. 215).

It is the skill of the practitioner in working with the offender to ensure that the potential for growth and pro-social activity is maximized, but enforcing as necessary the requirements of the court order or post-release licence. There has to be some trust and shared expectations between the supervisor and the supervisee or, as my former colleague Frank Treble commented, a shared higher aim.

The Conservative and Liberal Democrat coalition government came into power in May 2010 and in December 2010 they published a Green Paper, *Breaking the Cycle: Effective Punishment, Rehabilitation and Sentencing of Offenders* (Ministry of Justice, 2010a). This complained about the level of centralization within the criminal justice system, in particular the top-down approach in both prison and probation services, which focused on process rather than on results. This is considered in more detail in Chapter 8. It highlighted as its major innovation the notion of payments by results. This is considered further in Chapter 9. The new government seems to be seduced by the promise of new technology, with an exponential growth in the use of electronic tagging up from 3500 electronic tagging orders in 1999 to over 70 000 in 2010, with new contracts up for grabs in October 2011 to the value of over £1 billion. This is despite ministers admitting that the impact of tagging on reoffending is neutral (Travis, 2011).

Structure and Contents

In the following chapters I will be expanding on the themes that have been raised in this introduction. Chapter 2 begins with the early history of punishment and reveals the prerogative of mercy as a mechanism for mitigating the rule of law and establishing the absolute power of the monarch. This was also a time of fear of the vagrant and of popular uprising. In this chapter, the work of Rusche and Kirchheimer (1968) will be examined, as will that of authors such as Melossi and Pavarini (1981), Beattie (1986) and Weber (1948). Links will be made between punishments and 'economic and fiscal' forces. The homeless and rootless were subject to cruel treatment, but they were not seen as requiring imprisonment; rather, they were more likely to receive a whipping and to be sent back to their own parish. As society became more advanced, so the nature of punishment changed to exert the discipline needed to produce a more 'docile' workforce. Despite this, descriptive accounts of prisons, even in the early twentieth century, demonstrated brutality and cruelty. Women were treated differently to men and, during the time of transportation to British colonies, were likely to be sent out to the colonies to boost the future population.

Chapter 3 initially focuses on the changing nature of law as society became more complex. This was characterized by the shift from a *Gemeinschaft* to a *Gesellschaft* society. In the former, individuals are motivated to work for the good of the community at least as much as for themselves. In the latter, individuals focus much more on their own self-interest, although this means that they cooperate with others, as it is in their interest to do so. Implications for work with offenders are drawn and key writers (including Hay (1975), Bonger (1916) and Foucault (1977)) who examined the move away from a generally punitive response to offending to one that was more individualized and took into account personal circumstances. The early history of the probation service, which was concerned with rescuing the fallen by using police court missionaries, will be discussed. I then describe how from this religious philanthropic beginning grew a professionally trained service which drew on 'casework skills'. There then followed a crisis in confidence when the notion that 'nothing works' began to take hold of the service. The structure of the service began to change with a growth in managerialism and from 1984 the Home Office began to assert increasing control after publishing its *Statement of National Objectives and Priorities* (Home Office, 1984). Before this time, individual probation officers held almost complete autonomy over what they did with offenders and this was no longer acceptable to the Home Office or probation management.

Chapter 4 continues the theme of the changing nature of probation practice and ethos, when the groundwork was laid for a 'Taylorist approach'. We shall see that the interventions in 1989 of the National Audit Office (NAO) and Audit Commission introduced the notion of 'efficiency, economy and effectiveness' to the service. In 1991 the Criminal Justice Act introduced the notion of 'just deserts' and the intention was allegedly to move the probation service to centre stage as a community penalty enforcement agency. Probation orders became a sentence of the court for the first time, and no longer a recognizance to be entered into. A further Audit Commission report that year found that the probation service was developing a more managerial approach. In 1992 the first edition of 'National Standards (NS) for the Supervision of Offenders in England and Wales' was published, although NS for community service were published in 1989. The NS recognized the (social work) skills of probation officers and could be seen as a tightening up of the supervision of offenders. In 1993 a further Criminal Justice Act removed much of the progressive elements of the 1991 Act, and further punitive and regressive Acts were to follow in 1994, 1997 and 1998. In 1995 the Conservative Home Secretary removed social work training as a requirement for probation officers. A second version of NS in the same year was firmly rooted in the notion of punishment. The notion of probation officer discretion and professionalism was also absent. Finally, the changing nature of probation practice is considered, with a move to the management of risk and the strict enforcement of supervision. In this respect the move from a Conservative to a Labour administration was seamless.

Chapter 5 focuses on the textual and visual analysis of National Standards for supervising offenders. Versions started in 1992 and were revised in 1995, 2000, 2002, 2005 and 2007. These are important as they demonstrate how the language and presentation of these formal documents affect both the status and power of professional staff and how the ethos of their intervention changed from a skilled activity to one of administering punishment. Having established this, the third version of National Standards (Home Office, 2000) further tightened the reporting conditions of offenders. It is somewhat ironic that, having spent so many years making national standards so inflexible, the 2007 version includes a diminution of contact for offenders convicted of less serious crimes, maintaining the procedural ethos rather than a professional risk-focused one. Finally, the power balance between probation officers and offenders is analysed in terms of how probation officers can use language in reports to give a positive or negative image of the offender. Ironically, with the squeeze on resources the last version, which is not readily understandable to the lay person, represents a lessening of contact between offender and supervisor, compared to earlier versions as pragmatism replaced oversight.

Chapter 6 outlines and analyses interviews with a number of front-line staff and other informants over a period of time. The theoretical questions to be answered concern issues of bureaucracy, control, therapeutic work and the value base of probation; changes in probation practice and its skills base; changes in the knowledge base of the service, whether the offender profile was changing, effective practice initiatives, and finally why the changes were taking place. Issues of enforcement received much comment from front-line and other staff, as did the increase in bureaucratic tasks. The time taken to produce electronic assessments was a frequent source of concern, as this took probation officers away from direct contact with offenders.

Chapter 7 is a case study of a specialist probation unit that operated between 1965 and 1990, offering resettlement to homeless and rootless offenders in the inner London area. Chapter 7 describes how the unit was born out of the old Discharged Prisoners' Aid Societies and how it adapted imaginatively to provide the services needed by the offenders. It also describes how the unit changed from the mid-1970s to try to fit with the changing nature of the wider (probation) service. A management report completed by headquarters staff in the ILPS in 1988 recommended that homeless offenders who chose, on their own volition, to move to London would have to make contact with the nearest probation office and seek a service from them. The service would no longer provide a service for them in advance of their move. The unit closed two years later, as probation officers who left were not replaced and new offenders were no longer accepted by the unit.

Chapter 8 looks at the development of through-care and after-care of offenders by the prison and probation services, and how the importance of prison resettlement has fluctuated over time. This area of practice has declined in recent times as it has been deemed to be less important. Yet many reports, such as the Social Exclusion Unit (2002), *Reducing Reoffending by Ex-Prisoners* and the National Audit Office (2010) report, *Managing Offenders on Short Custodial Sentences*, show that this group is very vulnerable and highly likely to reoffend. It seems bizarre that they do not get as much assistance from the probation service as they did in the past.

Chapter 9 critically discusses contemporary issues around rehabilitation as probation became centralized and management moved from local control to a national organization and then to NOMS. The story is still unfolding with the creation of Probation Trusts, and the implications this has for the resettlement of offenders will be examined. It will conclude by drawing together the themes from the earlier chapters and will reflect on the future direction of offender resettlement. Will the rhetoric of punishment, protecting the public and moving the victim to centre stage turn the probation service into an enforcement agency that is irrelevant to offenders, especially those wanting to change and needing assistance and guidance in order to be rehabilitated? The wheel has turned full circle, with much work with offenders returning to organizations located outside the state.

If there is a key lesson to be learned, it is that over time there have been numerous examples of the reinvention of the (criminological) wheel. This book, which is not polemical in tone, will highlight examples of this, including the positive conclusion that the pendulum is swinging back from over-centralized control to a professional service that can utilize the skills of its workers to both rehabilitate offenders and protect the public.

The probation service is tiny in size compared to the other agencies in criminal justice, and receives a much smaller amount of the budget. However, its responsibility to protect the public should give it a central role.

2

The Early History of Punishing Offenders

Punishments and Help Offered to Those Incarcerated

The history of crime and punishment highlights the changing purpose(s) of imprisonment and how the state dealt with the spectrum of crime from serious to petty offenders. Punishment was used to give prostitutes and vagrants the experience of using their labour in the wider world so they were not a burden on the state (Godfrey, Lawrence and Williams, 2008).

It demonstrates that much of contemporary concern is not new, that community service was being practiced hundreds of years ago, and that the violent and cruel nature of earlier society can obscure the fact that philanthropic concern existed before John Howard's generation. Garland in *Punishment and Modern Society* (1990) warns against adopting any 'reductionist' arguments to explain the changing nature of punishment, meaning that single arguments that focus on areas such as economics (e.g. Scull, 1977), morals or control will not be sufficient. Instead in arguing against a functional approach, he prefers the more complex explanation of 'multiple causality, multiple effects, and multiple meaning' (Garland, 1990, p. 280).

The role of religion, including the complex relationship between the church and the judiciary, can be linked to the nature of punishment as it changed from an ethos of inflicting pain to one of instilling discipline in the offender. We shall see that even in the twentieth century religion did not prevent the possibility of corporal punishment (Paterson, 1951) and that the earlier device of 'benefit of clergy' could be used to mitigate the worst excesses of a savage criminal justice system and the maintenance of a moral order.

Civil unrest and disobedience was a regular problem from before Tudor times and this is linked in this chapter to how the most impoverished citizens, namely beggars, were treated. Responsibility from the time of the Middle Ages for the relief of the destitute was undertaken by the church and there is evidence that citizens were

Rehabilitating and Resettling Offenders in the Community, First Edition. Anthony H. Goodman.

prepared to donate money and food to avoid prisoners starving. Philanthropic support for the disadvantaged is not therefore a recent phenomenon and will be shown in Chapter 4 to have been instrumental in the formation and growth of the probation service.

The use of transportation as an alternative to capital punishment had the advantage of mixing mercy with the economic advantage of populating the colonies (with both men and women). For the homeless and rootless beggar there was still vicious corporal punishment and imprisonment. As transportation came to an end, so hard physical labour was substituted in a strictly regulated and individualized regime. The notion of transportation is still present in other advanced Western societies. Ash commented that the United States has deported 'hundreds of thousands of American residents to "homelands" that many have not seen since early childhood' (Ash, 2000, p. 5). Recent legislation removed judicial discretion to mitigate and offenders have been transported to countries such as Haiti where they are incarcerated, probably illegally, in appalling conditions as they are seen as being at high risk of reoffending.

The fear of the working class 'underclass' has been present from feudal times and, as seen above, is still present in some countries. This chapter will focus on what happened to those in England who were perceived as both 'workshy' and 'unrespectable'; namely the young were to be socialized during childhood, whereas adults were to be punished. It is remarkable that in the punitive atmosphere which prevailed that the Gladstone Report of 1895 on prisons could be so progressive in its argument for rehabilitation. It would coincide with the view of Max Weber that 'rational conditioning and training of work performances' became more important than the precise metering of punishment to offenders, which came to be seen as inefficient and not effective or economic (Weber, 1948). There was also a fascinating development throughout this period of policing, which progressed from an 'old' amateur or semi-professional system in around the mid-eighteenth to nineteenth century to a professional service after the formation of the Metropolitan Police in 1829, the 'new' police (Godfrey and Lawrence, 2005).

The Role of Religion and Offenders

Émile Durkheim was one of the founders of sociology as a discipline. He considered the place of punishment in both primitive and modern societies, concluding that it was not just a progression from retribution to protection of self-interests, but that there needed to be a balance between the harm caused by misdeeds and the pain inflicted on the transgressor (see Ruggiero, 2010, p. 67). Durkheim made links between primitive societies and religion, whereby the penal process took on a religious meaning (for a full discussion on this see Ruggiero, 2010, pp. 69–71). The two most important cultural influences on penal policy, according to many historians, are religion and humanitarianism. According to Potter (1993) there was a strong relationship between the church and the judiciary. He pointed out that the first recorded execution was in AD 695, when it was ordered as an 'exemplary punishment' for theft to 'discourage others' (1993, p. 2). This symbiotic relationship grew because 'homicide ... struck directly not only at the human but at the divine order' (p. 3). Mercy could be used on occasion to temper justice, and the myth of 'benefit of clergy' is described later in this chapter. The influence of religion in the rehabilitation of offenders was strong and consistent. Even in the twentieth century, key reforming officials, such as Sir Alexander Paterson, Commissioner of Prisons in the 1930s, and founder of the Borstal system, mixed compassion with religion, but also underpinned rehabilitation by the threat of corporal punishment as a sanction:

> 'Why are so many burglars bowlegged? ... The two phenomena of bowleggedness and burglarious habits are apt to emerge from the same environment. It is in the overcrowded home that rickets may commonly be found, and rickets are a common cause of bowlegs; it is in the overcrowded home that habits of honesty are with most difficulty taught, and hence also the greater danger of a burglarious career.' (Paterson, 1951, p. 30)
>
> 'A prisoner who ceases on discharge from prison to break the law has changed his life, and such a thing can only proceed from a change of heart. To religion, therefore, which touches the deepest springs of human conduct, we look for the redemption of the individual, for it can furnish to the weak and unstable the highest ideals and the sternest inhibitions.' (Paterson, 1951, p. 123)
>
> '...when its [corporal punishment] occasional use is contrasted with the likelihood of indiscriminate punishment if it is abolished, even the optimist will vote for its retention.' (Paterson, 1951, p. 138)

Techniques for Gaining Control of the Population

Foucault argued in his influential book *Discipline and Punish* (1977), after a lurid description of the dismembering to death of Damiens, who was convicted of regicide in France; that punishment changed from a disciplining of the body to the disciplining of the mind. Instead of the public spectacle of punishment, it was taken behind the anonymous gates of the prison, where offenders were given either precise amounts of physical pain via a certain number of strokes of the lash, or made to carry out pointless tasks such as walking on the treadmill 'grinding the air'. This was important as a measure for the general population to accept the disciplinary control of the state. For Foucault the aim of prison was not to punish less but to punish better and to 'penetrate more deeply into the social body' (Matthews, 1999, p. 12). While Foucault was interested in examining the changing politics and nature of society, he has been criticized for being more descriptive than analytic in how punishment changed and for failing to draw on archival material (Godfrey and Lawrence, 2005, p. 79). This may seem to be an unfair criticism: for critical observers like Foucault (1977), and Melossi and Pavarini (1981) the similarities between the prison and the factory in terms of their working conditions were significant, such as their control over the individual temporally and spacially (Godfrey, Lawrence and Williams, 2008, pp. 129–130). Foucault's analysis has served as a source of inspiration for many contemporary critical thinkers, such as Garland, who commented that if critical theory was to have relevance, it had to 'first engage with things as they actually are' (Garland, 2001, pp. 2–3). For Garland, the study of crime and crime control reveals the problems of government and social order, although he applied this in the context of 'late modern society' (p. 26).

Rusche and Kirchheimer (1968) in *Punishment and Social Structure* mentioned that:

> 'Every system of production tends to discover punishments which correspond to its productive relationships. It is thus necessary to investigate the origin and fate of penal systems, the use or avoidance of specific punishments, and the intensity of penal practices as they are determined by social forces, above all by economic and then fiscal forces.' (1968, p. 5)

Thus in times of slavery, penal slavery existed; in times of capital there was the introduction of the fine. For those unable to pay, corporal punishment was the imposed alternative, which allowed the cost to be expunged. Hence the system could be flexible in how deviants were punished. Prison fulfilled a disciplinary role, but this did not necessarily mean being locked up, away from the public eye: 'For custodial purposes, at least, the stocks is probably our oldest prison' (Pugh, 1968, p. 1). It is interesting to note that Pugh's comment on the stocks as a mechanism that deprived the offender of her liberty could broadly apply to any punishment that had this effect, including day centres, community service and so on. The stocks were used mostly used by local courts and, as well as immobilizing the offender, there was an element of 'reintegrative shaming' as it left 'them open to public display… Other evidence shows how the stocks could, on occasion, be used to give very full publicity to the offence being punished' (Sharpe, 1990, p. 20).

Melossi and Pavarini (1981) commented that in the sixteenth century, English parishioners paid a social tax to look after the needs of the 'impotent poor', but there was not a system to help the unemployed who were repressed. Houses of correction were later introduced to systematize this, especially for those refusing work. Their comment that '[l]abourers were obliged to accept the first available job on whatever conditions the employers cared to establish' (1981, p. 15) has an uncomfortable resonance with the recent policies of New Labour under their 'New Deal'.

Jonathan Simon (1993) in *Poor Discipline* commented that in the sixteenth century, prosecution was almost entirely dependent on private prosecutors, who were often the victim of the crime. To prevent abuse of power, recognizance bonds were used to release suspects on bail, thus known individuals even on serious charges could be released, when strangers on lesser charges might remain in custody. Peace bonds were used for lesser acts that threatened the peace, to ensure good behaviour. Using private citizens to act as sureties ensured that elements of control were exerted to maintain good order in the community.

The Threat of the Destitute

The violence of the Tudor era (Elton, 1985, p. 5) also affected the actions of central government. Throughout this era each monarch faced at least one serious uprising and there were correspondingly regular Acts which were intended to give relief to the poor and suppress vagrancy (Pound, 1986). Furthermore, until 1576 the government did not distinguish between the 'professional beggar' and the involuntary unemployed. The Act of 1531 stated that the:

> '...Justice of Peace shall cause every ... idle person ... to be tied to the end of a cart naked and to be beaten with whips throughout the same market town or other place till his body be bloody by reason of such whipping; and after such punishment and whipping had, the person so punished ... shall be joined upon his oath to return forthwith without delay in the next and straight way to the place where he was born, or where he last dwelled before the same punishment by the space of three years and there put himself to labour like as a true man oweth to do.' (*Statutes of the Realm*, iii, p. 328, in Pound, 1986, p. 96)

The intention of this Act was obvious. It was an attempt to ensure that citizens were to conform and that deviants, as a sanction, would be publicly shamed and punished. This can be compared with the twentieth century response to vagrancy which was to regard the homeless as 'invisible'. The state could then ignore its obligations to provide assistance to the homeless. Lea (2002) described this time as one when strangers were seen as suspicious, to be denied rights.

A further theme that can be traced from Elizabethan times, through the era of the Poor Law to the present day, is the concern to ensure that people did not become dependent on the state to provide for their needs. The government introduced a compulsory tax in 1572 and the Act also introduced the principle of the involuntary setting to work of the unemployed, either in the form of public works or working with materials supplied by the parish. The Act of 1601 extended this and nominated overseers of the poor of the same parish:

> 'who were churchwardens or substantial householders, who with the consent of two or more justices of peace as it is aforesaid, for setting to work of the children of all such whose parents shall not ... be thought able to keep and maintain their children; and also for setting to work all such persons married or unmarried having no means to maintain them, [or] use no ordinary or daily trade of life to get their living by ... it shall be lawful for the said churchwardens and overseers ... to bind any such children as aforesaid to be apprentices, where they shall see convenient ... And the said justices of peace or any of them to send to the House of Correction or common gaol such as shall not employ themselves to work, being appointed therein to as aforesaid.' (*Statutes of the Realm*, vol. iv, part ii, pp. 962–965, in Pound, 1986, pp. 98–99)

Thus the concept of parental responsibility is not new, nor is the notion that the state should have the right to remove children that were not well cared for. However, the church played a much more active role and the responsibility for the relief of destitution throughout the Middle Ages was 'assumed and accepted' by the Church (Webb and Webb, 1963, p. 1).

The Growth of the Prison System

According to McConville (1981), in addition to secular prisons the Church also owned prisons and maintained its own system of justice under the authority of bishops and abbots. Pugh (1968) provided a detailed analysis of the growth of prisons, and also described various statutes that demonstrated that imprisonment was a punishment *per se* (pp. 36–37), listing those which imposed a custodial sentence for a variety of crimes. Furthermore, 'franchise prisons were held by ecclesiastical and secular Lords and served a group estates, hundred, a manor or even a soke or liberty within a town, and varied in capacity from a single room in a manor house to specially constructed part of a monastery' (McConville, 1981, p. 7).

These prisons did not constitute a national system but certain establishments were recognized as having national significance, for example, the Newgate and the Fleet (McConville, 1981, p. 7, quoting from historical sources on the Fleet prison). He added, 'For the involuntary debtor and criminal prisoner without resources, imprisonment could be a virtual death sentence. Besides the risk of disease, many must have starved to death as whatever may have been the previous position, by the thirteenth century prisoners were expected to find their own keep' (McConville, 1981, p. 17; examples also given in Pugh, 1968, p. 319).

By the fourteenth century it was generally assumed that prisoners could not exist without alms; that is, clothing, food or money given to them by other people. Thus one of the arguments used for closing the jail of Berkshire in Windsor in the fourteenth century was that the local community was not large enough to contribute sufficient money to avoid starvation among the inmates. There was little evidence that 'nourishment of prisoners' was a task undertaken by the 'brethren of hospitals'. However, by the fourteenth century, bequests and legacies to prisons and prisoners became very common – for example, there were 70 legacies for Newgate prison (Pugh, 1968, p. 323) and the citizens of London donated 1.84 per cent of their charitable wealth to the relief of prisoners (Jordan, in Pugh, 1968, p. 323).

There were financial incentives to keep defendants in prison, even if acquitted: 'arrest once affected, the financial advantages of detaining prisoners unjustly were powerful, while the fee system made it difficult to ensure that prisoners were released from prison the moment their presence there was no longer warranted' (Pugh, 1968, p. 389).

The Export of Offenders

From the thirteenth century onwards, the 39th clause of the Magna Carta effectively declared that arrest had to be for justifiable reasons. It is fair to conclude that in medieval times, prisons were nasty, barbaric places, but that the rich could buy more comfortable surroundings and possibly even choose which prison they went to. Even if there was partial protection against false imprisonment for those accused of felonies, if an individual had offended against the Crown, either personally or politically, then it was likely that he would remain in prison for a very long time. Prison overcrowding is not just a recent phenomenon, and in order to contain the numbers held in prison and to remove beggars, transportation was introduced in England, Scotland and Wales. The first people to be transported, in 1648, were Scottish prisoners sent to the plantations in Virginia after being defeated by Cromwell (Cameron, 1983, p. 29). Transportation was not available to the courts in England and Wales as a regular punishment in the mid-sixteenth century, but convicts had been sent to the American colonies and to the West Indies over the previous 60 years (Beattie, 1986, p. 472). There was a connection between the introduction of transportation and the galley service in France and Spain (an attempt was made to introduce this sentence into England in 1602).

The 'middle' stage in transportation began in 1654 when a group of convicts had their death sentence commuted to transportation 'to some English Plantation'; however, if they returned to England during the following ten years the pardon was to be considered null and void (Beattie, 1986, p. 472). Transportation became a common alternative to the death sentence when offenders could be sent to the colonies for committing 'capital but not vicious' offences, mixing royal clemency with public advantage.

The Bridewell opened in the City of London in December 1556. It was the first House of Correction in the country to cater for the able-bodied poor, as opposed to the 'succourless poor child, the sick and the impotent' (McConville, 1981, p. 29). There had already been institutions opened for the poor, sick and orphans, but no institutions for the 'vagabonds and runnagates'. At a time when savagery was slowly being replaced by reason, the beggar was doubly reviled as they were not stakeholders in 'a society which ranked, not cleanliness (of which it had scarcely heard) but industry, next to godliness and loyalty and which condemned idleness as both a sin against God and crime against the Commonwealth' (Bindoff, 1978, p. 293).

The savagery of punishment and its 'essence of … irrational, unthinking emotion … was the emotional reaction contained within it, the authentic act of outrage' (Garland, 1990, p. 32). In a Durkheimian sense, punishment was a reaffirmation of common beliefs to strengthen social cohesion within the 'collective conscience'. Durkheim saw the move from hanging to imprisonment and/or transportation as resulting from two different phenomena: first, the evolution of society from a 'simple' to a more 'advanced' or modern social type with a new 'moral faith'; second, he distinguished between 'religious criminality' and 'human criminality', where in a simple society all crimes against the 'collective conscience' were of the 'religious criminality' type and invited a savage response (Garland, 1990, p. 38). The role of punishment was to reassert moral order.

Positive Custody?

The Bridewell grew; the first example (coupled with the Houses of Correction) of a system of imprisonment to supplement the savage imposition of community sentences: branding, whipping and hanging, as well as the predecessor of community service – cleaning out the city ditches which also served as the city sewers. Entry into the Bridewell could be prefaced by a public flogging, coupling retribution with the reformation (McConville, 1981, p. 33). However, there were also productive trades (25 by 1579) and a number of young apprentices were trained. Prisons at this time had a purely custodial function, and this allowed the gaolers to engage in transactions with their prisoners. The Bridewell did not suffer the degree of 'corruption and extortion' that characterized the later Houses of Correction (McConville, 1981, p. 36). There was a difference in function between the Houses of Correction and the earlier prisons in that, as the name implied, detention was for a longer period and was '[s]ystematic, [the] positive confinement was directed at creating a new individual, one who had been corrected, trained and transformed into an ideal encompassing the qualities [of] docility, malleability and hard work. Such labourers would meet the needs of a nascent capitalism' (Dobash *et al*., 1986, pp. 22–23).

They described a patriarchal system in the Middle Ages that reinforced the subjugation of women (80–90 percent of those accused of witchcraft were women; Dobash *et al*., 1986, p. 17). Thus women could have a 'scold's bridle placed on their heads with a spike or pointed wheel inserted into their mouth … this spiked cage was intended to punish women adjudged quarrelsome or not under the proper control of their husbands' (Dobash *et al*., 1986, p. 19).

Women could also be ducked into the village pond fixed to a ducking stool, and these public humiliations were designed to reinforce the power, right and ability to punish of the patriarch, church and Crown.

Circumventing the Gallows

One anomaly in the courts dating back to medieval times was the possibility of claiming 'benefit of clergy'. The intention, by the fourteenth century, was that if an offender could prove clerical status then he could avoid the gallows. Over the centuries the 'proof of literacy' became very liberal, so that 'the demonstration … usually took place in the court just before sentence was to be pronounced, by the prisoner being asked to read a verse of the Psalms. That was to be the means by which clergy became a massive fiction that tempered in practice the harshness of the common law rule that virtually all felonies were capital offences' (Beattie, 1986, p. 141).

This escape clause was progressively restricted as the practice was usually to release the offender after its successful pleading, and the linking with the ecclesiastical courts was broken in 1576. The judge could imprison clergied prisoners for up to a year, but this rarely happened. In the eighteenth century the reading test was abolished and the ability to use the 'benefit of clergy' depended on the nature of the offence. It could only be used once, but in a century that was notoriously bloody, it saved many illiterate men who would not have previously qualified from the death sentence (Beattie, 1986, p. 143). Transportation began to be used seriously from 1718, when 'a discretionary power was given to judges to order felons who were entitled to the benefit of clergy, to be transported to the American plantations … [this] continued … till the commencement of the War of Independence, 1775' (Mayhew and Binny, 1971, p. 92). After the outbreak of the American War of Independence, a plan for penitentiaries was considered by Parliament but not followed through, and in 1784 an Act was passed, allowing the King to transport offenders and transportation resumed. In 1786 future colonies were fixed, by an order in council, to be the east coast of Australia and the adjacent islands (see Hughes (1987) and Shaw (1998) for more detail on transportation). In 1787 an 'epidemic of whipping for vagrancy occurred' (Webb and Webb, 1963, p. 374), although there was not a regular pattern to the punishment. It would appear to have varied according to the whims of the local Justices of the Peace. Occasionally the Lord Mayor and Aldermen of the City of London would clear the street of prostitutes, sending them to Bridewell for a whipping and possibly hard labour. There were 60 whipping posts (and 18 prisons) in an area of approximately nine square miles, implying a whipping post every few hundred yards. The Justices of the Peace had a terrible dilemma of whether to subject a poor unfortunate beggar to the public humiliation of a vicious and bloody whipping or to send them to prison: 'The physical horror and moral contamination of the gaols, of which John Howard had rendered the more intelligent Justices acutely conscious, made them loath to sentence mere beggars or poor travellers to imprisonment' (Webb and Webb, 1963, p. 375).

Thus the dislike of one punishment implied the other by default. It was unclear if the judges were consulted before the introduction of the Transportation Act, but they gave it their enthusiastic endorsement: 'At a session of the Old Bailey in 1719, for example, 25 of 27 prisoners convicted of clergyable offences were sentenced to be transported' (Beattie, 1986, p. 506).

Beggars and vagrants might also be 'warned off' and could be provided with a 'pass' to get to their own parish. The Act also significantly transferred power from juries to judges because it abolished the distinction between grand and petty larceny. Hitherto the maximum sentences had been, respectively, hanging and corporal punishment. The jury had the discretionary power to find a defendant guilty of simple larceny of under a shilling, which ensured a maximum sentence of a whipping. Subsequently a prisoner convicted of any noncapital offence could be dealt with as the bench decided. This transfer of power was no accident, and of the noncapital sentences imposed in Surrey in the 30 years after the Act:

> '60 per cent of the men convicted of clergyable offences or petty larceny were allowed their clergy and were branded on the thumb and discharged, in the generation after

> 1718 that same proportion was sent to the American colonies and fewer than one in ten were granted clergy … The effect on the treatment of women was … significant, for it ensured that the largest proportion of the women convicted of noncapital property offences would be banished from the country.' (Beattie, 1986, pp. 507–508)

There was a further sanction available in the country to reinforce the power of the court, if the twice a year assizes or Quarter Sessions (four times a year) failed to impress the local populace. The offender could be summoned to Westminster, or 'the full panoply of the law' could be employed for 'exemplary hangings or at least exemplary trials … deemed necessary for the public peace' (Hay, 1975, p. 31). It is interesting to note that transportation did not become the automatic sentence for noncapital offences. It was still possible to be given the 'branding of clergy', with or without a period in a house of correction. Petty larceny could still result in a whipping and discharge. In eighteenth century England when the masses were excluded from political representation, 'food riots, machine smashing and much poaching can indeed be seen as proto-political resistance' (Lea, 1999, p. 309).

Transportation was the most severe sentence available and the judge would consider 'the seriousness of the offence and to the character of the prisoner, as far as they could learn about him in court or from his friends and enemies in the locality' (Beattie, 1986, p. 509). Lea, drawing on Foucault, also made the point that illegality as well as resistance could be seen as 'tolerated illegalities' a concept from even feudal times (Lea, 1999, p. 309). For those who could no longer be tolerated, it would appear that transportation was a convenient way of getting rid of petty persistent offenders and problem families, although the Act itself had commented on 'a great want of servants' in America. Transportation filled a gap between hanging and the granting of the branding of benefit of clergy. It thus created a middle ground for the punishment of petty and serious offenders, which encompassed the majority of defendants appearing before the courts. In addition, many offenders sentenced to be executed had their punishment mitigated to transportation (Johnston, 2009, p. 128).

Gatrell (1994) in *The Hanging Tree* offered an explanation for the rapid move away from hanging in the 1830s. He believed that prosecutions became more effective and too many executions were taking place to be sustained. McGowan (2000) was not convinced of this explanation, which he saw as too functional and mechanical. While he proposed no alternative explanation, his article is a timely warning not to simply accept arguments based on emotion, psychological causation or the responses of the middle or lower classes as articulated and recorded by individuals such as Byron.

What is clear from the figures is that the British government relied heavily on transportation as its principal secondary punishment (after hanging) until 1852, when 'the Australian colonies declared their final intention of ceasing to accept Britain's criminal dregs' (Tomlinson, 1981, p. 127).

Ensuring Punishment

It has previously been indicated that vagrants were not necessarily transported, though they were likely to be driven out of the larger towns without thought of what would happen to them. Parliament grew so alarmed at the practice of sending vagrants away without punishment that in 1744 power of searching vagrants' bundles was given to the developing system of parish constables, in order to ascertain whether they had any money to pay towards the cost of their journey to their parish. Furthermore, the Act of 1714, which stipulated that no parish need receive a vagrant before giving them a whipping was expanded in 1792 to ensure that vagrant males were given a public whipping (Webb and Webb, 1963, pp. 381–382). It should be recalled that transportation had ceased in 1776 and as Howard commented: 'Parliament had suddenly discovered, in the face of rebellion in the colonies, that '[t] ransportation to His Majesty's colonies and plantations in America [is] … depriving the Kingdom of many subjects whose labour might be useful to the community… (16 Geo. III)' (Howard, 1960, p. 14). An Act was then passed which had the effect of substituting hard labour for transportation, with Blackstone and Eden's proposal, adopting John Howard's principles of solitary cellular confinement when at rest and hard physical work. John Howard had stressed four main points, namely: 'systematic inspection, adequate sanitation, security of buildings and abolition of fees' (Howard, 1960, p. 15).

Sir Robert Peel, Conservative Home Secretary, had been unhappy at the laxity of transportation which he wanted to see as a more severe sentence if it was to replace the death penalty. Even solitary confinement was not seen by him as offering a severe enough punishment to offenders, as individuals would respond in different ways to the deprivation. The Victorian prison system was constructed around strict individualism (Garland, 1985). Long terms of imprisonment were available in prisons like Millbank, which held 800 inmates. For Peel:

> 'When they lived well, their lot in the winter season was thought by people outside to be rather an enviable one. We reduced their food, and from the combined effect of low but ample diet, and … depression of spirits … there arose a malignant and contagious disorder, which emptied the prison, either through the death or removal of its inmates.' (cited in Shaw, 1998, p. 145)

Inmates had to attend compulsory religious services. Although Howard is credited as a major penal reformer, he was still a product of his time and held strong views on prison regimes including religious instruction alongside solitary confinement and punishment. The quotation above serves to inform that other options could not be considered as 'soft'. John Howard insisted that the prison had to be built in Islington and when this proved contentious he resigned from the supervisors team set up by the 1779 Act. The delay, followed by the resumption of transportation to Australia, held back the growth of imprisonment, instead of transportation (Howard, 1960, pp. 15–16). The idea of cellular confinement, envisaged in the Act of 1779, was instituted in the building of Pentonville Prison in 1842, which used as its model a prison in Philadelphia. It should be recalled that until this time conditions in prisons were scandalous.

In 1775, John Howard published *The State of the Prisons in England and Wales* (Howard, 1929). The abuses were described as being 'physical and moral'. The first referred to bad food, bad ventilation and bad drainage; the other referred to lack of prisoner classification, and the lack of separation between the different groups of inmates. Hinde (1951) mentioned that there was an Act in 1776 which suggested that, instead of offenders being sentenced to death or transported, they could be sentenced to hard labour, dredging the River Thames. These prisoners were to be housed in prison hulks moored on the Thames, and this form of punishment started three years later. Many of these prisoners were to perish of cholera and other diseases before the hulks were scrapped. This was not to happen for many years and as late as January 1841 there were 3552 convicts on board the various hulks in England (Mayhew and Binny, 1971, p. 198). Conditions were appalling, with stories of the unfortunate prisoners having vermin-infested clothing and also of a chaplain carrying out a burial service for hulk inmate victims of cholera at a 'distance of a mile from the grave and letting fall a handkerchief … as a sign that they were to lower the bodies' (Mayhew and Binny, 1971, p. 200).

Prisoners were locked into the holds of the hulks where there was no oversight from the authorities and inmates were at the mercy of fellow inmates. The concept of through-care was thus totally lacking, survival literally being the only hope. It is surprising to learn that, according to the official records, prisoners that survived to be released did well:

> 'It should be remembered, let us add, by the opponents of the ticket-of-leave system, that although it is from these condemned hulks, where the men are herded together and are well pretty free to plot and plan as they please, that they are turned upon society, nevertheless according to the director's report … of five hundred and forty-four convicts discharged in 1854 from the Woolwich hulks only, and one hundred and six discharged before that period – in all, six hundred and fifty convicts – there have been but six received back with licences revoked for misconduct.' (Mayhew and Binny, 1971, p. 201)

This underlined the difficulty in linking the concept of through-care to after-care. There was clearly no assistance offered to prisoners during their sentence, yet official records indicate a low failure rate while prisoners were on licence. The ticket-of-leave scheme, the predecessor of the parole system, was introduced reluctantly in 1853. According to Bartrip (1981), it was the completion of the Portsmouth Convict Prison in 1852 which allowed a reduction in the use of the prison hulks. There was a somewhat emotive reaction in 1995 by many penal affairs groups to the Conservative government's decision to buy an American prison ship which was to be used as an expedient way of coping with the rising prison population in the aftermath of Michael Howard's 'Prison Works' policy.

It was under the Conservative–Liberal Democrat coalition in the aftermath of serious rioting in London and other major cities in England in the summer of 2011 that the prison population has again increased, reaching 87 501 at the end of September 2011 (83 245 males and 4256 females), 2000 more than at the same point the previous year. The usable operational capacity is 88 533, so there is little slack left in the system. As will be discussed in Chapter 7, new prison places will be located in the private sector.

Dealing with the Children: Reformatories

The early nineteenth century was also an interesting time for youth justice, as it was in 1837 that Parkhurst Prison, on the Isle of Wight, was opened as an establishment for boys (Cornish *et al.*, 1978, p. 42). Until this time, the treatment of young offenders had generally been regarded as a disgrace. Parkhurst received 1200 boys in its first eight years, who were mostly incarcerated for two to three years before being sent to Australia, to private masters. Courts were given the power to sentence youngsters under sixteen 'first to 14 days or more in prison, then to a period of two to five years in a reformatory school' (Cornish *et al.*, 1978, p. 43). The regime in these establishments was described as stern and rigid, and there was a rise in numbers sent from about 6000 in 1864 to 24 600 in 1894. It is instructive to learn that the Molesworth Committee (1837) regarded juveniles as a poor source for transportation, rendering this unworkable and costly (Shaw, 2008).

Shaw (2008) also commented that by the late nineteenth century many working-class children had been institutionalized, with the respectable ones catered for by educational legislation dating from 1870. She continued by highlighting the scandal of prison training ships, from the mid-nineteenth century, that could be used either as a punishment by the courts or as part of the reformatory or industrial school system. Some of these ships experienced mutinies by the young men and there were also inquiries into excessive violence and poor treatment.

Historically, concern for children's welfare has been relatively recent, with a distinction being made between the poor and the destitute: '[i]nitially the Court of Chancery was not the guardian of *all* children: those without property were considered outside its jurisdiction' (Morris *et al.*, 1980, pp. 1–2).

The reason why the state started to move from accepting child labour to perceiving that children needed care and protection has been linked to a fear of working class rootlessness and disobedience. Thus the young working class needed a proper childhood, and the family became the vehicle for exercising a socializing experience on its children; when it failed, the state would take its place. Children were perceived to be 'at risk' morally far more than they were seen as criminal: '[b]y 1894 over 17 000 children from the "perishing classes" [children growing up exposed to cruelty and poverty, and without the moral influences of education and religion] were held in industrial schools, compared with a mere 4800 delinquent children in the reformatories' (Morris et al., 1980, p. 5).

At the beginning of the twentieth century the 'experiments with probation' and the ability to give the courts details of individuals' backgrounds, coupled with the new Juvenile Courts (from 1908) gave an impetus to noncustodial sentencing (Cornish *et al.*, 1978, pp. 44–45). Winston Churchill, as Home Secretary, unhappy at the cruel treatment meted out on training ships, held a full inquiry that led to a Departmental Committee being formed in 1913 to look into reformatory and industrial schools to examine punishment and welfare practices (Shaw, 2008). In essence, the nineteenth century was a system where reformatories and industrial schools represented a *penal* response to young people deemed deviant, which was to be replaced in the twentieth century (see Chapter 9) by a multi-agency approach focused on family and the community (Shaw, 2011).

Dealing with Adults: Prison and Punishment

In 1877 prisons were nationalized and local prisons began to operate in a more uniformly rigid way. Peel's Gaol Act of 1823 had had the effect of separating prisoners according to their status, and the Prisons Act of 1865 required local authorities to build separate cells in jails (Shaw, 2011, p. 37). However, Johnston (2008) commented that there was a variation in practices within local prisons. The two major systems, known as *separate* and *silent*, required a high level of staffing, but Johnston cited evidence to show that staffing levels were extremely varied.

Penal servitude, a sentence started in 1853, consisted of three stages, the first for approximately nine months: solitary confinement coupled with work in the cell, prayers and exercise; second, sleep and meals in a separate cell, but working with others; third, conditional release under police supervision. There were also four classes which allowed a regime of progressive rewards for good conduct (Priestley, 1985, p. 194). Testimony from inmates between 1830 and 1914 gave graphic testimony to the brutality of prison regimes. What is of particular interest is the role of the prison doctor at this time. Prisoners believed to be malingering could be given severe electric shocks or be plunged into boiling hot baths (Priestley, 1985, pp. 176–177). Finally for ex-prisoners, the reality of discharge was of starvation, the workhouse or a return to previous bad habits. The alternative was emigration and the Discharged Prisoners' Aid Society assisted 655 out of 2217 men to emigrate between 1860 and 1962 (Priestley, 1985, p. 286). Summing up this time, Wiener (1990) eloquently made the point that a Lombrosian form of logic applied, drawing on the work of Mayhew and Binney. This was because there was a perception of 'a work-evading population of the "unrespectable", in which deviance blended imperceptibly into criminality' (Wiener, 1990, p. 25). There was a fear of the underclass as being 'deeply rooted in human nature, in the natural man (and woman) who lay underneath the thin crust of civilization' (Wiener, 1990, p. 25). In the circumstances it was remarkable that the Gladstone Committee (1895), 33 years after Mayhew, expressed faith in the rehabilitation of offenders, rather than of punishment and fear of the underclass: '[t]hat some of (the community's) worst and most dangerous products, and that many of those who would lead honest lives under different surroundings, can be reclaimed by special and skilful prison treatment is emphatically maintained by many of the most capable and experienced witnesses' (Gladstone Report LVI, para. 29, cited in Cornish *et al.*, 1978, p. 38).

Unfortunately this view of 'special and skilful prison treatment' did not translate into the prison regime. Hobhouse and Brockway (1922), in their now relatively neglected *English Prisons Today: Being the Report of the Prison System Enquiry Committee*, produced a damning indictment of a cruel and rigid regime. 'Hard labour' was described as sleeping on a plank bed without a mattress for the first fortnight; solitary confinement and no work for the first month; and a ten-hour working day. After this the working day, as for all other prisoners, was 8 3/4 hours (Hobhouse and Brockway, 1922, pp. 100–101). Work was picking oakum or horsehair, a very monotonous task; the workshops were typically low grade and deliberately deterrent in nature. Prison was more than just the physical reality of the regime: 'Freedom is not achieved by making the prison beds increasingly comfortable' (Gallo and Ruggiero, 1991, p. 273). They continued by analysing the purpose of prison which they saw as being two-fold: the 'institutional function' of the 'destruction of bodies' and the 'material function' of the 'productive use of the bodies themselves' (Gallo and Ruggiero, 1991, p. 273). This was a change from the ethos of Pentonville (Ignatieff, 1978) where the use of the crank and the treadmill was deliberately to 'grind the air', was an unproductive, but precisely measurable, punishment. This centralized system of control was described by Beatrice and Sydney Webb as 'the fetish of uniformity', with David Garland describing it as 'classical criminology', where individuals operate through free will, making rational decisions (Godfrey and Lawrence, 2005, p. 82).

There was a concern that drunkenness was becoming an increasing problem for women from the 1860s. Consequently, the Inebriates Acts 1879–1898 sought to offer a more constructive sanction than short periods of imprisonment (Morrison, 2008). Morrison described this as a gendered system where inebriate institutions were set up to contain the problem, with a tougher regime than the local prisons. Indeed, women could be transferred there from penal institutions where they could reside for three years. They were all eventually closed by 1921.

Sir Evelyn Ruggles-Brise, president of the International Prison Commission, wrote that there was a move, internationally, to make incarceration more humane. In the meeting of the Commission in 1902 the following countries were represented: France, America, Belgium, Holland, Spain, Greece, Norway, Switzerland, India, Japan, Hungary and Sweden. In his book, *Prison Reform at Home and Abroad* (1924), he highlighted seven areas of interest that still have resonance today: substitutes for imprisonment, recidivism and its cure, the right of the injured party to compensation, the right to wages, patronage, limited responsibility, and those who have experienced a childhood of guilt and abandonment.

He gave details of criminal laws that were not punitive in intent. The 1887 Probation of First Offenders Act allowed the court, in cases where the defendant was of previous good character and due to 'youth, character, and antecedents or to the trivial nature of the offence' (Ruggles-Brise, 1924, p. 60), could be released on entering into a recognizance. This meant that the defendant agreed in court to be of good behaviour and was not then charged (later repealed by the Probation of Offenders Act 1907, discussed in Chapter 3, the early history of the probation service).

An Act that actually kept offenders out of prison was the Act for the better administration of Criminal Justice (1914). This made it obligatory for courts to allow time for fines to be paid. Ruggles-Brise said that in the year before the Act, out of approximately 130 000 convictions, 80 000 people went to prison for fine default. In the year after the Act, the number sent to prison for this reason fell from 15 per cent to 2 per cent, to around 15 000 per year.

Physical punishment could also be measured. In 1937 George Benson MP produced a paper for the Howard League for Penal Reform entitled 'Flogging: The Law and Practice in England'. In the introduction, Cicely Craven, Honorary Secretary for the League, commented that England 'maintains her ancient faith in the power of the lash to induce morality' (Benson, 1937, p. 3). She was vehemently opposed to physical punishment and Benson described the hysteria whipped up by campaigners to justify its continued use.

I once visited an elderly offender sentenced to life imprisonment in the mid-1980s who claimed to have received the 'cat o' nine tails' in prison and, in view of his age and offending history, could well have done so. He expressed great anger and at this punishment many years later, and it had had no effect on his offending behaviour in a positive sense.

Punishment was there for those the system had not been able to control. Foucault, like Weber, viewed the changing nature of punishment, not in terms of excess, but rather that traditionally punishment was irregular and/or inefficient and did not have what Foucault referred to as 'disciplinary power'. It had to become both 'efficient and rational' in order to produce 'docile bodies' (McNay, 1994, p. 92). There was one core essential element that had to be present: discipline.

> 'The discipline of the army gives birth to all discipline. No direct historical and transitional organisations link the Pharaonic workshops and construction work...with the Carthaginian Roman plantation, the mines of the late Middle Ages, the slave plantation of colonial economies, and finally the modern factory. However, all of these have in common the one element of discipline.' (Weber, 1948, p. 261)

Weber added that 'hospitals and prison cells were not absent' (Weber, 1948, p. 261) but he made two further points which are relevant to contemporary analysis of criminal justice thinking on policy. First, that 'the American system of scientific management enjoys the greatest triumphs in the rational conditioning and training of work performances' and, second, in terms of the effect that this had on people:

> 'The individual is shorn of his natural rhythm as determined by the structure of his organism; his psycho-physical apparatus is attuned to a new rhythm through a methodical specialisation of separately functioning muscles, and an optimal economy

> of forces is established corresponding to the conditions of work … This universal phenomenon increasingly restricts the importance of charisma and of individually differentiated conduct.' (Weber, 1948, pp. 261–262)

What is of interest is the time scale of Weber's observation on the changing nature of the individual's 'rhythm'. In this respect the observation is more pertinent to methods of control being applied to offenders at the end of the twentieth century, when cognitive programmes are in vogue to be applied across the board without considering individual differences. Offenders are given anger management courses, alcohol awareness programmes and other courses according to a set agenda which must not be deviated from, to maintain programme integrity. But this analysis 'jumps' the growth and decline of the 'treatment' model, common in probation in the 1960s. Chapter 3 will therefore consider in detail the formation of and changes in probation during the twentieth century, when the criminal justice system did not apply a moral justification but a managerial one (Garland, 1990, p. 72).

Summary

This chapter has sought to introduce a number of key themes, namely that historically there has been a fear of those people who do not have a stake in society, notably the homeless and rootless, who have been dealt with severely and unsympathetically. Crime was a threat to the moral order and, as society became more advanced, so the nature of punishment changed with it.

In terms of gender, patriarchal society was well established and formalized in the Middle Ages and when it became an attractive proposition to export deviants to the colonies, as a source of cheap labour and to provide a population for these areas, both women and men were sent. Young people were seen as feckless; in Victorian times this was dealt with in institutions, but this later changed to control within the community and within the family.

In terms of punishment, the 'uneven' savagery was replaced by a measured response, arguably violent, but with the intention of exerting a disciplinary force on the population. This 'economy of power' was 'more efficient and less costly in both economic and political terms' (McNay, 1994, p. 92). Seminal writers including Ignatieff, Rothman and Foucault have been called revisionists (including by Ignatieff himself), in that they exaggerate the importance of the role of the ruling class and issues of class (Matthews, 1999, p. 24).

Chapter 3 discusses the age of enlightenment and the rationalization of punishment through progressive thinkers such as Cesare Beccaria. This might be a rather rose-tinted view of these philosophers who were comfortable with the notion of eugenics and forced labour for life instead of capital punishment (Emsley, 2005). What this chapter has highlighted is that, as prison became an important and much-used deterrent for offenders, the use of the treadmill, crank and other physical measures forced prisoners to expend much energy and go through pain for no productive reason, simply 'to help them realize the error of their ways'; and the introduction of disciplines such as medical science did not necessarily mitigate this. Forcing men to endure sensory deprivation, such as the absence of contact and communication with others, not being allowed to speak and being hooded when outside their cells, had the unfortunate side effect of driving men mad (Emsley, 2005).

3

The Probation Service from its Inception until 1984

From Rescuing the Fallen to a Centrally Managed Organization

From a Primitive to an Industrial Society

The early part of the nineteenth century was characterized by political and social crises as vast numbers of people moved from living in the countryside to living in cities, in the search for work (Melossi, 2008). This led to the fear of the crowd (discussed in 'Issues of power: from control of the body to control of the mind', later in this chapter) as capitalist development evolved and the Industrial Revolution led to huge changes in work practices. Philosophically, positivist notions of humanity took root as classical criminological ideas began to be aired. Durkheim was a proponent of the view that punishment was not to be considered on a micro-level, that is, what should happen to the individual offender; rather, it was intended to restore the 'sacred moral order' for all lawful citizens (Whitehead, 2010, p. 34).

The Weberian idea of scientific management techniques and centrally determined and defined behaviour might seem a long way from the nascence of a late-nineteenth-century probation service steeped in the idea of 'reclaiming' offenders and their redemption or salvation. The time before the inception of probation can be characterized as a *Gemeinschaft* society (where the individual is part of a family, neighbourhood, community or association underpinned by a common tradition). Kamenka, although denoting the concept a Weberian 'ideal type', described this as a period when the 'emphasis [was] on law and regulation as expressing, internalized norms and traditions of the organic community, within which every individual member is part of a social family … Justice is … substantive, directed to a particular case in a particular social context and not to the establishing of a general rule or precedent' (Kamenka, 1979, pp. 5–6).

Rehabilitating and Resettling Offenders in the Community, First Edition. Anthony H. Goodman.

Thus in this period we can envisage the need for the prerogative of mercy rather than the embodiment of universal rules and regulations. This traditional form of justice was later replaced by what Kamenka referred to as the *Gesellschaft* society (where individuals are more impersonal, acting in their own self-interest; the division of labour is more complex). In this time, linked to the rise of commerce and social mobility, justice was 'oriented to the precise definition of the rights and duties of the individual through a sharpening of the point at issue and not the day to day *ad hoc* maintenance of social harmony' (Kamenka, 1979, p. 8).

However, changing offenders' behaviour has at its heart a number of dichotomous pressures. If, as the nineteenth century progressed, there was a growth in progressive criminal justice regimes, why was there also a resurgence in punitive responses to crime? Criminals were seen as rational and could therefore be taught how to make the right choices but, as fear of the feckless working classes grew (for example, as a response to the fear of garrotting considered in 'Issues of power: from control of the body to control of the mind', confidence that rationality would triumph waned, to be replaced with the notion that behaviour could be modified by fear; that is, punishment, rather than understanding. This lent credence to the notion of moral degeneracy, rather than a distorted or underdeveloped understanding of lawful behaviour (Rawlings, 1999, p. 100). This was the year that Pentonville Prison opened, with its punitive silent system and use of the pointless treadmill (Ignatieff, 1978); and Edwin Chadwick produced a report on the insanitary conditions that existed for the poor, showing that these conditions precluded people from bettering themselves (Rawlings, 1999, p. 101).

In terms of criminal justice, 'shaming' punishments disappeared during the nineteenth century, public whippings early on in the century, the pillory by 1815, the stocks by 1860 and public executions were abolished in 1860 (Pratt, 2003). In an interesting analysis of the loss of shaming, Pratt highlighted the beginning of bureaucratic state control of penal matters and the letting go of more primitive methods. The antithesis of this is that shaming was reintroduced in England at the end of the twentieth century, with offenders on community punishment being made to wear high-visibility vests, thus making them obvious to the public. Pratt has attributed this to Garland's (1996) argument about the loss of authority in the central state and the decline in the faith (and status) of criminal justice experts (Garland, 1996, pp. 190–191). The analysis in Chapter 5 on national standards for the supervision of offenders is an exemplar of this latter element, with a systematic attack on the professionalism of probation officers. It sought to remove professional discretion and substitute a set of rules to be followed without deviation. This will be discussed further in Chapter 9.

Making Offenders Productive

Early criminologists, like Lombroso, believed that the criminal was a 'moral degenerate' or 'throwback' and this concept was referred to as *atavism*. Van Swaaningen, describing the work of another founding criminologist Willem Bonger, commented that the peaceful handling and resolution of conflicts in more primitive societies than those of capitalism disproved this theory. Bonger believed that the growth of capitalism instead had a depressing effect on the working class as a 'social climate was created which incites egoism and increases the opportunity to commit crime' (van Swaaningen, 1997, p. 52). Van Swaaningen also linked this to the work of the probation service because Bonger argued that the 'workers' movement' should support the work of the probation service to 'socialize the workers' by working on 'social politics and education'. In furthering this aim, private enterprise would need to be compensated, presumably as they would not be maximizing their profits at the expense of the workers.

In order to place the probation service in an historical context, we will begin the analysis from the eighteenth century, the period before probation started, although passing reference will be made to earlier times. Cesare Beccaria (1738–1794), a seminal writer on criminological law reform, put the formation of criminal laws into context, incidentally anticipating the notion of the stakeholder society:

> 'Let us open our history books, and we shall see that laws, which are or ought to be agreements among free men, usually have been the instrument of the passions of a few persons. Sometimes laws arise from a fortuitous and transient necessity, but they have never been dictated by an impartial observer of human nature who can grasp the actions of a multitude of men and consider them from this point of view: the greatest happiness shared among the greatest number.' (Beccaria, 1986, p. 5)

Garland commented that Hay developed a theory of punishment in the eighteenth century in England to make sense of the paradox that the judiciary retained, indeed expanded, the range of capital statutes, while the number hanged decreased (Garland, 1990, pp. 118–119). The second paradox to exercise Hay was, how did the ruling classes exercise their power after feudalism had ceased to exert the tie between master and serf? Hay's response was to conclude that contemporary historians argued that a penal policy built on terror would not work. Indeed, he contended the death penalty was more a deterrent to judges and juries than to criminals (Hay, 1975, p. 23). He also commented that:

> 'The prerogative of mercy ran throughout the administration of the criminal law, from the lowest to the highest level. At the top sat the high court judges, and their free use of the royal pardon … [discretion] allowed the paternalist JP to compose quarrels, intervene with prosecutors on behalf of culprits, and in the final instance to dismiss a case entirely.' (Hay, 1975, p. 40)

Issues of Power: From Control of the Body to Control of the Mind

Foucault, in his seminal work *Discipline and Punish*, argued that a change occurred between 1750 and 1820 when there was a shift in the balance of power. This power was exercised by control of the mind rather than of the body: 'The carceral network does not cast the unassailable into a confused hell; there is no outside … The delinquent is an institutional product … Prison continues, on those entrusted to it, a work begun elsewhere, which the whole of society pursues on each individual through innumerable mechanisms of discipline' (Foucault, 1977, p. 301–303).

According to Pratt (2003) Foucault started with the Bentham 'blueprint' of the Panopticon Prison which had all-seeing control within its radial prison structure, so the prisoner was never sure when he was being watched and hence had to assume he was being watched at all times. This vision of control was later developed by Stanley Cohen (1985) in his seminal work, *Visions of Social Control*, where he discussed the blurring of control and benevolence: today, measures for dealing with offenders might seem to be benevolent, but they incorporate increasing levels of control. Thus, community supervision might seem preferable to prison but when it is coupled, for example, with curfews, electronic tagging and so on, in reality it is akin to home custody.

Morris (1999) commented that it had been eighteenth century Age of Enlightenment philosophers who had moved the nature of penal opinion away from its punitive origins. While acknowledging that the law was less directed towards the needs of the 'propertied and the powerful', he noted that the recipients 'still come from the bottom of the social heap' (1999, p. 8). It is helpful to retain the dichotomy and tension between punishment and rehabilitation, when considering the birth and development of probation as a criminal justice sanction in England and Wales. This is very pertinent today, as the increasingly punitive response to offenders on supervision invokes the public as the reason for breaching offenders who do not comply with probation conditions. It could be argued that offenders who manage to keep to the high reporting level required probably do not require that level of oversight in the first place.

Pragmatism in the mid-nineteenth century forced the British government to consider other methods of dealing with offenders than the imposition of long prison sentences: 'From the 1850s Britain was faced with the problem of finding an alternative for the punishment of transportation and dealing with its serious offenders at home. The size of this task should not be exaggerated … transportees constituted only a relatively small proportion of all convicted offenders' (Bartrip, 1981, pp. 172–173).

The Penal Servitude Act 1853 included ticket-of leave provisions which allowed prisoners to be released early. Responsibility for supervision, the predecessor to parole, was given to the police. Bartrip made the point that enforcement relied on 'sanction' rather than 'effective detection'. Many men just disappeared without trace.

There was a widespread public panic over an outbreak of garrotting in the mid-nineteenth century, which led to the Garrotters Act of 1863 which added 50 strokes to the sentences of armed robbers or garrotters. In the same year, there was a Royal Commission which thought that the crime rate was '… at least partly attributable to defects in the system of punishment now in force, and to the fact that there has been an accumulation of discharged convicts at home, owing to the comparatively small number sent to a penal colony since 1853' (Bartrip, 1981, p. 169).

Garland commented that Foucault viewed the 'leniency of punishment' as a 'ruse of power' which allowed for the extension of control. This leniency could be both authentic and based on religious conviction, but the combination of 'humane treatment' and increased control was not incompatible (Garland, 1990, p. 159).

Stedman Jones stated that in the 1880s there was a resurgence of fear about the 'dangerous classes' with the fear that they would spill over into the 'respectable working class'. He told of how the poor had been ruthlessly displaced in London for urban improvement and street clearance. This fear was exacerbated by the disturbances of 1886 and 1887, culminating in 'bloody Sunday' when the police and the poor clashed in Trafalgar Square. The consequence, according to Bailey, was the appointment of Sir Charles Warren as Chief Commissioner of Police who in turn appointed ex-army men as Chief and Assistant Chief Constable. It was forbidden to hold any public meetings in Trafalgar Square, and the police dispersed any demonstrations. Barbara Weinberger, researching into police activities in Warwickshire at this time, stated that the working class felt a deep-seated antagonism towards the police. This was in part due to the enforcement of the licencing laws and the tightening up of the Poor Law, as there were so many vagrants requiring relief in the 1860s. This made it harder for able-bodied people to get assistance, making work more attractive to them. The Poor Law still helped the old and the 'feeble-minded'.

In this context the opening of Pentonville Prison in 1842 represented an attempt to cope with the crisis of what to do with offenders after transportation to the colonies had been attacked from two fronts; first, as the colonists did not want more criminals and second, that this did not constitute moral justice (Tomlinson, 1981). Transportation had been a useful method of ridding England of offenders since 1717, when the American colonies were first used for this purpose. Between 1775 and 1787, during and after the War of Independence, this outlet temporarily closed, but it reopened in 1787 when Australia became the new venue for disposal of criminals. Pentonville, operating a regime of silence, had the unfortunate effect of sending many men insane and the details of its ethos and purpose are described in fine detail by Ignatieff (1978). It was intended that offenders would spend a period of time in Pentonville before being shipped to the colonies, but this did not satisfy those in Australia and eventually prison was the sanction that remained for serious (and not so serious) offenders. A temporary expedient (renewed in the 1990s) was the use of prison hulks moored in the Thames for offenders. The fact that conditions were appalling might not have changed the situation but the reality that 'gaol fever' could also be caught by respectable people did. Between 1847 and 1849, in addition to the 2000 prison places in Pentonville, Millbank Penitentiary and Perth Prison (in Scotland), a further five establishments were constructed to house 1200 inmates.

The Early History of the Probation Service

The probation service, legitimized in the Probation of Offenders Act 1907, was the formal vehicle for the judiciary to be able to sentence offenders to supervisory guidance. Many books have been written on the probation service (e.g., Jarvis, 1972; Page, 1973; Bochel, 1976), but they have tended to concentrate on the history as a narrative, without analysing why these changes occurred. The probation service has undergone a number of major changes and indeed this chapter is being written at a time of great uncertainty, far removed from its original quest to reclaim drunks and then to help other 'fallen souls', using police court missionaries (Jarvis, 1972, p. 3). The first missionary was appointed in 1876 and the fascinating history of the growth and development of the service highlights some of the dilemmas still facing the probation service today, including how to engage with resistant offenders.

Preparation for work as a police court missionary appeared to require a background of active church participation and temperance. One such wrote, rather amusingly:

> 'Rescue them,' said my employers, 'and the last day of every month a small cheque shall be your reward.' 'How am I to do it?' 'Here's a temperance pledge-book; take pledges.' 'But there are others.' 'Give them tracts.' 'But there are the hungry and homeless to feed.' 'Give them tracts.' 'There are the poor wantons.' 'Take them to rescue homes, and let them work out their own salvation at the wash-tubs.' (Holmes, 1900, p. 40)

Later in Holmes (1900), the author described his first day, visiting a police court and getting the full flavour of the stench of the cells, in semi-darkness; and the misery of the prisoners, where a woman could be locked up with her child awaiting the payment of her fine and the sexes were not separated before being brought into the court. All the Court staff were male. He clearly felt overwhelmed at the prospect as he described walking into Kennington Park and, once there, sat crying like a child. Many of the offenders described in the book, had drink problems and there was a major related problem of domestic violence: 'Scan the [court] list, and you will see the part drink plays in it. "Drunk and disorderly", or drunk and something else, is appended to fifty out of the sixty names on the list' (Holmes, 1900, p. 36).

A good example of the state of the art was provided, vis-à-vis the type of assistance that could be given apart from money, using the example of a woman with a drink problem and a history of violence. She had been thrown out of lodgings and a rescue home. The magistrate, having decided that prison had not helped her, discharged her to the support of the police court missionary. He decided to take her into his home and give her the support of his wife's 'gentleness and sympathy'. However, unsurprisingly, she began to drink again and became insolent, insulting his wife:

> 'I heard you insult my wife.' 'Well, what of it?' 'Don't do it again, or it will be the worse for you.' 'I am going to do it now. I want to see what you will do,' she said. 'What do you think I will do?' 'Send for a policeman, give me into custody, charge me, charge me. You are no better than the others. I should like you to do it.' 'No,' I said, 'I shall want no policeman for you. I can settle you myself, and this is how I shall do it.' I took her by the throat and gave her a good shaking. When I let go of her, she looked at me and I looked at her. I don't think she was the least bit afraid of me, but to say that she was surprised is to put it mildly.' (Holmes, 1900, p. 180)

Magistrates referred women with matrimonial problems to the police court missionaries, although Holmes complained that the law 'gave no relief or redress to husbands possessed of drunken wives' (Holmes, 1900, p. 29). A shelter for women which 'received drunken women from the police courts *free of charge* … admitted there are many discouragements' (Holmes, 1900, pp. 29–30). The Inebriates Act 1898 allowed the Courts to compulsorily detain repeat drunken offenders in special reformatories.

These police court missionaries, like Holmes, may have been compassionate, but they also had some strong beliefs about moral degeneracy. Vanstone (2004) makes a convincing case that many held eugenicist beliefs, Holmes for example writing that drunken wives (described by him as 'criminal inebriates') needed to be kept in reformatories possibly for the rest of their lives (Holmes, 1900, p. 37). He even welcomed the practice in Holland where the government had established a colony 'for the permanent segregation of these helpless people [the deaf and dumb, the cripple, the hunchback, etc.]' (Holmes, cited in Vanstone, 2004, p. 39).

Leaving work with offenders to untrained, even if well-meaning, people, clearly invited the possibility of a response, which could be described as somewhat violent. A probation officer at the time of transition from the old mission described himself as 'police court missionary, probation officer', straddling the divide between the old and the new. His first chapter, entitled 'What is a police court missionary?', provided the following description of the qualities needed to be a probation officer:

> 'He should be a twentieth century replica, in a modest degree at least, of Solomon of biblical fame, possess the patience of Job, be not too thin skinned, able to keep his temper under control … and possess sufficient courage not to quail at threats of physical violence … To all and sundry he should be a peacemaker.' (Stanton, 1935, p. 15)

Concluding on the satisfaction of being a probation officer, he lapsed into lyricism, however his prose usefully pinpointed the redemption of the probationer as the object of his intervention :

> 'As the earth breaks into loveliness at the touch of spring, when the trees send forth their leaves, and the landscape rings with the glorious songs of the feathered world making all things bright and beautiful, so the heart of the Probation Officer is filled with gladness when success in his work has been given him [sic]. It becomes a pleasure to him to know that he has been able to influence his probationers for their good, that in some small measure he has helped to rescue them from the dangers of falling into the pit of moral self-destruction and that they have found there is something better worth living for than the gratification of self's lower instincts.' (Stanton, 1935, p. 82)

The original ethos of the service, as exemplified by Holmes, was one of taking pledges. Female missionaries soon joined their male counterparts and were employed by the Church of England Temperance Society (CETS). The 1907 Probation of Offenders Act, which was heralded as a Act that would empty the prisons, did not have this result. The probation order was not a sentence in its own right but was a recognizance entered into, at court, by the offender. The Samuel Committee of 1909 recommended 'that in future legislation the term "probation" should be applied to only refer to release under supervision, and not to binding over without supervision or dismissal' (Bochel, 1976, p. 147).

One further worry of the Samuel Committee was regarding the probation order and the media, highlighting the fact that concern over the power of the media is not a recent phenomenon:

> '... it would mean an end to the appearance in newspaper reports of the phrase "dismissed under the Probation of Offenders Act" which helped to encourage in the public mind the idea that probation was equivalent to being "let-off". This "unfortunate" idea was further fostered, the committee reported, by the words of the 1907 Act which suggested that probation might be used when "it is inexpedient to inflict any punishment, or any other than a nominal punishment".' (Bochel, 1976, quoting from the Samuel Committee, p. 147)

A contemporary writer outlined the sensitivity to publicity and its ability to affect legislation:

> 'Law-making opinion is merely one part of the whole body of ideas and beliefs which prevail at a given time. We therefore naturally expect first, that alterations in the opinion which governs the province of legislation will appear in other spheres of thought and action and will be traceable in the lives of individuals, and next, that the changes of legislative opinion will turn out to be the result of the general tendencies of English or indeed European thought during a particular age.' (Dicey, 1905, p. 397)

Criticism of Dicey's hypothesis 'that public opinion equals legislation and legislation equals public opinion' (Bartrip, 1981, p. 151) focused on its tautological nature. It did not accord with the earlier notion of changing the focus of punishment by exerting 'control of the mind', rather than the body. Denney commented that the 1907 Probation of Offenders Act did not see probation taking on a central role within the criminal justice system. Rather, it was the Criminal Justice Act 1925 which created probation areas and the Probation Amendment Act 1926. May (1991) argued that this was a period of change when probation became an 'expert' within the criminal justice system, echoing the work of McWilliams who characterized distinct periods in the genesis of probation work. Denney further pointed out that probation training changed after the implementation of parole and the implementation of the Seebohm Report.

The Seebohm Report, published in 1968, recommended the formation of an 'enlarged social service department' for each local authority which would be generic to replace the old separate 'children, welfare, health, housing and education departments' (Denney, 1998, p. 13). Probation entered the mainstream of social work and the training of probation officers passed from Home Office run courses to the umbrella of the Central Council for the Education and Training in Social Work (CCETSW), alongside the much larger number of social workers being trained. The Certificate of Qualification in Social Work (CQSW) was introduced by statutory instrument in 1971 and this established social work as a discipline within higher education (Denney, 1998, p. 13).

From the Mission to Social Work with Offenders

The early stages of probation were directed at the redemption or salvation of the individual. I have been fortunate to meet Guy Clutton-Brock, the first Chief Officer of the London Probation Service, in 1936. He told me that Alexander Paterson, Head of the Prison Commission, plucked him from obscurity when he was working as an assistant governor in a borstal to take on this role. He had no preparation nor training for the task. He saw this as integrating casework-trained probation officers from university social studies courses with former missionaries. These staff had been taken over by the Home Office in 1938 from the Church of England Temperance Society (CETS). The state of the art for many probation officers at this time was to give their probationers 'five bob' and a bible and to leave them to their own devices! This marked the start of a process of centralization and the slow growth of Principal (later Chief) Officer grades. This highlights two further paradigms, *contact with offenders* and the changing nature of the *contact, communication and relationship* between main grade probation officers and their middle and senior managers.

From their religious origins (as late as 1936, CETS would only appoint practising Christians) probation officers (POs) were given social work training and had the task of helping individuals to change and cease offending. As mentioned earlier, the ethos of the service was based on 'casework'. The Criminal Justice Act 1948 stated: 'It shall be the duty of probation officers to supervise the probationers and other persons placed under their supervision and to advise, assist and befriend them' (Criminal Justice Act 1948, Schedule V).

In 1936 the Report of the Departmental Committee on the Social Services of Summary Jurisdiction was established to enquire into the administration of justice in the summary (magistrates') courts. This included the work of probation officers, actual and potential. It recognized the need for a trained probation workforce but commented that their status vis-à-vis the Bench, the Clerk, the police and others was not clearly defined. The term probation was defined as those on supervision, and not those bound over without supervision. In 1933 there were nearly 19 000 people on probation, with over 10 000 adults, but there were huge differences around the country, with indictable offences dealt with under the Probation of Offenders Act varying between 63.2 per cent and 21.2 per cent in different districts. Probation supervision varied between 43.8 per cent and 5.0 per cent, while those bound over without supervision varied from 31.6 per cent to 3.3 per cent. These variations led the report to state that more offenders should have been placed on supervision than bound over, and many sent to prison and/or borstal should have been placed on probation too. The governor of a girls' borstal in Aylesbury in 1933 stated that of 49 receptions during 1933, only 15 had had previous probation supervision.

The report blamed the variations on misunderstandings: that it was more for young offenders, that it was for first-time offenders, as set out in the Probation of First Offenders Act 1887; more worryingly, that it had become confused between case dismissal or a bind-over: 'The failure to discriminate between these methods has undoubtedly contributed to the not uncommon opinion that to be placed on probation is to be "let off" ' (Home Department, 1936, p. 43). It also commented on the lack of uniformity in what constituted a breach of recognizance. In some courts a probationer was not breached unless he reoffended rather than failing to keep to the terms of the order. This was a collection of conditions that could be included at the court's discretion: to be of good behaviour, not to associate with (named people), not to frequent (certain places), to lead an honest and industrious life, abstain from intoxicating liquor, reside at (named place), be placed under the supervision of a probation officer, receive home visits at a time fixed by the probation officer and truly answer all questions put to them with regard to their conduct, employment or residence. They could also have further particular conditions attached as appropriate.

Probation officers were recognized even at this stage as requiring trained social work skills; personality alone was not enough. Employment support was seen as significant but it needed to be suitable: 'the object of probation is the ultimate re-establishment of the probationer in the community and the probation officer must accordingly take the long view' (Home Department, 1936, p. 58). This was still a time of transition with some areas having only part-time staff who did not attend court, many also being untrained. Age-wise, many probation officers were over 65, indeed over 75 and 80 years of age. They were of both sexes and it was believed that female officers were needed to supervise women offenders. Caseloads were recommended to be 60–70 for men and less for women, but examples were given of 124 and 131. As probation expanded, bureaucracy failed to keep up, with some Benches failing to appoint Probation Committees or having ones that did not meet. Thus some probation officers complained 'that they have never met their Committees, and that they carry out their work without supervision, criticism or encouragement' (Home Department, 1936, p. 95).

In the prisons, the origins of prison welfare can be traced back to 1936, when the National Discharged Prisoners' Aid Society appointed its first welfare officer to undertake prison visiting in regional prisons. In the same year a full-time prison welfare officer was appointed to Wakefield, the regional training prison (Appleyard, 1971, p. 107). An important point regarding the relationship between the public and private sectors at this time was that the Police Court Missions and the Discharged Prisoners Aid Societies 'submitted to a considerable degree of state regulation, in return for which the state provided them both with funding and with a new kind of power over their clients, backed with the threat of imprisonment…[or] of with being compelled to report to the police' (Ryan and Ward, 1989, p. 89).

The consequence of this was the service becoming more scientifically based under the auspices of the Home Office. It is interesting to note the later replication of this as probation services, after the Criminal Justice Act 1991 (backed up with cash limits), were forced to devolve from 5–7 per cent of their budget to the voluntary and private sectors. These sectors took the money and in return had to conform in their contact with offenders to national standards contact and sharing of supervision contact information.

McWilliams, in a quartet of essays (1983, 1985, 1986, 1987), traced the history of the probation service from its evangelical roots and the desire to 'rescue' the fallen through the golden age of the 'treatment' model to today's 'managerialist' model.

The casework model held that interpersonal relationships were of unique importance (Biestek, 1961) but working on faulty relationships did not necessarily lead to lower reoffending rates. The IMPACT (Intensive Matching of Probation and After-Care Treatment) experiment was a project carried out by the Inner London Probation Service, which was evaluated by Folkard *et al* (1974). It failed to demonstrate that more intensive support to offenders would result in a lower reconviction rate. McWilliams examined the role of the probation officer in court, which described as changing from 'friend to acquaintance' and he described the importance of the Court as an independent entity, separate from the executive. One example of their power was their ability to apply pressure leading to the overturning of 'the legal requirement to suspend a sentence of imprisonment in the absence of excepting circumstances. This provision, introduced by the CJA 1967, was repealed by the CJA 1972 due to the unpopularity of the courts' (McWilliams, 1987, p. 98).

The Middle Period of Probation

The history of the probation service has been catalogued by Jarvis (1972), Page (1992) and Bochel (1976). Literature written before and during the 1960s focused on the social work (psychological) needs of offenders, for example, see King (1969) or Foren and Bailey (1968). An earlier report by the Butterworth Committee (Home Office, 1962) had stated the need to 'protect society' and 'ensure the good conduct of the probationer'. In 1958 Radzinowicz, produced a report called 'The results of probation' which gave a very positive outcome for probation supervision. For first offenders it stated the rate of success was 76.8 per cent (males) and 89.2 (females), 64.1 (boys) and 79.1 (girls). Overall for all offenders it revealed an 81.2 per cent success (non-reoffending) rate for adults and 65.7 per cent for juveniles. For those with one previous conviction the figures were 67.3 per cent and 55.3 per cent, and for those with two or more previous convictions the figures fell to 51.5 per cent and 42.1 per cent (Radzinowicz, 1958, pp. 5–7). Probation appeared to work less well after a period of imprisonment, but almost as well if given again after a first order had been completed. In 1962 (reprinted in 1966) the Report of the Departmental Committee on the Probation Service began by giving its brief as 'examin[ing] all aspects of the probation service'. Probation was described as 'the submission of an offender while at liberty to a specified period of supervision by a social caseworker who is an officer of the court: during this period the offender remains liable, if not of good conduct, to be dealt with by the court' (Home Office, 1962, p. 2).

The idea of the offender's consent was acknowledged to be 'conditional', as other sanctions were likely to be 'less congenial'. The report did not question the value of 'casework' with offenders, indeed it stated that: 'Rare sensitivity may be needed in establishing and developing this relationship'. In an acknowledgement that the background of the offender may well include social disadvantage, it continued:

> 'Failings, anxieties and problems are the outcome of diverse causes which may be understood and altered. There may, in the first place, be scope for altering external

influences by helping the individual to change his home or economic circumstances, his habits or companions. Here, although the need may sometimes be for direct material assistance, the caseworker's aim will be to encourage people to help themselves rather than be helped; to co-operate rather than obey.' (Home Office, 1962, pp. 24–25)

The report was not critical of the composition of probation committees, other than that the term of office of the chairman should be limited. It did not want a residential 'Probation College' for training officers but envisaged an apprenticeship-type model through two placements where the first was to give a general insight into the job, and the second was to be more hands on, with responsibility for supervising offenders. The link with social work was clear, as students with previous social work experience 'will, no doubt, be given responsibility from the beginning for a small caseload' (Home Office, 1962, p. 123). What is of interest is the criticism of the role of the Home Office in relation to the probation service:

> 'We have already indicated that the Home Office should, in our view, exercise a degree of control and guidance which reflects the legitimate national interest in the service. But we are satisfied that the present apparatus of control, which was devised in 1926 on the inception of probation committees, is now wholly apt for the purpose … Home Office control should serve one or both of two ends – the efficiency of the service; and the safeguarding of a substantial Exchequer interest.' (Home Office, 1962, p. 76)

Foren and Bailey (1968), in an important book, one of the few published during the period that could be used in social work training, started a chapter in the book entitled 'Casework in probation' by quoting from the 1936 Report of the Departmental Committee on the Social Services in the Courts of Summary Jurisdiction. This stated: 'The need for a trained social worker in summary courts is being more and more recognized' and led them to state that 'the probation officer is generally regarded as the social worker of the courts' (Foren and Bailey, 1968, p. 80). They made a distinction between the formal authority of the probation officer and their personal authority, which they described as 'personal prestige and influence'. They believed that 'whenever the personal aspects of the authority relationship are more marked, the formal aspects, though still present and effective, become secondary in importance … the aim must always be to strengthen the client's ego' (Foren and Bailey, 1968, p. 94).

The Incompatibility of Breaching Orders with Traditional Notions of Casework

They further stated that probation officers used the sanction of 'breach' sparingly, both because it was difficult to prove but also as they wanted to try all other methods first, so offenders were written to, visited and generally cajoled into returning to the probation office. Probation orders generally contained three requirements, in addition to the threat that a further offence would see the offender back in court to be resentenced for the offence for which they received probation: first 'to be of good behaviour and lead an honest and industrious life; second, to notify the probation officer of any change in residence or employment; third, to keep in touch with the probation officer in accordance with such instructions as may from time to time be given and in particular receive visits from the officer at their home. The ambivalence to the authority nature of the role and the interest in a psycho-therapeutic relationship was evident in the language:

> 'The necessity to report to the probation officer in accordance with his instructions may be interpreted by a client in a punitive way. It is, however, a convenient way of providing for the personal contact which is the very essence of the helping relationship … To put a little pressure on a client, or to strengthen his resolve to continue treatment can often be helpful to him…The majority [of probation officers] are probably fairly easy-going about occasional failed appointments so long as reasonable excuses are given, while others regard the attitude of the client toward reporting as a reflection of his attitude toward them both as persons and as fantasy-figures and use the resistance or dependency thus revealed as an area of emotional behaviour to be explored in the interviews themselves.' (Foren and Bailey, 1968, p. 99)

The above quotation encapsulates the 'essence' of casework, the analytic tool probation officers typically employ in their day–to-day work with offenders. King, writing at a similar time about probation practice, also described what she saw as the skill base of the caseworker. It confirmed the need to delve into the past history of the offender to bring about change:

> 'Comment by the caseworker can also help the client to see the connection between certain parts of his story which had hitherto eluded him, thus clarifying the issue and throwing fresh light on his situation, so enabling him to see it more clearly. The caseworker has learned to recognise that the problem which brings the client to his attention, or about which the client expresses most concern, may or may not be what is really troubling him but is often an expression of unsatisfied desires or unsolved conflicts.' (King, 1964, p. 66)

Without wishing to labour this point further, it is interesting to note two further books from this time, by Monger, entitled *Casework in Probation* and *Casework in After-Care* (working with prisoners and ex-prisoners). This was the apex of the ideal of 'treating' offenders, with Monger asking the rhetorical question: 'to what extent is it possible for him [the offender] to become motivated in the direction of social conformity, unless some attention is given to unconscious forces?' (Monger, 1972, p. 69). It was interesting to note, however, that probation officers wrote similar reports on offenders, whether they were casework-oriented or held a radical view that society's inequalities were largely responsible for triggering offending (Hardiker, 1977). (The antithesis to casework was to occur more than a decade later with rational choice theory when offenders were to be viewed as knowing actors fully responsible for their actions.)

From the Pessimism of 'Nothing Works' to 'What Works?'

There has been a continuing debate about the changing nature of the service in the literature for almost twenty years. Haxby (1978) discussed the possibility of a correctional service and Bottoms and McWilliams (1979) discussed a 'non-treatment paradigm' whereby offenders would report to see their probation officer, but 'treatment' would be optional. Haxby began his book by acknowledging where the probation service had moved to, in terms of ethos. The Morrison Committee in 1962 had described the probation officer as a 'professional caseworker' and had located probation practice as a specialized field within social work. In this sense there was an implication of the need to form a relationship with the offender and to use this to bring about positive change.

According to Bottoms and McWilliams, there were four aims for the probation service:

1. The provision of appropriate help for offenders.
2. The statutory supervision of offenders.
3. Diverting appropriate offenders from custodial sentences.
4. The reduction of crime.

They did not assume empirically that the successful pursuit of the first three aims would lead to the fourth being achieved (Bottoms and McWilliams, 1979, p. 168). The publication of their nontreatment paradigm was given much attention within the probation service as it replaced the 'treatment' model with a 'help' model. They reminded the service that the 1907 Probation of Offenders Act also listed the duties placed on the offender 'to visit or receive reports from the person under supervision at such reasonable intervals as may be specified in the probation order or, subject thereto, as the probation may see fit' (S.4 (a), cited in Bottoms and McWilliams, 1979, p. 175).

Thus in 1907, there was an expectation of regular supervision and it was later in the 1948 Criminal Justice Act that the treatment ethos was highlighted, with its statement of 'advise, assist and befriend'.

Harris (1996) believed that the probation service, which he described as marginal historically to the criminal justice system, and which dealt with marginal people, had a premodern approach until the 1960s when it took on responsibility for the supervision of ex-prisoners on parole licence, following the Criminal Justice Act 1967 (numbers then increased year on year). This was the exercise of *executive*, rather than *judicial*, decision-making. According to Harris, in the early 1970s, after the Criminal Justice Act 1972, the imposition of pilot projects for community service and the introduction of four day training centres, and the massive expansion of hostel places over a five-year period, these measures exerted direct control over the lifestyles of offenders and their ability to lead their lives without explicit control from the probation service. These measures were very time-consuming for the offender and a lack of cooperation from him would be immediately noticed and breach proceedings initiated. Harris located this as the time that: '*Gemeinschaft* came to an abrupt end … with the attempt of government to introduce rational planning into criminal justice generally and probation specifically' (Harris, 1996, p. 124).

In this context it is instructive to determine who are the criminals in society, and do they constitute a particular stratum of society or class? We may never know whether people are good or evil, but what is of more importance is whether people are capable of making moral judgements. To teach or coerce people to change required them to learn and obey the ethical code that underpinned morality (Bauman, 1994). In terms of the work of the probation service, historically charged with the task of redeeming the drunk and the fallen, the change from *Gemeinschaft* to *Gesellschaft* coincided with a change to targeting more serious offenders.

Martinson (1974) was famous for his statement that 'nothing works' when it came to working with offenders. His commissioned research was originally repressed; indeed, he had to go to court to get it published. He wrote 'that even if we can't "treat" offenders so as to make them do better, a great many of the programs designed to rehabilitate them at least did not make them do *worse … the implication is clear: that if we can't do more for (and to) offenders, at least we can safely do less*' (Martinson, 1974, p. 48; italics in original).

However, Martinson recanted this only five years later:

> 'On the basis of the evidence in our current study, I withdraw this conclusion. I have often said that treatment added to the networks of criminal justice is "impotent", and I withdraw this characterisation as well/ I protested at the slogan used by the media to sum up what I said – "nothing works". The press has no time for scientific quibbling and got to the heart of the matter better than I did.' (Martinson, 1979, p. 254)

'Martinson's paper is the most cited in the history of evaluation research' (Pawson and Tilley, 1997, p. 9). However, it has been described as having a 'loaded logic' with an 'impossibly stringent criterion for success … He is thus able to discount successful experiments by dint of them being "isolated" and thus producing an "inconsistent" pattern of outcomes' (Pawson and Tilley, 1997, p. 9). His work triggered an attack on conventional probation practice with a backlash against the treatment model in favour of 'just deserts' and punishment (reflected later in the 1991 Criminal Justice Act, discussed in Chapter 4).

The Professional Identity of Probation Officers

The work of the probation service should not be seen in isolation, but in the wider context of social work in general. In the late 1960s and 1970s, as social work became an important part of the 'welfarist project' so, in Britain, this approach began to experience strains 'in both its political rationality and technological utility'. Social work was associated with all that was deemed wrong with welfarism (Parton, 2000, p. 458). With the demise of welfarism, social work became marginalized in influence and this was true of the probation service within the criminal justice system.

The major confidence-raising rejoinder to the negative message of 'nothing works' occurred many years later with the cognitive approach to work with offenders. Haxby, writing in 1978, felt that this was 'a crucial time in its development' (1978, p. 15). He detailed how the management structure within the probation service had grown between 1966 and 1974 when middle managers (then assistant principals) had grown four-fold. He linked this and other events to 'encroachments upon the autonomy of the probation officer' (Haxby, 1978, p. 36) as new tasks were imposed on the service (e.g., parole was introduced in the Criminal Justice Act 1967). The major cause for this was statutory after-care which included parole licences and supervision of young people from detention centres and borstals. This involved probation officers being in contact with the Executive, for example, the Parole Board, via the Home Office, rather than the judiciary. Under the Probation Rules 1965 (and earlier Rules), the Home Office were obliged to inspect the work of probation officers. In 1968 the Probation Rules were amended to allow the task to be undertaken by the Services themselves. Thus the probation management took on an inspectorial/managerial role (see Haxby, 1978, pp. 46–47). The other important aspect of 'probation history' discussed by Haxby concerned the 'professional identity' of probation officers. In 1970 the British Association of Social Workers (BASW) was formed, incorporating seven different 'trade' organizations. The National Association of Probation Officers (NAPO), although involved in the setting up of the Standing Conference of Organizations of Social Workers in 1963, decided not to join it but rather to maintain its separate identity.

In June 1970, the membership decided by a margin of two to one not to join BASW but to maintain NAPO. Probation officers joined NAPO and/or BASW or opted out of both organizations. There was a discussion about whether NAPO was a professional organization or a trade union or both. Haxby was writing in the aftermath of the Younger Report (The Advisory Council on the Penal System: 'Young Adult Offenders'), which recommended that probation officers be given the right to have young offenders locked up for three days if they felt that they were 'at risk' of offending and a cooling off period was required. This proposal was fiercely contested by NAPO, particularly the London branch, but for Haxby it signalled the changing nature of control. He compared the requirements of the proposed 'supervision and control order' with the probation order and argued that the lack of consent for the proposed order marked a further change which 'could effect a subtle and undesirable change in the nature of the relationship between supervisor and client' (Haxby, 1978, p. 163).

Fielding, in 1984, conducted 50 interviews with probation officers of various grades which were written up into a densely argued book. This started off by putting the debate on practice into context, in a manner still pertinent today:

'As one of the earliest treatment-oriented sentences, probation had an early concern with rehabilitation. Rehabilitation has come under fire as a rightful object of the state's handling of criminal offenders … It is also under continual suspicion from another quarter, the social work establishment, for its confused posture as part of the social control system overtly operating on social casework methods while being charged with a significant control function.' (Fielding, 1984, pp. 1–2)

This suspicion of the 'social work establishment' is an interesting issue. Clearly Fielding felt there was a question to answer, whether the social work establishment (as exemplified by the Central Council for Education and Training in Social Work (CCETSW)), wanted to retain responsibility for probation training. At the time that the Home Office was considering severing the link of probation training with the Diploma in Social Work (DipSW), and it was interesting to note that 'work with offenders' was missing from the redrawing of the social work competences; the framework through which social work practice, or competence, was tested. Hurried work on this by a CCETSW adviser with probation sympathies, and a NAPO trade union official reinforced the notion that CCETSW did not want to take probation with it. Indeed, the Home Office was very dismissive of the role of CCETSW.

The Home Office and Probation: Turning the Screw

The Home Office was not heavily involved in setting priorities for probation until 1984 when it published its Statement of National Objectives and Priorities (SNOP) (Home Office, 1984). May commented: 'Nowhere was the attempt to control local variations more clear than in the 1984 SNOP for the probation services in England and Wales' (May, 1995, p. 872).

What SNOP did, for the first time, was to set central priorities for the probation service, rather than leave it to the services themselves. First, SNOP put this into a wider criminal justice context, under the heading 'Purpose, Objectives and Priorities of the Probation Service':

I 'The probation service, together with others involved in the criminal justice system, is concerned with preparing and giving effect to a planned and coordinated response to crime. It must maintain the community's confidence in its work, and contribute to the community's wider confidence that it is receiving proper protection and that the law is enforced.

II The main purpose of the Service within the criminal justice system is to provide means for the supervision in the community of those offenders for whom the courts decide that it is necessary and appropriate.' (Home Office, April 1984)

This changed the ethos from work with 'clients' in terms of their social need/inadequacy, to one of working with the courts. It introduced the idea of catering to the public in terms of maintaining its confidence (assuming it had gained this in the first place), and the notion of 'protection of the public', not incompatible with working on the needs of the offender, but a change of emphasis.

It listed the principal tasks of the service: working with the courts, supervision in the community, through-care, other work in the community. and then came the 'crunch' paragraph:

> VI In the allocation of resources towards these objectives, the following broad order of priorities should be followed:
> (a) The first priority should be to ensure that, wherever possible offenders can be dealt with by non-custodial measures and that standards of supervision are set and maintained at the level required for the purpose.
> (b) Resources should be allocated to the preparation of social enquiry reports on the basis that standards will be similarly set and maintained, but that reports will be prepared selectively in accordance with the objectives set out above.
> (c) Sufficient resources should be allocated to through-care to enable the Service's statutory obligations to be discharged (including the minimum qualifying period of parole). Beyond that, social work for offenders released from custody, important in itself, can only command the priority which is consistent with the main objective of implementing non-custodial measures for offenders who might otherwise receive custodial sentences.
> (d) The service should allocate sufficient management effort and other resources if necessary to ensure that each area probation service is making an appropriate and effective contribution to wider work in the community. The scale and pace of development will depend on local needs and the opportunities available.
> (e) The proportion of resources allocated to civil work should be contained at a level consistent with the circumstances and the foregoing priorities. (Home Office, 1984)

SNOP for the first time charged the 55 probation services with the priority of working with offenders in the community and downgrading voluntary work with prisoners and community projects. Lloyd (1986) analysed the initial individual services' responses to SNOP, in their Statements of Local Objectives and Priorities (SLOPs). He noted that they largely ignored what they had been asked to do, and they also included 'values' statements which had been absent in the SNOP document. He interpreted this as providing three main points of conflict between central government and the Home Office and local service managements. These focused on: 'the autonomy of probation officers; the control implications of taking on more serious offenders on probation and the need to respond to human plight' (Lloyd, 1986, p. 72). The reaction of the Home Office in subsequent White, Green, Blue and Peppermint (coloured) Papers was to threaten probation management with outside direct entrants and the implementation of 'cash limits' to the services to force through the proposed changes.

Probation staff lost their autonomy as managers began to dictate priorities. The ethos changed from welfare issues to 'just deserts' and punishment (Garland, 2000). In particular, prisoner resettlement ceased to be seen as a priority. This did not go down well with many chief probation officers: 'We publicly stated that the Home Office had completely got it wrong, that their lack of investment in decent through-care made after-care very much more difficult … [so] we continued to build up specialist through-care' (CPO (Chief Probation Officer) in Rutherford, 1993, p. 108). Another CPO interviewed by Rutherford explained that he tried to work with the Home Office, but this was not easy: 'what I do find difficult is the Home Office view that they know best, and how it should be done. The Home Office are determined to take a very central approach, and therefore it is much better that we work with them at it, rather than just taking what comes' (CPO in Rutherford, 1993, pp. 109–110).

The aftermath of SNOP, discussed in the next chapter, demonstrated that the Home Office, criticized back in 1962 for leaving the probation service alone, was about to take a considerable 'hands on' approach which was to change the service from being a social work, social casework agency, into being a correctional service.

Other important papers were published in November 1988, one of which, at the time, was seen as a non-event. This was the Parole System in England and Wales: Report of the Review Committee and was chaired by Lord Carlisle. It included an excellent review of the history and philosophy of parole and remission and it came to the conclusion that the system needed to be overhauled. Sentences needed to be linked more closely to the sentence passed by the judge and parole would be abolished for sentences less than four years when the offender would be released at the mid-point. Offenders serving under one year would not receive compulsory probation after-care supervision, but all longer sentences would include time on compulsory licence. It rejected the use of electronic tagging for those released from custody and wanted 'a more consistent approach to the supervision by the probation service of prisoners released on licence' (Carlisle Committee, 1988, p. 93). The report was not afraid to tackle the Home Office head-on over SNOP and the effect on probation services:

> 'It seems clear that the 1984 statement was taken by some [probation services] to reduce their commitment to working with offenders in prison. That indeed is the signal which the Statement seems designed to give. We very much regret that. Reducing the priority for work with prisoners does not seem to us to be consistent with the overall objective of preventing further offending … Establishing a rigid hierarchy between objectives in the way attempted by the 1984 Statement does not seem to us to be helpful.' (Carlisle Committee, 1988, p. 90)

'Just Deserts' and the Increase in Compulsory Supervision

The proposals in the report were included in the 1991 Criminal Justice Act. The overarching effect of the Act was two-fold. First, offenders should be sentenced in a manner commensurate with the seriousness of what they had done and second, probation became a community sentence in its own right; defendants no longer had to agree to be placed on the order. All offenders sentenced to twelve months or more in prison would have a period of time on release on licence to the probation service.

Thus offenders who had previously been seen as poor candidates for parole, such as sex offenders and other violent offenders, who received long sentences but then disappeared without compulsory oversight on discharge, would now go on to probation caseloads. The probation caseload changed from being predominantly voluntary to compulsory.

Many offenders on traditional caseloads are poor and consider themselves relatively deprived compared to most of the population (Young, 1998). This has been associated with the problem of boredom which is difficult to eradicate on a low income (Bauman, 1998). The move to an administrative criminology and crime prevention rationale fitted in with the changing political climate and a move away from explaining crime in terms of social causes (Mooney, 2000). In fact, the toughening of the response to crime became a metaphor for a number of assertions by the New Right focusing on 'the mugger, the scrounger and other folk devils...' (Blagg and Smith, 1989).

The other two papers from 1988 were the Green Paper *Punishment, Custody and the Community* (Cm 424) which set out ways in which the courts' and the public's confidence could be strengthened by more community penalties, also how existing penalties could be made tougher; and *Tackling Offending: An Action Plan* which looked at how this could be implemented and required probation services to set out their implementation plans. These included intensive probation programmes and, for inner London, the resources required were to be diverted from the After-Care Unit, which was seen as a repository of very experienced staff undertaking non-core work. It is ironic that at the time Lord Carlisle was advocating making through- and after-care a specialism, the pressures of the Action Plan forced services to cut back on these area to release resources. The result was the closure of the After-Care Unit in 1990. Lord Carlisle had visited the After-Care Unit and was impressed at the serious work it carried out with 'heavy end' offenders. This was not just my personal observation from meeting Lord Carlisle and his colleagues there, but in the report he wrote:

> 'We saw in some places the very successful way in which specialist through-care and resettlement units were operated by the local probation services … specialist units or specialist officers working in general teams do have the great advantage of giving a clear focus and priority to through-care and after-care work.' (Carlisle Committee, 1988, pp. 90–91)

The response of NAPO to Carlisle was reported in *NAPO News* in February 1989 under the subheading, 'an opportunity lost'. The thrust of the criticism was that prison sentence lengths would have to be reduced by 5 per cent for the scheme to break even on numbers in prison, while a 10 per cent reduction would reduce the population by 3600. Although Carlisle wanted the reasons for parole refusal to be given to inmates, NAPO was critical that there was not to be an appeals system. In the same monthly news bulletin, figures were given from a NACRO briefing paper 'Imprisonment in the 1980s' which demonstrated how the prison population had increased:

'Twenty-one per cent of adult men and 8 per cent of women convicted of indictable offences were imprisoned in 1987, compared with 17 per cent of men and 3 per cent of women in 1977. The average length of a prison sentence rose from 10.9 months in 1983 to 15.1 months in 1987. Four out of five people sent to prison are non-violent offenders … Twenty-one per cent had committed offences involving violence, sex or robbery … 55 per cent of males and 34 per cent of females are re-convicted within two years of release … the highest rate (80 per cent) is for 15- and 16-year-old boys leaving youth custody centres.' (*NAPO News*, Feb. 1989)

Summary

This chapter has examined how probation started as a voluntary philanthropic exercise, overseen by the Church, but as the need for greater consistency and professionalism was recognized, there was a (contested) change to a professional 'casework' probation service from its missionary roots. As Fielding (1984) commented, casework and control were not necessarily seen as compatible by all in the social work establishment, although casework was concerned with personal growth and understanding.

The probation service grew in confidence and size as the 'treatment' model began to influence the thinking of the Home Office and the service took over responsibility for prison through-care and after-care tasks. As the Home Office began, somewhat belatedly, to take an active interest in the work of the probation service, it started to set priorities for the work to be completed which were not compatible with the voluntary tradition of the service. In particular, voluntary contact with prisoners was given a very low priority.

4

The Probation Service after 1984

From Social Work to Social Control and Punishment

The Probation Task and 'Taylorism'

The first survey of how probation officers spent their time took place in 1977 and was titled the National Activity Recording Survey. In 1990 there was a second survey (National Probation Survey, NPS) of the way that the probation service managed its workload, when 25 Chief Officers and 2400 probation staff kept a log of their time. These comprised seniors, POs and unqualified assistants (PSAs). The probation services did not have a record of the time that POs spent on their different tasks (May, 1990, p. v). This type of information was essential for a 'time and motion' approach to the job tasks.

The first study was obsolete as soon as it was conducted, as it coincided with the introduction of community service. The second study had similar problems as it coincided with the implementation of the 1991 Criminal Justice Act and National Standards. In the time between the two surveys, probation caseloads had fallen and it was assumed that the service was dealing with more 'serious' offenders as the service started to move from a 'welfare' model to a 'justice' model, as the Conservative political mantra of 'punishment in the community' and 'just deserts' impacted on the probation service. In the week the survey was carried out, POs spent 23 per cent of their time supervising offenders, 15 per cent on court duty, 14 per cent on pre- and post-release work with prisoners, 11 per cent on Social Inquiry Reports (court reports produced for the judiciary to give them more personal information on offenders and why they offended, to assist them in deciding on sentencing), 8 per cent on civil work, 8 per cent on community service supervision, 3 per cent on office duty

Rehabilitating and Resettling Offenders in the Community, First Edition. Anthony H. Goodman.

and 18 per cent labelled 'other'. In hindsight, it could be seen that starting to ascertain how probation officers worked opened up the route for a Taylorist managerial intervention (whereby all work tasks are broken down into simple component parts to minimize skill requirements), the 'efficiency, economy and effectiveness' wanted by the National Audit Office (NAO) and Audit Commission (AC) (National Audit Office, 1989; Audit Commission, 1989).

The Audit Commission report looked at overhauling and 'improving' the management of the service and it entered into the jargon of tackling/challenging offending behaviour. The middle section was called 'The Service Today: In Search of a New Role'. It engaged with the new perceived scientific approach of utilising risk of custody scales, was liberally spattered with graphs to show the links between the 'level of cover' and resources, and made the point that increases in probation orders had been made against a drop in the use of fines. The final chapter was entitled 'Delivering Good Value for Money'. It was steeped in the language of performance indicators, financial management, lines of accountability and revenue proposals by the Home Office. The National Audit Office report focused on the performance of the Home Office and was critical of the limited Home Office response, believing that there was insufficient information on how 'resources [were] deployed to achieve value for money, and that targeting and priorities are reviewed accordingly' (National Audit Office, 1989, p. 2). (Raine and Willson (1993) highlighted the consequences of this, namely that the probation service responded to this pressure by adopting a more businesslike approach (as mentioned).

Punishment in the Community

The NAO report was critical of the probation response to SNOP, and made it clear that 'value for money' was important. It also commented that the Home Office was ineffective in exerting influence over individual probation services. The AC report started by stating that 'The criminal justice system is under considerable strain' (Audit Commission, 1989, p. 5). The report took the view that 'offenders are punished by giving up their free time while on probation, but at the same time they gain from the experience. So probation can satisfy the call for a just deserts approach while retaining its main objective of helping the offender' (Audit Commission, 1989, p. 20).

This could be seen as an attempt to ameliorate the pure form of a 'just deserts' model by holding on to the concept of rehabilitation when 'just deserts' implies that the punishment must be commensurate with the severity of the offence, without regard to issues of rehabilitation. Key performance indicators (KPIs) were seen as essential tools, as was the imperative to develop a Financial Management Information System (FMIS). The Home Office was mandated to take a more influential role (presumably to take control of the individual services which had chosen to ignore the injunctions in the SNOP document).

In April 1990 a Green Paper was published by the Home Office entitled *Partnership in Dealing with Offenders in the Community* (Home Office, 1990c). This was to complement the White Paper *Crime, Justice and Protecting the Public* (Home Office, 1990a) and the Green Paper *Supervision and Punishment in the Community: A Framework for Action* (Home Office, 1990b), which were both published in February 1990. The White Paper proposed a bifurcation whereby there should be 'a sharper distinction in the way the courts deal with violent and non-violent crimes' (Home Office, 1990a, p. i). The courts were required to consider probation reports before passing a custodial sentence except in 'the most serious offences', and in general the severity of the punishment should match the seriousness of the crime. Fines were to match offenders' means, and prison sentences were to follow Carlisle's recommendations. Curfews were proposed for young offenders, and parents were to take more responsibility for the actions of their children.

The Green Paper began with a number of bullet points under the heading: 'The working practices of probation officers will have to change' (Home Office, 1990b, p. iii). It is worth producing these points in full:

- probation officers are officers of the court, and must respond to the wishes of sentencers
- they must supervise orders in a way envisaged by the courts, and enforce firmly any conditions attached to orders
- in supervising offenders they must take full account of the need to protect the public
- they must gear their work towards crime prevention in its broadest sense
- they must work in closer cooperation with the police, local authorities and the rest of the community
- probation officers must see themselves less as exclusive providers of services and facilities, and more as managers of supervision programmes. They must make greater use of skills and experience of the voluntary and private sectors
- probation officers must show that they can produce results to justify the extra money being spent on the probation service. (Home Office, 1990b, p. iii)

This last paper was permeated with the language of punishment and how probation officers could administer punishment. In marketing language, if the probation services did not deliver what the courts wanted, they would go out of business. Probation managers had to be attracted from a wider field, the link with a social work qualification for them was to be broken, and the appropriateness of this in any case was questioned for all staff. The concept of empowerment is central to social work practice and depends on the experience of individuals in relation to society as a whole, and in the circumstances and conditions in which services are accessed (Barnes and Warren, 1999). The client in this case is the court, with the offender adopting a passive role, which does not allow the notion of offender empowerment to operate. Finally, cash limiting the services to force compliance was clearly spelled out. The third part of the trilogy focused on where the voluntary and private sectors could take on tasks that were previously done by the probation service, including crime prevention, tackling drugs, bail and remand information, and helping with supervision programmes, specifically job finding, help with literacy and numeracy, accommodation advice, equipping offenders with the skills they needed to avoid getting into trouble, addiction support, sport and physical activities and constructive use of leisure (Home Office, 1990c, p. 12). With regard to prisoners and ex-prisoners, it envisaged a bifurcation whereby probation officers dealt with reports and offending behaviour, and volunteers with the rest.

In 1991 the government published a peppermint-coloured paper entitled *Organizing Supervision and Punishment in the Community: A Decision Document* (Home Office, 1991). This started by stating that the government valued the probation service and would increase the resources allocated to it. Court reports were to become more important, the profile of community sentences was to be raised, and it flagged up that National Standards were to published. Carlisle's recommendations were accepted and in the wake of Lord Woolf's report on prison disturbances, so was the necessity for closer cooperation with the prison service. Partnerships for probation were to be encouraged and cash limits would be a disciplining force for compliance. The linking of public order and accountability put huge pressure on the probation service, not least because the Conservative government had a public commitment to be both tough on crime and on public-sector professionals (McLaren and Spencer, 1992).

The proposals were enacted in the 1991 Criminal Justice Act. This Act would allegedly place the probation service 'centre stage' as a community penalty enforcer. The National Association of Probation Officers produced a set of guidelines after the Act, but these were not well received by the Home Office. The guidelines sought to ameliorate the punitive aspects of National Standards, for example by stating:

> 'Be reasonable about missed appointments. They only count towards breach action if the explanation given is deemed unacceptable … A domestic crisis, a DSS problem and a myriad of other aspects of people's normal lives (never mind lives that are in difficulties) reasonably take priority over a normal appointment. The client is the best judge of what is a priority in their life.' (NAPO, undated, p. 19)

The report also stressed the anti-discriminatory aspects of practice and the need for sensitivity toward ethnic and other minorities. NAPO had been more successful than the Prison Officers Association in resisting change (Ryan and Sim, 1998). NAPO argued against 'fast-track reports' and other attempts to speed up criminal justice favoured by the Home Office and Audit Commission who saw the Courts as the client, not the offender. Many of the far-reaching aspects of the Act were overturned in the Criminal Justice Act 1993, which allowed the courts to again consider all of the offender's previous convictions when sentencing and to decide on the level of fine without being tied to set scales, according to income. Faulkner, who served in the Home Office until 1992, wrote about the 1991 Act and its implications for probation. He questioned the need for the social work qualification; rather, he felt that a multiplicity of skills was required. He saw partnerships as a major future theme for the service. He was cautious about the new managerialism, but he raised a very interesting point on complaints:

> 'The Citizen's Charter provides a wider view of public accountability with its emphasis on published information and on responsiveness to the customer, consumer or user ... It enables the customer to complain if the service is not provided to the advertised standard, but not to demand higher standards or a different kind of service, and its principles are not easily applied to criminal justice functions.' (Faulkner, 1995, pp. 67–68)

It raises the point that if the courts are the probation services' clients, where does this leave the offender? The notion of punishment and control is imposed on probation officer and offender, with limited potential for discretion. Higher standards of supervision are not wanted if the bottom line is simply one of compliance.

The first set of National Standards, implemented in 1992, forced services to take reporting much more seriously and devolve 5 per cent of their budget to the private (voluntary) sector to carry out core probation tasks. This was the start of changing probation officers from caseworkers to case managers. This could be interpreted as a move to hive off tasks to leave the probation service as a 'correctional agency' to enforce statutory orders.

Control Over Probation: The Role of Her Majesty's Inspectorate of Probation and Themed Inspections

The HM Inspectorate of Probation (HMIP) was started in 1992 with a dual role of conducting thematic reviews and inspecting individual probation services. However, it also instigated work on producing effective practice initiatives, under the theme of 'what works'. The first annual report by the chief of HMIP (HM Inspectorate of Probation, 1993b), and its initial overview, resembled a mission statement. It started with an acknowledgement that it was 'a difficult time to write a report' (1993b, 1.1) as the probation service 'must win and maintain the community's support and respect ... ineffectively supervised community penalties will increase crime costs and prison numbers' (1993b, 1.2). If this generated a suspicion that the report was addressed more to the government than to the service and the public, this was confirmed in the very next paragraph. 'It is essential that this Inspectorate and probation services generally, listen closely to what *users* of their services want from them' (1.3, my italics). It would be a very naive person who assumed that a service user referred to the offender. Rather, it was the courts, as the National Audit Office (NAO) had suggested back in 1989, that made use of probation and were therefore its primary customer, plus the government's decision to make compulsory prison after-care standard on automatic conditional release for sentences of twelve months and longer (see HM Inspectorate of Probation, 1994). The report, as well as mapping out the way that HMIP would operate, made two very important other points. First, where should the probation service be located? Certainly not in social work. 'I have already made use of the phrase *community corrections* to include probation services and all other agencies and organizations who receive public money and operate in the field of offering rehabilitation in the criminal justice system' (1.6, my italics). Second, he continued, 'This inspectorate has a role with the *voluntary and private sectors* which are expected in the future to play a greater part in the delivery of community based penalties' (1.6, my italics). Thus 'creeping' privatization was on the cards. In terms of the inspections it is useful to note the emphasis laid on statutory reporting, although 'good practice' was also emphasized.

A New Report: *Probation Services Working in Partnership: Increasing Value for Money*

The Inspectorate produced the above report in 1996 (HM Inspectorate of Probation, 1996a) which had two significant findings. First, partnerships were developing over a short period of time despite 'numerous competing demands made on probation services' (1.1). Partnership agencies apparently were very positive about these links made with probation. Second, requirements in this area laid down by the government and developed by Home Office officials 'were successful in providing a developmental framework and encouraged services to take action' (1.1). Continuing the business language, probation committees had to ensure that by April 1997 partnership plans were incorporated into local service plans to ensure value for money (VFM). Service-level agreements with partnerships, partnership data compatibility with computerization, and the fact that probation supervision plans and accordance with National Standards had still to be met if the offender was being seen by a partnership agency meant that these agencies, if they wanted probation money, had to toe the probation line on regularity of contact and record/information sharing. At this time partnerships were to have 5 per cent of the probation budget, which rose to 7 per cent by the end of 1999.

The Work of Prison Probation Departments Report

The above report, published in 1996 (HM Inspectorate of Probation, 1996b), was positive about the work of the prison department and criticism was couched in terms to make it seem minor, for example, 'It was regrettable that a number of establishments have been unable to implement fully the requirements of the National Framework for Through-Care, almost two and a half years after its publication' (2.4). It then unveiled a number of things that had failed to happen: delay in agreeing business plans between chief probation officers and prison governors, coupled with 'considerable variations in their quality' (2.4), a failure to carry out reviews in most prisons visited by the report reviewers, a lack of 'through-care policy groups' in many prisons, the 'piecemeal' implementation of sentence planning, and finally probation departments in prisons had an uncertain future after the Prison Service became a 'Next Steps' agency in April 1993 (see HM Prison Service, 1995). Instead of a firm statement that probation departments needed to know their future (size, at least), the report mentioned: 'the pressures on governors' budgets creating an atmosphere of uncertainty … and the inevitable effect of this on morale and possibly on the [probation] department's ability to recruit good staff' (2.4).

Any discussion of the state of the prison estate must consider the serious disturbances in 1990 that led to the Woolf Report. The disturbance at Manchester Prison Strangeways started on 1 April 1990 and was the largest single disturbance in the history of the English Prison Service. For the rest of that month, there was a series of disturbances in 25 other prisons. The riots were ferocious and led to loss of life. The causes of this were clearly linked to severe overcrowding, poor regimes, bad industrial relations between prison staff and prison management, and poor medical care. It was a disaster that could have been predicted; when a prison 122 years old built to hold 970 prisoners had 1625 crammed into tiny cells. The probation inspectorate did not consider the multi-problematic nature of prisons.

The report identified 'considerable difficulties' which could stop effective prison and outside probation liaison. Probation officers did not visit inmates or attend sentence planning meetings when invited; adequate notice of these meetings was not always given; many prisons were remote from the prisoners' home area and made travelling difficult (there was no comment on the implications of this for the families of prisoners); some probation services restricted probation officers from visiting due to budgetary constraints; field officers did not always communicate information into the prisons; sentence plans did not include tasks for field officers; pre-release forms about inmates' progress and/or post-release forms were not returned to the prisons or were of poor quality and hence could not help the prisons shape change for future practice. Finally, few prison probation officers were given training prior to taking up their prison probation post, and many prison probation officers were critical of this, and the isolation from the rest of the service. This was the author's experience in Holloway Prison many years earlier, of being forgotten by the service, and largely left to get on with the work.

Exercising Constant Vigilance: The Role of the Probation Service in Protecting the Public from Sex Offenders, Report (1998)

The above report (HM Inspectorate of Probation, 1998b) was completed at a time described as being 'of unprecedented public debate and concern about the dangers posed by sex offenders' (1.3). Some of this was as a result of hysteria in the media and the consequence of the 'talking up' of ways of dealing of serious offenders by Conservative and Labour politicians before the general election. In June 1996 the Conservative government produced a consultation document, 'Sentencing and Supervision of Sex Offenders', which included the proposal for a sex offenders register. After-care was going to include inter-agency cooperation, surveillance and control. This was translated into the Crime (Sentences) Act 1997, and later the 1998 Crime and Disorder Act would add to the level of control. This made a life sentence mandatory for a second serious offence (murder or attempted murder, manslaughter, wounding, or grievous bodily harm (GBH) with intent, rape, sex with a girl under 13, firearm offences, robbery, etc.). The report commented on the extension of treatment programmes, challenging offenders on the harm caused to victims. It appeared that there was a huge variation in programmes offered, and this was assumed to be a bad thing. This was probably pre-empting the later change to what are being called 'pathfinder projects'. These were evaluated during the period 2000/01 with the chosen programmes delivered, without variation, throughout England and Wales. The rationale of this is 'programme integrity'. Nash (1999) cited Worrall's concern regarding the way that sex offenders were to be worked with. They were no longer clients to believed, but were to be challenged, not within a humane social work discourse, but in a way that was dismissive of them as individuals. Multi-agency panels were to 'manage risk' on these offenders but a problem shared between professionals was not necessarily a problem minimized. Nash extended the argument to consider whether the dismissal of what had gone on before in probation, when risk was managed, might lead to the public being put *more* at risk:

> 'It is important for the probation service to keep in mind that it has a much longer tradition of working with offenders, many of whom have also posed significant risk to the public. It must run away with the idea that a programme of group work is a panacea ... Offenders are notoriously good at quickly working out what is required of them in certain situations and delivering accordingly. The good probation officer who develops a close relationship with an offender may well be in a better position to spot the trigger signs of potential danger.' (Nash, 1999, p. 67)

Two further issues raised concern for the report writers. First, the high number of prisoners being released who had not gone through a prison sex offender treatment programme (SOTP). Furthermore, when a SOTP had been provided, the link was not made to programmes in the community. Most offenders post-discharge were seen individually by the service and not in groups. Second, 'There was a surprisingly high number of community service orders made on offenders convicted of sexual offences ... three quarters involved ... indecent exposure' (HM Inspectorate of Probation, 1998b, 11.11). Because the new managerialism had led to senior staff losing their casework supervisory skills the report recognized 'there was a need for a better understanding of work with sex offenders among non-specialist SPOs' (1.20). Finally, the problem of adolescent sex offenders was raised as they appeared to fall through the net: 'it was disturbing that responsibility for tackling sexual offending for those aged under 17 was not clearly assumed by one agency, nor was there any indication of such work attracting high priority when competing for resources with other work' (3.20).

Towards Race Equality (2000)

This report (HM Inspectorate of Probation, 2000a) was completed in the aftermath of the Macpherson Report, which had been written after the murder of the black teenager Stephen Lawrence and a flawed police investigation. Macpherson, it was stated, had raised expectations by ethnic minority staff in the probation service that there would be changes. It was worrying that the Inspectorate Report found that '29 per cent of minority ethnic staff rated the quality of supervision from their line manager as unsatisfactory or poor' (p. 19) which is a very high percentage.

The report stated that 60 per cent of pre-sentence reports on white offenders and 63 per cent on Asian offenders were considered satisfactory or good, compared to only 49 per cent African/African-Caribbean offenders, with a focus on welfare rather than offence-related problems for this group. Just as worrying was that equal opportunities had been translated into 'treating everyone alike' (p. 22). This could be seen as an attempt by the Inspectorate to be even-handed but it is somewhat duplicitous. On one level the latter point acknowledged that ethnic difference exists, but when it came to report writing, notions of risk of reoffending were to be decontextualized from the life pressures and disadvantages suffered by minority ethnic individuals, so that this should not be a sympathetic consideration when it came to sentencing. Instead, linking this to notions of risk perversely raises the risk of reoffending and increases the risk of custody.

The Growth of Managerialism

McWilliams criticized the managerialist position, arguing that procedural codes and handbooks only offer a minimum standard, they relocate professional discretion up the hierarchy and they removed the spotlight from individuals (McWilliams, 1992). A major problem was that the growth in management, who did not have responsibility for carrying out the work, could create a split with those who did (Coker, 1988).

The concern of management to adopt private sector language and techniques had potential ethical consequences, according to Vanstone. 'My point is not that modern probation managers are unethical but ethics have been largely ignored as a basis for management practice' (Vanstone, 1995, p. 49). Management by objectives required outcomes consistent 'with Drucker's aims of result-achievement, cost-effectiveness and measuring the return on funds invested' (Parry-Khan, 1988, p. 9). There was also a danger of privatization to sectors of the probation service such as hostels and/or community service. This was occurring within the prison service which became a 'Next Steps' agency; certain prisons were privatized (see Ryan and Sim, 1998) and rumours circulated within the probation service.

Wade, a senior probation manager, looked at the impact of managerialist culture on the probation service with management by objectives, key performance indicators, supporting management information needs, better quality services; and inspections based on: efficiency and effectiveness, quality and effectiveness and now performance inspection programmes. She expressed concern that management was becoming efficient at carrying out tasks on behalf of others, and debates would become focused on the 'how' rather than the 'why' probation was working in a particular way. May commented that probation officers criticized their managers for the loss of social work in policy initiatives, which he attributed to 'Home Office directives … and the use of Home Office Inspectors' (May, 1995, p. 34). This was not surprising as the report by the HM Inspectorate of Probation in 1993 conveyed the stark message that 'deliberate failure by probation staff to comply [with National Standards] would lead to disciplinary action' (HM Inspectorate of Probation, 1993b, p. 10 iii).

The change of government from Conservative to Labour in 1997 which included a change in Home Secretary, from the right-wing Michael Howard, who espoused a 'prison works' philosophy, to Jack Straw, did not lessen the pressure on the probation service to demonstrate a 'toughness' towards offenders, utilizing the language of punishment. Lord Williams, Minister of State in the Home Office with responsibility for both prisons and probation, spoke at a debate at the annual general meeting of the National Association of Probation Officers in October 1998. While trumpeting a change in funding that the Labour government intended to give the probation service an extra £18 million for the financial year 1999/2000, when the Conservatives had intended to cut the service by £6 million, he indicated that the government supported the view of a recent Home Affairs Committee report:

> 'In the main the Committee's concerns are our concerns, and the report majors on ensuring the effectiveness of community punishment … The Home Affairs Committee commented that National Standards are a minimum basic set of requirements, and said that they were "alarmed" to discover that how frequently National Standards are not adhered to. They went on to observe – quite rightly – that strict enforcement of community sentences is vital if they are to represent a credible alternative to prison.' (Home Affairs Committee, 1998, p. 4)

The probation response was voiced in the comments of the new Deputy Chief Probation Officer of the Inner London (the largest) Probation Service, David Sleightholm, who provided the continuity of ethos and purpose with the previous political regime. The probation service could be the social control agency to provide half of the Labour Party mantra 'tough on crime', if not the second half of the mantra 'tough on the causes of crime': 'the public see us too much delivering services to offenders, and not enough as delivering effective punishment, control and surveillance' (Sleightholm, 1998, p. 12).

From Casework to Corrections

An increasingly tough response from the probation service would place the agency into a correctional context, not capable of creating change in offenders because of the need to ensure compliance. Althusser would have described this as a move from being part of the 'ideological state apparatus' to that of the 'repressive state apparatus'. Ward highlighted this danger in the conclusion of his edited book: 'The signs of a gathering momentum towards greater injustices are clear … a criminal justice system geared towards crime management through containment and punishment, and a Probation Service reduced to servicing community corrections will not work' (Ward, 1995, p. 309).

Harris neatly encapsulated the dilemmas: 'We are left … with the problem of a profession which strives towards sensitive individualized judgements, and which has an in-built sympathy for its "clients" being asked to manage a form of community punishment which will inevitably discretion shrinkage and increased routinization' (Harris, 1989, p. 32).

There has been a growing debate about social work values and the probation service (e.g., Nellis, 1995; Spencer, 1995; James, 1995; Williams, 1995). Other probation academics have been determined to discuss the need to practice in an anti-discriminatory manner (Denney, 1992). Nellis did not believe that there should be a link between social work, seen as too generic, and probation training. Instead he favoured 'anti-custodial', 'restorative justice' and 'community safety' as appropriate values for probation. Harris argued for the separation of 'care' from 'control' within the probation service and the reinvention of something akin to the old Police Court Mission for vulnerable offenders with welfare and 'coping' problems. The service would then be free to take on a case management role (Nellis, 1995).

There were two major reviews of probation training during the time it was linked with social work. Coleman (1989) recommended concentrating probation training into courses whose probation stream were better than the substandard ones. Dews and Watts (1994) found considerable support for the maintenance of the partnership between the probation services and the social work courses with probation streams. Both organizations appeared to have heeded the criticisms of Davies and Wright (1989) in their research on newly qualified probation officers (see Wood, 1999). Dews and Watts reported that the training had become more skills-based and probation-focused, but the political timing of the report needs to be considered, as this was at a time when both major political parties were trying to show a tough approach to law and order issues, with probation being a 'soft' target. The report was presented to the Home Secretary, Michael Howard, in September 1994, and made public in February 1995, together with a Home Office discussion paper. (For a defence of the links with social work, see Williams, 1996.)

Dews and Watts recommended removing probation from social work education and replacing it with in-house training and a higher qualification, based in higher education. The report commented that probation recruits were over-represented by women, the young, ethnic minorities (8 per cent of the intake), and the single, divorced and separated. Howard accepted the break with social work, but rejected a university qualification of any sort (for a detailed discussion of the politics of this review, including the role of the media, see Aldridge and Eadie, 1997). Thus formal links with social work training came to an end. The final debate, which I attended, revealed that neither political party was committed to continuing the link with social work, but Labour wanted to retain a professional qualification (House of Commons debate, 1995). In the Lords, a number of Conservative peers lined up to speak against the government (House of Lords, 1995). When the

Conservatives lost the general election in 1997, there was no alternative qualification in place. Although probation values continued to be debated, the original Diploma in Probation Studies was very much a skills-based qualification. It was difficult to ascertain whether Nellis's values had a place in the reconstituted probation training. Acknowledging difference is present, but predominantly the emphasis is on working to the effective practice agenda.

The qualification, a Diploma in Probation Studies (DipPS), was announced by Joyce Quinn, the incoming Minister of State in the Home Office in August 1997. In a letter dated 29 July 1997 from Joyce Quinn to the Chair of Chief POs (ACOP), she made it clear that the DipPS, to be based in higher education, must be located outside social work departments. However '[It] should include knowledge and disciplines from other faculties, such as psychology, law, criminology and so on' (Quinn, 1997). Besides demonstrating an ignorance of university structure, it was apparent that this new qualification drew on the same core theoretical base as social work, but it may not include the depth on providing the theoretical underpinning as before – the 'how' to do the probation task, rather than 'why' practice follows its particular course. Nellis argued that the qualification was not at degree level and included insufficient theory, and was too vocational. This view was challenged by Senior, who was heavily involved in the formation of the qualification (see Senior, 2000).

Harris ably summed up the terrain of the debate on the future of probation around this time: 'the Probation Service deals with far more complexity than is generally appreciated, but the agenda for the public debate today is not drawn up by the service's friends, and the debate does not do credit to an advanced European liberal democracy' (Harris, 1996, p. 133).

In terms of who set the agenda in criminal justice and contributed to the difficulties in effectively working with offenders, the role of policy makers was also seen as relevant: 'It is time that criminologists and penal reformers add[ed] government to their list of variables that make up the "social problem" of prisons and in general the machinery of discipline and punishment which includes community penalties' (Vass, 1996, p. 178).

Changes to the Influence of Probation in the Court Setting

Research by May (1995) revealed the tensions present in the probation role, if it included the notion of responsibility towards the offender to ensure 'just deserts'. Many probation areas used 'risk of custody' scales to calculate possible outcomes of court appearances, also drawing on the personal history and previous conviction(s) of the offender. He described a situation where a PO had been shocked that one of her offenders had received a prison sentence when the 'risk of custody' score had been zero. The PO had got her senior to ring the solicitor to check on whether they would be advising the offender to appeal, and was told that the police had overheard the PO discussing the appeal with the offender and had informed the magistrates, who were 'displeased'. The PO regarded this as his 'right' to do so (May, 1995, pp. 114–115). This tension between the PO and the judiciary was ignored by the Audit Commission in the report (Audit Commission, 1991) which stated that the courts were the 'customer' for the probation service, in terms of requesting pre-sentence reports and taking up probation options for offenders. This presumably left the offender as the passive recipient of whatever sanction the court decided to order. Thus both the probation officer and the offender were rendered powerless to alter events. This scenario is discussed further in Chapter 5 in the context of National Standards.

Probation, which traditionally had been the caring side of the criminal justice system, was under pressure to demonstrate that it was effective, but what this actually meant was confused (Mair, 1997a). McGuire (1995) recommended neither being punishing towards offenders nor indulgent: what was needed was constructive action, typically drawing on the cognitive-behavioural approach. The Home Office in *What Works: Reducing Reoffending Evidence-Based Practice* (1999a), gave the principles used to evaluate the pathfinder projects that would become the model throughout England and Wales for delivering all (evidence-based practice) programmes. This would become central to the way that offenders were to be worked with. Each programme had to have:

1. A clear model of change backed by research evidence (This was to include how the programme was intended to work)
2. Targeting criminogenic need (Changing factors closely linked to the offending of the participants)
3. Dosage (Amount, intensity, sequencing and spacing of intervention, related to seriousness and persistence of offending and typical participant criminogenic factors)
4. Responsivity (Methods to target criminogenic factors should be ones offenders will respond to)
5. Effective methods (Methods used in programmes should have been demonstrated to be consistently effective with offenders)
6. Skills oriented (Programmes should teach skills to make it easier to avoid criminal activities and engage successfully in legitimate ones)
7. Selection of offenders (Offenders' criminogenic needs and risk levels should be at levels targeted by the programme)
8. Case management (There had to be clear links between the programme and the overall community supervision package)
9. Monitoring and evaluation (There should be a built-in commitment to monitoring the quality of delivery and the long-term evaluation of outcomes)
10. Programme construction, manuals and change control. In order to replicate programmes, clear documentation was essential to run the programme in the manner it was designed. This had to be maintained over time.

In many ways the proposition that practice should be 'evidence-based' was hard to argue with, but it was the context that was important, rather than the decontextualized statistical power (Smith, 2000b). Smith was concerned that 'a great deal of evaluative research was not very good. Positivism must … take some of the blame for this' (2000b, p. 4). He despaired that many papers submitted to him, while he was the editor of the *British Journal of Social Work*, 'showed a preoccupation with statistical testing combined with very little understanding of what statistical tests are for and in what circumstances they are useful' (2000b, 4). His article read as a strong warning to be careful in naively believing the scientific promise of this approach.

Looking at the above ten points, issues of discrimination are absent, as offenders are atomized into their criminogenic and non-criminogenic elements, the former being the parts to be worked on. It ignored social factors, despite the research of the Home Office highlighting the influence of these. The message of young people in custody (Lyon, Dennison and Wilson, 2000) enjoys a foreword by Paul Boateng, Home Office Minister, which urged the reader to listen to what the young people had to say, and the message spelled out in the Executive Summary from the young people was that 'many had had to struggle to survive in difficult and disrupted circumstances. They talked about "rough, nasty areas" where violence, crime, drug use, unemployment and poverty were just part of everyday life' (Lyon *et al.*, 2000, p. viii). A further edited Home Office paper *Reducing Offending* (Goldblatt and Lewis, 1998) made the unsurprising discovery that risk factors for later criminal behaviour included: 'poverty and poor housing; poor parenting …; association with delinquent peers, siblings and partners; low measures of intelligence, poor school performance and persistent truancy; high levels of impulsiveness and hyperactivity; and being brought up by a criminal parent or parents' (Goldblatt and Lewis, 1998, p. 123).

The limit in the usefulness of this (rather obvious) shopping list of problems approach is exposed, as the narrative continues: 'Although we *cannot predict accurately which individual will become an offender on the basis of the risks to which they are exposed*, we do know that children exposed to multiple risks and those who engage in anti-social or criminal behaviour at an early age are more likely to end up as serious or persistent offenders' (Goldblatt and Lewis, 1998, p. 124, my italics).

The offender was damned by his personal circumstances: the more unfortunate, the more he is labelled as being at risk. The more he is targeted by the programme, the higher the level of intervention as he will have a more criminogenic level of risk. The higher risk was of failure. In the past, probation officers would take on bureaucracies like the Department of Social Security or Housing Departments, to ensure that the rights of offenders were met. This was missing from the ten points. This was also the nub of anti-discriminatory practice, to challenge racism and other issues relating to unfairness when they are exposed: 'For the Probation Service to have the right to expect its clients to assume some responsibility for their lives, it has to accept its responsibility to make interventions on behalf of those clients and stand alongside them' (Drakeford and Vanstone, 1996, p. 106).

The danger with a centrally orchestrated and tightly managed system, even allowing for Smith's concerns, that it was difficult to research the effectiveness of programmes; the needs of the individual are assumed to be dealt with by the programme. The problems are located within the offender, rather within wider society, and are therefore ignored if they require structural challenge and change.

Probation research has shown that offenders find it difficult to maintain a decision to abandon crime, and need guidance from POs, who they see as being concerned about their wellbeing (Rex, 1999). It remains to be seen whether group-work programmes, at a time when individual offenders are receiving less time with POs each month and when community orders are backed up with more punitive sanctions, will allow this concern for offenders by POs to be demonstrated. Will there still be scope for individuality by POs?

Probation and New Labour

The Labour election campaign was unprecedented as it sought to establish itself as the party to be tough on law and order and this was carried out in its practice (Brownlee, 1998b). The Labour government elected on 1 May 1997 inherited a rapidly rising prison population and the new Criminal Justice Act, The Crime (Sentences) Act 1997, which abolished automatic release from prison and parole and substituted a 'discount' system for good behaviour and cooperation. It also imposed mandatory life sentences for second convictions of a serious sexual or violent offences, and minimum sentences on third-time Class A drug offenders and domestic burglars. It allowed fine defaulters to be given community service orders and/or be electronically tagged. Thus the penal climate continued along its punitive trajectory; indeed, the Labour government implemented from the Act automatic three-year sentences for third cases of burglary.

Jack Straw, Home Secretary in the first Labour Party administration for eighteen years, continued a seamless theme with his Conservative predecessors, placing responsibility for offending firmly with offenders and having no time for 'strain theory' explanations for offending. Speaking on how to make 'prisons work', he commented that the first priority was that: 'we should be directly challenging the underlying attitudes and behaviours that propel inmates back into crime. Most offenders lack respect for themselves and others' (Straw, 1999, p. 11).

The Labour government placed on record its intention to increase the use of electronic monitoring and in 1999 there were four pilot projects with the purpose of evaluating the use of tagging to ensure compliance to curfew conditions as laid down in the Criminal Justice Act 1991, but not implemented. Paul Boateng, Minister of State at the Home Office, confirmed this in his keynote speech to Chief Probation Officers and Chairs of Probation Committees in October 1999. He commented that the 'Home Detention Curfew scheme' had started in January 1999, whereby prisoners were released on discretionary controlled release (parole). He saw this as 'an effective means of easing the transition from custody back into the community'. A more cynical response would be that tagging represented a cheap way of ensuring home confinement and a way of reassuring the public that the prisons were not being emptied in a 'soft' manner. He continued by stating that 'it provides an element of stability, which can help to disrupt offending patterns', and he hinted that this would be useful for prisoners serving sentences of under one year who were not subject to compulsory probation post-release supervision. Thus Stan Cohen's warning of the blurring of the boundary between prison and the community became more apparent. Boateng postulated about the future and had a further possibility which was not mere conjecture. He considered the use of what he described as 'reverse tagging' whereby people could be excluded from certain areas. He linked this to a 'comprehensive response to domestic violence', but it was clear that this was not the sole possibility as he continued, 'our work is at an early stage, but this is an exciting and growing area.'

The above would constitute the ultimate break with probation's social work past, with a sole concentration on reporting for its own sake. Combining police and probation resources makes twenty-four-hour supervision a 'highly accountable reality' (Harding, 2000b).

Giddens helpfully located the possibilities available in a post-traditional society, where tradition was described as the mechanism whereby disputes are settled 'between different values and ways of life' (Giddens, 1994, p. 104). In multicultural (and class) terms, it is more accurate to talk of traditional societies, each with its own culture and customs, each existing within its own space. He continued: 'Looked at analytically, there are only four ways, in any social context or society, in which clashes of values between individuals or collectives can be resolved. These are through the *embedding of tradition; disengagement* from the hostile other; *discourse* or dialogue; and *coercion* or *violence*' (Giddens, 1994, p. 105; italics in the original).

Clearly the modus operandi within criminal justice is one of embedding the values, not just of a law abiding society, but also in terms of what is defined as 'good parenting', not indulging in 'anti-social behaviour', and in ensuring the compliance of young children or else risking the imposition of 'child safety orders' (all part of the state armoury legitimized in the 1998 Crime and Disorder Act). The dominant force of the new orthodoxy entitled 'what works' is to engage with offenders in a cognitive skills way. The absolute imperative to conform to National Standards is a coercive tool aimed at ensuring compliance. Giddens stated that 'Tradition, plainly, is bound up with power, it also protects against contingency' (Giddens, 1994, p. 104).

The cognitive approach to dealing with offenders is a valid method of helping them to change, by working on the 'here and now', rather than focusing on what has happened to offenders in their past, which is the traditional psychodynamic approach. However, the overriding focus and preoccupation with reporting and the use of, and mechanical dependence on, actuarial risk assessment scales in assessing individuals decontextualizes offending, its causes, notions of fairness, oppression, indeed all the traditions of society, leaving the individual as an entity to be reprogrammed, or at least to be trained in methods designed to stop him reoffending. In an interview with Celia May, the Permanent Under-Secretary at the Home Office, David Omand, since January 1998 a career civil servant, previously Director of GCHQ and with most of his working experience in the Ministry of Defence, put across his opinion of how the probation service had to change: 'the crucial element of the [prison/probation] review centres on convincing the public that the Probation Service has a "hard edge" to its work and that a community sentence is not short-hand for "getting off scot-free"' (Omand, 1998, p. 7).

Just Deserts

In this context the White Paper of 1990, broadly translated into the Criminal Justice Act (CJA) of 1991, represented an attempt to provide an epistemological break with all previous criminal justice legislation:

> 'at the heart of the White Paper and of the 1991 Act is the idea of "desert" – that the severity of the sentence of the court should be directly related to the seriousness of the offence ... It is predicated on the idea that the level of seriousness of each offence and the severity of a particular type of sentence can be gauged accurately enough to allow some sort of scale or "hierarchy" of punishments to be established, so that punishments can be "traded", as it were, against offences of equivalent seriousness.' (Brownlee, 1998a, p. 18)

The concept of proportionality, according to Brownlee, meant that sentences like probation could no longer be considered as 'alternatives to prison', rather they needed to consider how far, for example, the community sentence represented a restriction of liberty – how punitive was the sentence when applied to the offender it referred to? All sentences of the court had to be seen in terms of their degree of punitiveness, and any rehabilitative potential had to be regarded as a bonus.

The CJA 1991 was described by Worrall as the 'culmination of Thatcherite criminal justice policy' (Worrall, 1997, p. 36), with its emphasis on just deserts. As she pointed out, within six months the pressure of the legal lobby began to tell as the judiciary objected to the curbs on their sentencing powers. As McWilliams had pointed out about earlier legislation (the Criminal Justice Act of 1967), the government backed down and the Criminial Justice Act of 1993 overturned the restriction on considering the offence and 'one other' when sentencing, so all previous convictions could be considered when looking at the seriousness of the offence. In addition, unit fines, a measure to link the level of fine with the income of the offender, was also abolished.

In 1991 the Audit Commission produced a further document on the probation service which found 'that the service continues to develop a more managerial approach. Systems to target field team activities are being widely applied and information systems are being used to support the process' (Audit Commission, 1991, p. 13). Following the Criminal Justice Act of 1991, probation became a sentence of the Court in its own right, but there was a political sensitivity towards the public view of probation. Did POs see their role as one of punishment, acting punitively towards their clients, or did they feel a state of tension between how they were supposed to act and how they actually acted? Morris posed the question concerning the central purpose of the penal system:

> 'What is it we seek to do – to reform and change them, or control them? We could do well to challenge the simplistic notion that those who commit crime deserve to be punished because they have done wrong and know that they have done so. It is more complex than that, not least because a lot may depend upon how far those who commit offences see themselves as having an obligation to behave well. Alienation, combined with a sense of anomie … is a deadly cocktail, the effects of which are likely to take more than a simple incarceration to overcome.' (Morris, 1999, p. 8)

Despite the moulding of the probation service into a vehicle satisfactory for the Conservative Home Secretaries, Michael Howard changed the status quo dramatically as he espoused the mantra that 'prison works', in his view, rather better than probation did. This was at a time when the 'nothing works' mantra was being challenged abroad by researchers evaluating probation programmes that had adopted a cognitive framework. This was the development of a new practice question, 'what works?' In Canada, Ross, Fabiano and Ewles (1988) produced research which appeared to show that their approach could change the levels of reoffending. They reported a reconviction rate for the 'cognitive approach' of 18.1 per cent, nine months after the treatment programme, compared to 47.5 per cent for a 'life skills' approach and 69.5 per cent for 'regular probation':

> 'These data provide support for the view that cognitive training can lead to a major reduction in recidivism. Support for cognitive training as an effective method in reducing the recidivism of high-risk probationers is clearly observed. This type of training can be effectively conducted by well-trained and well-supervised probation officers.' (Ross *et al.*, 1988, p. 34)

Probation and the Punitive Tendency

The fanaticism with offender reporting was manifested in the Home Affairs Committee, Third Report (July 1998) entitled *Alternatives to Prison Sentences*. This carried the threat of privatization:

> '*Strict enforcement of community sentences is vital if they are to represent a credible alternative to prison and retain the confidence of sentencers and the public. If community sentences are to be credible they must be enforced stringently. It is therefore entirely unacceptable that local probation services are, on average, taking breach action in accordance with the National Standards relating to probation orders in barely a quarter of cases. The Home Office should set a minimum target for all local probation services to comply with these standards, ensure that the Inspectorate assesses each local service on this every year and that it requires publication of the results, and take action against those which fail to meet the target. Consideration should be given to reworking the funding formula for local services to provide an incentive for services to meet this target.*' (Home Affairs Committee, 1998, para. 87, p. xxvi, italics in original)
>
> '*It is essential that offenders who breach community sentences are returned to court quickly. It is not satisfactory that warrants take so long to enforce, and command so little*

> *confidence among sentencers and probation officers. We recommend that the Home Office institutes a new target and Key Performance Indicator for police services for the time taken to execute warrants, and that it monitors the amount of time taken to do so on a force by force basis. We also recommend that civil enforcement agencies be used to execute warrants on a trial basis and that their performance be assessed against that of the police in terms of speed and cost-effectiveness.*' (Home Affairs Committee, 1998, para. 91, p. xxvii, italics in original)

These two extracts together carry a strong message about the future of probation in a rigid way. The personal circumstances of the offender competed with the threat of redundancy for, as threatened above, the service faced a cut in budget if POs did not conform.

Social Exclusion

Finer examined the implications of Britain becoming a 'stakeholder' society where society was organized for the 'paying' or 'paid up members' (Finer, 1998, p. 155). She added that 'Stakeholders want bargains, not presents … Those without stakes or *sufficient* stakes in a world where stakes are everything will not simply go away' (Finer, 1998, pp. 169–170, italics in original). Furthermore, 'Probation looks out of fashion, save maybe to the extent it can be rendered more militaristic, simplistic and punitive in style' (Finer, 1998, p. 168). Rehabilitation was a lower priority than retribution and deterrence.

Earlier research by Smith and Stewart (1998) provided examples of the 'socially excluded' offender in terms of 'deprivation, poverty, stress and personal difficulties' (Smith and Stewart, 1998, pp. 97–98). To manage these offenders the technique of offender management turned to the actuarial language of probability. Supervision is not focused on punishment or rehabilitation, but on their identification and management (Feeley and Simon, 1992).

The punitive response of the Home Affairs Select Committee failed to take into account the research that black people were (and remain) disproportionately represented in the criminal justice system and women offenders are increasingly likely to be sentenced to prison. The permanently excluded segment of society has been labelled an underclass. In America this group was largely comprised of the black and Hispanic population, living in poverty in the centre of cities. Others might be poor and unemployed, but the underclass was permanently dysfunctional, unable to assimilate, and involved in a violent culture: 'Actuarial justice invites it to be treated as a high-risk group that must be managed for the protection of the larger society' (Feeley and Simon, 1994, p. 192).

Ulrich Beck commented that 1989 was a symbolic year in history as 'the year in which the communist world fell apart' (Beck *et al.*, 1994, p. 1). As mentioned earlier, it was the year that the Audit Commission and National Audit Office publications highlighted the need for the probation service to become economic, efficient and effective; that is, start using the language and structure of managerialism. Beck coined the term 'reflexive modernization' to mean 'the possibility of a creative (self-)

destruction for an entire epoch: that of industrial society' (Beck *et al.*, 1994, p. 2). He foresaw that it was not a Marxian interpretation of a crisis of capitalism; rather, capitalism was evolving into another modernity in the wake of '… industrial society becoming obsolete. The other side of the obsolescence of the industrial society is the *emergence of the risk society*' (Beck *et al.*, 1994, p. 5, my italics)

Beck *et al.* envisaged that within this new modernity the nuclear family would become a 'rare institution'. They added:

> 'There are increasing inequalities, but class inequalities and class-consciousness have lost their central position in society … Individuals are now expected to master these risky opportunities, without being able, owing to the complexity of modern society to make the necessary decisions on a well founded and responsible basis, that is to say, considering the possible consequences.' (Beck *et al.*, 1994, p. 8)

It is in this changing arena that the evolving nature of probation practice has to be considered. The early ethos of 'advise, assist and befriend' formalized in the CJA 1948 has been put to rest and in its place is the central importance of assessing and managing issues of risk. In June 1999 the Home Office published regulations for the Diploma in Probation Studies and, in the first section entitled 'Regulatory Framework and Guidance Notes', the role of the newly qualified probation officer was articulated. This qualification took its first intake in September 1998 and the first staff qualified in July 2000. The role was stated as follows:

> 'Working effectively within a framework of statutory duties and powers and alongside other organizations, particularly those in the criminal justice and community justice systems, the probation officer seeks to protect the public, promote community safety and prevent crime by:
>
> - evaluating information in order to make assessments and providing reports, in respect of risk and other matters of concern, to those organisations using the service in both criminal and civil jurisdictions
> - managing and enforcing both orders of the court and licences
> - working directly with offenders in order to bring about changes in behaviour which reduce the impact on victims and the risk of harm to members of the community
> - managing and coordinating the contribution of other services.' (Home Office, 1999b, p. 1)

The adage to replace 'advise, assist and befriend' from this list, can be articulated along the lines of: assess risk, manage and enforce legal sanctions, change/challenge offending behaviour, be a case manager. In order to assess risk, the Home Office has utilized several different assessment programmes, including Offender Group Reconviction Scale (OGRS), a predictor of offender reconviction based solely on 'static' risks; Assessment, Case Recording and Evaluation (ACE), which covers both criminogenic and non-criminogenic needs; Level of Service Inventory – Revised (LSI-R), it consists of a total of 54 factors linked to reoffending that are used to calculate the possibility of this occuring. Her Majesty's Inspectorate of Probation produced a report in

1998 entitled *Strategies for Effective Offender Supervision*, by Andrew Underdown, as part of the HMIP 'What Works' project. Several probation areas were due to test LSI-R, a Canadian assessment instrument. The report commented:

> '[LSI-R] seeks to support structured assessment of reoffending risk and offender-related need. It is designed to inform decisions on the level of intensity of supervision and allocation to programmes and services. It was also intended for ongoing use during the course of supervision to capture changes in likelihood of reoffending during the period of probation.' (Underdown, 1998, p. 78)

Underdown reported on a number of projects operating around the country and proposed a model whereby the fully qualified probation officer as case manager oversaw cognitive skills/social skills training at the highest level of involvement. This might include behaviour therapy for self-control and self-understanding. Unqualified or lesser trained probation service officers would then supervise less risky offenders. The next layer down included providing victim awareness, input on substance abuse and other problems, such as driver re-education, citizenship and health. The next layer down concerned resolving problems/meeting offenders' needs in his family and the community, such as family support, accommodation, financial advice, access to employment, education and health provision. This model was then breached by Paul Boateng's announcement that probation officers must engage with homelessness, the bottom rung of the model, typically worked with in partnership with voluntary, not-for-profit organizations in the community: the very organizations that probation officers used to work with before being told that these offenders were not high enough risk to justify probation contact! This represented a confused set of objectives for probation officers. Were they the front-line in dealing with high-risk offenders or was their level of knowledge, experience and skills needed to work with other offenders too?

The discovery from the rough sleepers' initiative that many of the homeless were offenders brought a new spin to priorities. The problem with the above is that one cannot atomize the offender and deal with discrete bits in descending order. There is a danger that new-style workers will not have the holistic knowledge and skills of their predecessors, and practice will not prove to be effective after all.

Buzz-words from a slightly later report by Chapman and Hough (1998) were 'effective methods'; effective programmes were to be 'multi-modal' (that is, using a variety of methods to address 'criminogenic needs'). It is worth setting this out in detail as it is the essence of 'what works': group-work for 'role play, peer education, challenge and support; cognitive and interpersonal skills training, reflection on common difficulties' (Underdown, 1998, p. 14). Individual work for: high levels of 'intervention and surveillance to protect others from serious harm, reflection on some personal disclosure, self-monitoring and self-instruction training, tutoring or applying learning outcomes from group-work to personal circumstances, managing personal obstacles to programme participation.' Family work, experiential learning, drama and other therapies to work on antisocial issues, skills acquisition, cognitive and behavioural psychology, prosocial modelling (explained as offering praise/reward so that the probation officer becomes a positive role model). The interesting thing about the above is that it is not incompatible with previous practice, but it has taken on the mantle of innovation. It is heavily linked to evaluation but not to the increasingly rigid nature of supervision and sanction.

It can be seen therefore that one likely future scenario is that offenders are given an assessment of their criminogenic potential and risk to the public. This is then used to decide the type of offending behaviour group they should attend, and what services they should receive. The programmes, to ensure quality and consistency, are then delivered, without variation, ongoing further assessments are carried out to check on possible changes to criminogenic potential. As programmes are delivered to script, it is unclear whether qualified probation officers would be needed – probably not. Thus the probation role becomes one of a case manager and overseer of compliance to court orders in line with National Standards.

Feeley and Simon (1994) described the institutionalization process of actuarial justice:

> '"Supervision" consisted of monitoring levels of risk as determined by several indicators, most prominently drug testing. Moreover, with large portions of the non-incarcerated population in some of the poorest and most crime victimized communities in the country, probation, parole or some other form of community supervision are becoming a lower end cost alternative to traditional justice.' (Feeley and Simon, 1994, p. 180)

Kemshall in her book, *Risk in Probation Practice*, described the assessment of risk as the core business of the probation service and 'supplanting ideologies of need, welfare or indeed rehabilitation' (1998, p. 1). Kemshall, while acknowledging the danger on basing assessments of risk purely on clinical judgement, was also aware of the shortcoming of actuarial assessment: 'psychometric tradition of risk assessment has been criticized for failing to incorporate a social dimension into its approach' (Kemshall, 1998, p. 31).

Despite her balanced approach, which places value on both aspects, the clinical approach has fallen out of favour with policy makers. The latest assessment tool, OASys, defines the level of risk, and ensuing 'treatment programme', from a repertoire of pathfinder agreed programmes which cannot be deviated from for the sake of programme integrity. This is linked to electronic tagging in some instances and multi-agency cooperation and surveillance for heavy-end offenders. Stan Cohen in *New Society* (Cohen, 1979a) called his trilogy of articles 'How can we balance justice, guilt and tolerance?' He commented that: 'The survival of conventional criminology cannot be explained in pragmatic terms alone. It has simply not produced theories or policies which "work"' (Cohen, 1979a, p. 476). He questioned whether 'just deserts' could work within an unfair society, maintained by the penal system.

Prisons did not have to justify themselves, unlike industry: when their product (the discharged prisoner) failed, the simplistic economic reductionist argument of Scull (1977) failed on this point. Cohen foresaw the changing nature of criminal justice and increasing 'community control' although the technology then was primitive. First, blurring referred to the 'increasing invisibility of the social control apparatus.' With electronic tagging ensuring compliance to home confinement, half way in or out of prison is unclear. Hostels operating curfews act in a similar manner.

Second, widening previous alternatives to prison were in reality alternatives to other non-custodial sentences, and fines dropped as probation orders rose. After the 1991 Act combination orders of probation and community service were made when previously one or other would have been ordered. Most dramatically, first-time young offenders can be given a 'cocktail' of activities by the youth offending panels. Third, masking is the process whereby new programmes are portrayed as helpful to the offender and not intrusive, certainly to be seen as less punishing than prison. Cohen advocated a moratorium on prison building, lowering prison sentences, mediation and a wariness of 'over-zealous probation officers' and other specialists. According to Williams, 'there is a widespread understanding among those who work in the system that punishment alone will not change offenders behaviour' (1996, p. 34). These factors both advance the possibility of a schism between probation managers and front-line staff as well as undermining the potential for preventing reoffending. This is a pity, as the STOP programme, evaluated by Raynor, Smith and Vanstone (1994), appeared to show good potential for a cognitive approach which allowed probation staff to work with offenders on issues such as how to manage anger and frustration.

The Labour government viewed the future of probation as a service working to tight guidelines, where professional discretion is limited. There is a mechanistic element in how programmes to offenders are delivered and the demarcation lines between qualified and unqualified staff blurred. This is because if 'treatment' programmes are rigid and deviation is not permitted for the sake of 'programme integrity', then it follows that staff can be trained to deliver set parts. This is not just conjecture, but evidence exists of these changes. In the field of youth justice, youth offending teams have now been formed, encompassing a number of different professions, including social workers, probation officers, education, health, police and the voluntary sector. All staff are eligible to write pre-sentence reports, not just those with a social work qualification.

This 'brave new world' had not impacted on the adult offender in 1997, when a probation satisfaction survey was published, which was a random postal questionnaire of 106 probation supervisees in Dorset, which yielded 93 'useable' responses or an 88 per cent response rate (66 per cent on probation, 22 per cent on post-custody licence). The respondents appeared very positive about their probation contact:

> 'Although probation officers' ability to assist with practical problems might be limited by scarce resources, they are clearly seen as competent with family problems, and the listening aspect of counselling. They help with boredom and loneliness, and when necessary refer people on for other kinds of help. Crucially they are considered trustworthy, helping people to help themselves, and in respecting their clients helped restore damaged self-esteem.' (Ford, Pritchard and Cox, 1997, p. 57)

There is a gap between what effective practice needs for a sufficient 'dose' of probation officer time to work effectively (Chapman and Hough, 1998), and what is actually offered. This has been blamed on the structure of probation supervision

(Smith, 2000a). McClelland (2000) calculated that in 1998 offenders were being seen for about 16 minutes per week, less than half the time available in 1992. The third version of National Standards (Home Office, 2000) became operational on the first of that month and the relationship between probation officer and offender has now even less scope for discretion. Hedderman and Hough, who carried out two national audits of probation compliance to National Standards 1995 for the Association of Chief Officers of Probation, first in early 1999 and the second six months later, found increasing compliance with the Standards, which they thought should increase public confidence in the probation service. Their article 'Tightening up probation: a step too far', warned:

> 'probation officers will [not] be able to use the breach process [to remind] recalcitrant offenders … to comply with supervision. There will be more breach proceedings … when demands on the police and the courts are already injecting unacceptable delays in serving warrants and listing cases; … probation officers will … avoid using formal warnings … where a prison sentence would be disproportionate; sentencers will be denied a constructive role in monitoring the progress of probationers; … sentencers are likely to pass nugatory sentences … where a prison sentence would be disproportionate, signalling a lack of confidence in the legislation.' (Hedderman and Hough, 2000, p. 5)

Tony Leach (2000) in an article in the probation managers' journal *Vista* came closest to criticizing the current drive to standardize programmes for all offenders, attacking it on a number of fronts. Although initially articulating his ambivalence to writing at all for fear of being misinterpreted (by fellow senior managers or the Home Office?), he started by questioning what was meant by effective practice and then turned to the courts, where orders are still being made on 'welfare grounds'. He argued that as the courts (to quote an old Audit Commission report) were the legitimate 'customers' of the probation service, it was their right to do this. Second, he stated that knowledge of 'what works' was still in its early stages and the jettisoning of earlier practices was akin to putting all one's eggs in one basket. Third, the complexities and differences between offenders could be underestimated and 'offenders will be made to fit willy nilly, even if it means stretching them a bit or lopping off bits here and there' (p. 145). Fourth, social factors were being ignored especially when programmes were seen as not only necessary but also sufficient. Finally, there was a danger of 'applying the effective practice approach in a very rigid, simplistic, centralized and monolithic fashion which would shut off other legitimate goals of supervision' (p. 148).

Harding, Chief Probation Officer for the Inner London Service, gave a coded warning in his article at the start of the millennium (Harding, 2000a). He took as his starting point the 1998 document *Joining Forces to Protect the Public* and I will consider some of the key concepts in the document before returning to Harding's concerns. This document was a review of the position of the prison and probation services and was seen as necessary, as 'a system of punishment which is effective, credible and therefore commands public confidence requires both community and custodial sentences to work, and to work well together' (Home Office, 1998, 1.1). The report acknowledged that as prison governors became responsible for their budgets so the number of prison probation officers declined. In financial terms £16.7 million in 1996/97, a fall to £15.6 million in 1997/98. Numbers of prison probation officers fell from 659 at the end of 1995 to 561 at the end of 1996. The report envisaged a: 'harmonization of NVQ's (training) for both services and a harmonization of the competence framework ... Joint commissioning of competence-based training involving the identification of common priorities for both services ... A target for joint training – provisionally 5 per cent in the first place ... Senior management exchanges and cross-postings' (Home Office, 1998, 4.12).

It is at this point worth restating the remit of the prison service which is: 'Her Majesty's Prison Service serves the public by keeping in custody those committed by the courts. Our duty is to look after them with humanity and to help them lead law abiding lives in custody and after release.' This does imply fertile ground for sharing, however as the prison service corporate plan 1995–98 made clear in its strategic priorities: 'Security is our top and overriding priority' (Home Office, 1998, 4.2). Thus the harmonization of the two services was more likely to involve issues of risk management, security and control, rather than rehabilitation. There was a danger that the training base of probation officers would be downgraded to match the much shorter training of prison officers. The report looked at the name of the probation service and this is worth quoting in full:

> 'It is important that the names, language and terminology used by the services should give accurate and accessible messages about the nature and aims of their work. Where there are mismatches, changes could be useful in marking a new start, and could have indirect benefit by influence culture and behaviour. The focus here is on probation work rather than the work of the Prison Service because there is no perceived problem in the terminology used about prisons. On the probation side some of the terms used have been criticized, for example because they are associated with tolerance of crime (e.g., "probation" which can be seen as a conditional reprieve and inconsistent with "just deserts" or even a rigorous programme aimed at correcting offending behaviour) or they can be misunderstood (e.g., "community service" which sounds like a voluntary activity), or they are too esoteric to be understood outside the two services (e.g., "through-care" which sounds more associated with the "caring" services.' (Home Office, 1998, 4.14)

This long quotation needs unpicking, and is typical of how New Labour put a spin on issues and concentrated on the packaging of measures, rather than their content. Who are the people/organizations who see probation as a tolerance of crime? Who is concerned about caring? The review then produced 17 potential names (not, incidentally, the later chosen *Community Punishment and Rehabilitation Service* or even *Community Rehabilitation and Punishment Service*) which sounded sufficiently macho with connotations of corrections, control, risk management, etc. A letter sent to me at Christmas 1999 from a former probation colleague mentioned to the self-deprecation whereby probation officers referred to themselves as the 'CRAPpies service', so the name change was having a – negative – effect on morale. The confirmation on spin was confirmed with the statement that court orders should also have their name changed and '*We recommend that the public consultation process be used to test attitudes to these options*' (Home Office, 1998, 4.19, italics in original). As Ryan comments, there has been an emergence of 'powerful media monopolies' and politicians use focus groups to gather opinion, rather than listen to those who suffer most disadvantage (1999, pp. 11–12).

The prisons–probation review was not concerned with the petty persistent offender, and Harding was concerned that the two services were not united by a common and overriding ethos:

> 'the thrust of Joining Forces is unbalanced, displaying a *flawed understanding* of probation's *traditions, values and strengths* as a series of *locally based services at the hub of criminal justice* with its point of reference focusing outwards towards a complex web of connections with local communities, local authorities and the independent sector … The probation service is more at ease in understanding the community context in which crime takes place, of playing a central part in the community safety planning arrangements which are enshrined in the Crime and Disorder Act 1998 … We are, as Paul Boateng suggests, "a law enforcement agency" but one whose conceptual roots lie in community justice.' (Harding, 2000a, p. 28)

For Harding, probation's strengths lay in its local base and its ability to work in a multidisciplinary manner. It was concerned with work beyond offender supervision, namely, crime prevention, working on troubled estates, working with vulnerable offenders and partnership work with the police (which was absent from the prisons–probation review). The review therefore involved a major realignment of probation practice away from a sense of community towards being a punishment, correctional and control agency.

The *Guardian*, in an editorial entitled 'Postcode sentencing: computers cannot deliver justice' (2000) quoted from the Chief Inspector of Probation, Sir Graham Smith: 'we have relied too much on nous, instinct and feel. In the past nous has been important, but people have used it in different ways.' The editorial stated that courts, as well as having a pre-sentence report written by a probation officer, would also have a computer-generated risk prediction. According to the *Guardian* this would be based on: 'criminal record, education, training, employability, lifestyle and associates; alcohol and drug use; emotional stability, relationships, attitudes to crime, general social behaviour and *postcode*' (my italics).

The *Guardian* was uneasy at the reliance on actuarial judgement as it brought in the danger of false positives. The prediction could only place a person in a risk category or not, so a 70 per cent chance of reoffending meant that 30 per cent of the total number would not be reconvicted. The civil rights of those wrongly assessed as likely to reoffend – the 'false positives' – needed to be protected. How good and subjective was each predictor, and why should postcode be included?

They were concerned, like the Law Society, that this represented a 'serious shift in sentencing – from what an offender *has* done to what he or she *might* do.' Their conclusion was that computers could aid but not be a substitute for human discretion.

They located this in the delivery of justice. This should include the way that offenders are dealt with by the probation service and not just the courts. Humanity and a personal knowledge of the offender, with proper controls, allows for a fairer criminal justice system than could be operated by an inflexible computer system.

In 2001 a small-scale study was published (May and Wadwell, 2001) that posited a link between enforcement and reconviction rates. This worked both ways in that appropriate enforcement lowered reconviction rates and the converse was also true. However, stricter enforcement of National Standards was leading to faster breaches of orders and consequently fewer opportunities to rehabilitate the offender. Offenders breach their orders for failing to comply with its conditions, not just because they reoffend. This has been referred to as technically violating the order. So when the offender fails to attend a first appointment, he is sent a warning letter and then automatically on the second occasion he fails to attend he is taken back to court. I was told that one probation office considered offenders who were more than 15 minutes late for their appointment to have 'failed to attend'! As probation officers lost their discretion to accept reasonable explanations for failed appointments, so the breach rate rose. This did not mean that offenders were offending more, but that the system was instead becoming more inflexible.

A further Home Office report examined the impact of variations in the breach rate across the country on reconviction rates (Hearnden and Millie, 2003). Over three-quarters of those breached were reconvicted within two years. This rate was higher than those who completed orders successfully or whose orders were terminated early for good progress. Their recommendation was that there needed to be an exploration of more positive ways to engage with offenders to avoid breaches.

A growing body of research on desistence began to form around this time. Academics such as Farrall (2002, 2004), Maruna (1999, 2000, 2001) and McNeill (2002) were putting across cogent alternatives to the orthodoxy of enforcement, compliance and reliance on accredited group work programmes. As the prison population grew there was more sympathy for the new ways of engaging with offenders. Farrall's research linked stopping offending to overcoming social problems linked to accommodation, employment, etc. These were the sort of issues that traditional probation officers had constructively engaged with in their work with offenders from the beginning of the twentieth century. Maruna's analysis was more complex in a way as it focused on the personal narratives of offenders. He commented that desisting ex-offenders looked back to their early life and experiences to find a time when they were happy and positive, to find the person they wanted to be in future, in order to stop offending (Maruna, 2001). The Home Office's own research on what works showed great inconsistency in results, which made coherent conclusions difficult (Harper and Chitty, 2005). Perhaps the best-known group programme was evaluated by Raynor and Vanstone (2001) entitled the STOP programme. This was not a Home Office inspired programme, it predated this and was inspired by Raynor and Vanstone's desire to find constructive ways of engaging with offenders. They were not in favour of centralized national programmes. Their findings were mixed, with a community-sentenced group of offenders performing better than a prison-sentenced group after one year, but after two years there was no significant difference. They have been criticized (Rex, 2001) for downplaying environmental factors and focusing more on cognitive ones instead.

After the failure of the 1998 prison–probation review to produce any change there was a period of respite before the government moved to change this. In 2000 there was a new set of more punitive National Standards (see Chapter 5) and a new Act, the Criminal Justice and Court Services Act 2000, which presumed that orders that were breached would lead to custody. The 90 per cent enforcement target was measured against these tougher standards (Robinson, 2011). More significantly, this Act brought in the change to a National Probation Service with areas coterminous with the police. This came into effect at the beginning of April 2001.

In February 2001 the government published *Criminal Justice: The Way Ahead* (Home Office, 2001). It was a blueprint to force probation further down the accredited programme route by confidently announcing that probation would reduce reoffending by those under supervision by 5 per cent, to be achieved by processing 30 000 offenders through programmes by 2004, leading to 20 000 fewer offences. Community sentences were to become more flexible, with the following components: a punitive component, a reparation component, an offending behaviour component and a proceeds of crime component (Home Office, 2001, p. 42). It could only have been dreamed up by a civil servant. Five months later the Halliday report, *Making Punishments Work*, was published (Halliday, 2001) which argued that the 'just deserts' principle should be modified to make sentences tougher to reflect the offenders previous offending history. Sentences were to become more seamless, in that they could contain both custodial and community supervision elements. The 2002 Social Exclusion Unit review of resettlement highlighted nine key factors: education, employment, drug and alcohol misuse, mental and physical health, attitudes and self-control, institutionalization and life-skills, housing, financial support and debt, and family networks (Social Exclusion Unit, 2002, p. 6).

It was time for a further Act – the 2003 Criminal Justice Act and a review – the Carter Report (Carter, 2003). This Act was radical. It brought in the generic community sentence envisaged by Halliday, and made the consequences of breaches more serious as the order had to be amended in some way, and not merely by a warning or a fine.

Carter was also radical in his report, recommending that there should be a National Offender Management Service linking the prison and probation services with a single higher management, while also bringing in the concept of contestability, increasing the potential for contracting out public services to the private and voluntary sectors (Nellis and Goodman, 2009). Carter also produced an ideal figure for the size of the prison population, 80 000 (the actual figure was 86 654 as of 19 August 2012, following the serious riots in summer 2011 in London). The government accepted the report in their response, *Reducing Crime – Changing Lives* (Home Office, 2004), but as Dobson (2004), a former Chief Probation Officer and Chair of the Association of Chief Officers of Probation had pointed out, it failed to consider issues of race, gender or the level of remand prisoners.

NOMS began in spring 2004, but the Home Secretary David Blunkett lost his job in the same year and his replacement was not as preoccupied with these changes (Nellis and Goodman, 2009). In November 2005 *Restructuring Probation to Reduce Reoffending* (Home Office, 2005c) was published, with the then Home Secretary, Charles Clark, stating that this was not about cutting costs or changing staff. However, it brought in Regional Offender Managers (ROMS), who were to become the purchasers for the new Probation Trusts that had replaced Probation Boards for the national service, which had in turn replaced the old Probation Committees. Charles Clarke in turn lost his job in May 2006, to be replaced by John Reid, who made disparaging comments about his new Ministry. Sadly there were some terrible tragedies after this time when offenders under supervision went on to murder members of the public, with very negative consequences for probation.

The Home Office then produced *The NOMS Offender Management Model* (Home Office, 2005a) which painted in glowing terms the future for offender managers. Diagrams within the document looked wonderful, if somewhat unreal, and the model was to be underpinned by the C-NOMIS communication system. Sadly, C-NOMIS was an expensive fiasco and was dropped. In July 2007 the Offender Management Act was passed and in the intervening period probation areas have been turning themselves into Trusts. The future remains very uncertain and the change to a Conservative–Liberal Democrat coalition has not made the future of probation clearer. The Green Paper *Breaking the Cycle: Effective Punishment, Rehabilitation and Sentencing of Offenders* (Ministry of Justice, 2010a) was strong on rhetoric and promoted payment by results. What is interesting is the active recruitment of experienced senior criminal justice staff by the private, for profit sector. According to Doward and McVeigh (2011) GS4 has recruited the first head of NOMS and former head of the prison service, Martin Narey and his successor as head of NOMS, Phil Wheatley. They also report that Andrew Bridges, the former head of the Probation Inspectorate, has been recruited by Interserve. This is likely to be the precursor of an attempt by the private sector for prison and probation work, with the potential to cherry-pick those parts likely to maximize payment by results (see Senior, 2011).

The probation service is not in good shape. The evidence for this comes from the Ministry of Justice itself. Turley *et al.* (2011) examined *Delivering the NOMS Offender Management Model (OMM Practitioner Views from the Offender Management Community Cohort Study)*. Staff liked the idea of continuity in their work with offenders, but the pressures on resources needed to be addressed. There was a high level of staff sickness (a good indicator of low morale), a high turnover of offender managers, high caseloads, a shift towards shorter supervision, an increasing transfer of tasks to less trained probation service officers (PSOs), including Fast Delivery Reports, and a lack of supervision of cases managed by POs, which could include the highest-risk, tier 3 offenders. There was evidence that PSOs were not always sufficiently trained for these tasks. Offender managers did not always have time to discuss offenders' needs with relevant agencies when preparing pre-sentence reports or to investigate whether specific interventions were available. This had led, on occasion, to the inclusion of unsuitable requirements. Substance abuse and other problems needed to be stabilized if offending behaviour programmes were to be effective, but the correct sequencing of events did not always take place. This was also a resource question.

Finally, if end-to-end management was to work, the offender manager had to be more than a 'broker' of services. Changing offenders needed time to give face-to-face contact, support or whatever else it might be called. As the report has spelled out, all these factors impact on staff retention and, it is clear, add to the danger of more tragedies and thus increased danger to the public.

Summary

This chapter has discussed the probation service, starting in the late 1980s, when it began to engage with managerialism and 'value for money', having been inspected by the Audit Commission and the National Audit Office. The role of the probation inspectorate was considered in relation to the reports it produced and their central theme of compliance to National Standards. Vass warned, back in 1984, (Vass, 1984) that changes to the probation service should not be seen in isolation but needed to be linked to what was happening to other criminal justice agencies in terms of creating a more coercive model of justice. Political comment, both from Conservative and New Labour politicians, has sought to give probation a hard edge and to move it away from a social work base.

Finally, this chapter considered the changing penal climate from New Labour, which continued the punitive trajectory of the previous Conservative government, to the Conservative–Liberal Democrat alliance. The punitive terrain started with National Standards being tightened further to allow only one unacceptable breach of the court order, and further Criminal Justice Acts that turned the probation service into a national organization and then into a joint organization with the prison service, NOMS. Alongside structural changes, there has been a continuing preoccupation with risk, with the danger that this would override all other considerations to the extent that offenders will simply be labelled and pigeon-holed, without an opportunity to move on and change. As this book is published, there appears to be a move afoot to lessen the inflexibility of National Standards, which might enable probation staff to regain their professional discretion; but it could also be the precursor to a move to privatize the work of the service, as envisaged in the Offender Management Act. However, the government's own research on offender management does not make comfortable reading, and this will be further considered in the final chapter, Chapter 9.

5

Deconstructing National Standards for the Supervision of Offenders in the Community

Historically, until 1992 (other than some piloting of National Standards in community service), probation staff could decide how often they should meet with their (offender) clients. This meant that nationally and locally there could be significant differences in the intensity of supervision, including giving offenders 'time out' and for probation officers to use their discretion for non-attendance. There is nothing wrong in codifying minimum standards for the supervision of offenders; after all, if the offender is not seen then no work can be done with them. However, if the implementation of the standards underpins a change of ethos, then the work of staff can change dramatically. When the author practiced as a probation officer, before the introduction of any standards, it was very much left to the discretion of main grade POs to decide how often they would see their 'clients' and when they would institute breach proceedings if the offender 'disappeared'. In Chapter 3 we saw that the casework relationship could override the requirement to take action against a non-cooperating offender. This chapter will examine the implementation of National Standards, in particular the implications on the ability of the practitioner to exercise discretion and make professional decisions about the offender. It will draw on semiotic analysis.

National Standards (NS), for probation officers (POs) and social workers (SWs) in youth justice, were introduced in August 1992, two months before the 1991 Criminal Justice Act was implemented (a major piece of legislation which had profound implications for probation practice). NS 1992 (Home Office, 1992b) cost £3, with free copies being given to all probation officers. The NS was the first formal codification of standards that probation officers had to follow and represented a break from the past when the 55 probation services were allowed much more discretion by the Home Office. In March 1995 a second edition of NS was published, which had major changes from the first version. The second edition was free.

Rehabilitating and Resettling Offenders in the Community, First Edition. Anthony H. Goodman.

This chapter will initially focus on the first three pages of NS 1995 and draw comparisons with NS 1992, pages 1–5 (up to the end of NS section 1.4). The implementation of the standards was reinforced within Parliament. The Home Affairs Committee (HAC) Report commented '*Strict enforcement of community sentences is vital if they are to represent a credible alternative to prison…*' (Home Affairs Committee, 1998, xxvi, para. 87, italics in original). The report continued to say that probation services were failing to comply with National Standards 'in barely a quarter of cases'. There was a threat that probation funds should be contingent on probation officers fulfilling National Standards requirements. This chapter seeks to investigate the message contained within National Standards, both overt and within its context.

NS 1992 acknowledged that POs utilized their social work skills in their work with offenders. There was a review of probation training in 1994, which had the remit of reviewing the need for the social work qualification as a prerequisite to practice. NS 1995 were published *before* the results of the review. The Home Office *subsequently* decided to end the requirement of a social work qualification for probation officers, despite the fact that 490 out of 504 responses had wanted the status quo to be retained. NS 1995 pre-empted this change by not referring to social work at all. What is referred to constitutes the central thrust of the early part of this analysis. The two sets of NS (1992 and 1995) set the tone for all that followed. The initial emphasis in this chapter will be on these editions of NS. The subsequent NS of 2000 (revised in 2002), 2005 and 2007 will be discussed later in the chapter. The power of semiotic analysis is that it can reveal the underlying message contained within the text and its implications (within the context of NS) for workers within the system, as professional discretion became the focus of scrutiny and central direction.

Worrall commented that 'Discourse analysis is concerned with the power and the production of knowledge' (1997, p. 26). In a section entitled 'Enter discourse analysis' she added that:

> 'Punishment in the community is the ejection from the discourse of rehabilitation of any legitimate concern for the welfare of the criminal. Instead, that concern is constructed as Other – the non-legitimated programme. The personal or social welfare of the criminal is explicitly detached from, and made discursively irrelevant to, the process of preventing recidivism. Offending is a matter of choice, not something determined by circumstances, and modern rehabilitation "addresses offending behaviour" – it is not concerned with the offender's address.' (Worrall, 1997, p. 27)

Background to the Analysis

The term 'semiotics' is derived from the Greek word *sèmeion* denoting sign (Martin and Ringham, 2000). Semiotics has a premise that meaning only exists if there is difference; that is, for good to exist there has to be evil (Martin and Ringham, 2006). The 'study of signs' was founded independently by Saussure in Switzerland and

Peirce in the United States who referred respectively to semiology and semiotics (Lacey, 1998). Saussure stated that the sign is the product of the signifier and the signified. In essence, the signifier is the physical object or form in the real world and the signified is the mental picture or concept the word evokes. Understanding is learned and denotation is the identification of the sign and the words attached to the perception of the signifier. Signs may or may not be arbitrary, they may describe a sound or be onomatopoeic.

For Saussure, the description of the sign is important as he emphasized that they are constructed. He distinguished between 'langue' (the rules of the sign system) and 'parole' (the articulation of signs), so that language is the product of both langue and parole. Thus he concluded, 'The linguistic sign unites, not a thing and a name, but a concept and a sound image … the psychological imprint of the sound' (Burke, Crowley and Girvin, 2000, p. 24). Language constituted a system and was not completely arbitrary, it could change over time, which could result in a shift in the relationship between signified and signifier. There need not be a 'quality' in the signifier or in the signified: what was important was that the interpretant understood the structure of the language, there was no need for further experience beyond this. The relationship between them could be 'fundamentally arbitrary' or in Peirce's terms 'imputed' (Hawkes, 1977). Meaning therefore did not rest in individual words, but rather 'in a complex system of relationships or structures' (Martin and Ringham, 2000, p. 2).

Finally, Roland Barthes commented that the relationship between signifier and signified was not one of equality but of equivalence, united by a correlation. A bunch of roses could signify passion, thus the bunch of roses was the signifier and the passion the signified. The relationship between them produces the bunch of roses as a sign; as a signifier it is merely a horticultural entity, as a sign it is full (meaning passion, romance, and so on) (Hawkes, 1977, pp. 130–131).

The Paris School of Semiotics is concerned with the relationship between signs, and the manner in which meaning is produced by them in a text or discourse. Semiotics, according to the Paris School, allows for the representation of a model that can enable the signifying object to be decoded and its meaning to be interpreted. This is possible, since any narrative structure can be reduced to three pairs of binary opposition, namely, subject/object; sender/receiver; helper/opponent (Martin and Ringham, 2000). The Paris School posits different levels of analysis at the discursive, narrative, and deep, or abstract, levels (for a more detailed explanation of the key terms used, see Martin and Ringham, 2006).

At the discursive level, there is a 'surface' level of meaning. Specific words and grammatical structures are visible within the text and examining the vocabulary allows words to be grouped together that have a common meaning ('isotopies'). These isotopies can be compared, dominant ones discovered and their distribution within the text discussed. Oppositions can be extracted and themes discovered from the text. Grammatical features can be investigated, namely the use of active/passive and how the text is organized to reveal strategies of manipulation of the reader, such as the use of pronouns, the narrative voice, modality (wanting/having/being able to/ knowing how to), to trace the relationship between speaker/author and listener/reader.

At the narrative level, which is more general and abstract than the discursive level, 'it is the level of story grammar or surface level syntax' (Martin and Ringham, 2006, p. 9). There are two narrative models: the actantial narrative schema and the canonical narrative schema. The former accounts 'for all relationships within a story', where the subject/object is the most fundamental relationship, whereby the former goes on a quest for the latter. The helper/opponent helps or hinders the subject in his quest and in the sender/receiver relationship the sender provokes the action and turns the receiver into the subject, ready to embark on the quest.

In the canonical narrative schema, there are three tests, the qualifying test, the decisive test and the glorifying test. In the first the subject acquires the competence to carry out the planned action. The decisive test represents the principal action or event for which the subject has been preparing, typically a confrontation between the subject and anti-subject (opponent to the quest). Finally the glorifying test reveals whether the subject succeeds or fails and is rewarded or punished.

The deep or abstract level is where the fundamental values of the text are articulated and can be presented as a semiotic square. The corners of the square are opposite one another, but each term presupposes the other.

This analysis will be applied to the aforementioned versions of NS and will draw on the contemporary School of Critical Linguistics, especially the work of Fowler (1988) and Fairclough (1989, 1992), and the relationship between language and power; and the Paris School of Semiotics, and the concept of 'deep level' grammatical structures and the work of Greimas (1987). This analysis works on the premise that prose cannot have meaning without structure and opposition (e.g., good/bad). The concept of opposition is particularly significant within the context of the supervision of offenders, with the oppositions of punishment/rehabilitation, victim/offender, and so on. This type of analysis can be applied to other documents, enabling the underlying message in each text to become apparent.

The differences between the versions of NS will be highlighted. The Paris School of Semiotics, according to Martin (1995; Martin and Ringham, 2000, 2006), 'postulates the existence of three levels of meaning: the discursive level, the narrative level and the deep level' (Martin, 1995, p. 2). These three levels of meaning within the context of NS will be discussed, starting with describing the NS and putting it into context.

Context

Each version of NS was written at a significant point historically and politically. Deconstructing these versions can therefore 'unpack' the ethos of the criminal justice system at the time. The second version of NS (Home Office, 1995a) was written at a time when 'law and order' was high on the political agenda. The Home Secretary at the time, Michael Howard, had an aggressive style and a very high public profile. He introduced 'boot camps' for young offenders, raised the recommended sentence on young killers from 8 to 15 years (the Jamie Bulger case) and sacked the Director of the Prison Service. He made no secret of his desire to end the social work qualification for probation officers, and this occurred in 1995. The analysis will investigate how the changes to NS affect the public, offenders and probation staff. At the time of the implementation of the second edition of NS in an address to Chief POs, Howard commented: 'Society looks to you [the probation service] to provide punishment and public protection, but also to provide guidance and help in turning offenders away from crime' (Howard, 1996).

Was this rhetoric present in NS 1995?

The typographical layout of NS 1992 and NS 1995

Both editions of NS were produced in a soft cardboard-covered book 15 cm wide and 21 cm long, with a metal ringbinder. NS 1992 (Home Office, 1992b) included much background detail of the 1991 Criminal Justice Act and comprised 123 pages. There was a further volume published concurrently, which was a reference guide to the 1991 CJA and was of similar structure. The detail of the 1991 Criminal Justice Act was necessary as it was a fundamental break from what had gone before, as it had an underpinning ethos of 'just deserts'. In contrast, NS 1995 comprised only 64 pages. The front cover has the Royal Coat of Arms and the emblems of the Home Office (HO), Department of Health (DOH) and the Welsh Office. The title and year are enclosed in a coloured box – bright green for 1992 and purple for 1995. The 1992 edition contained the signatures of the three ministers from the relevant departments. Both versions of NS use copious amounts of emboldened sub-headings in larger type. The 1992 NS highlighted key words in emboldened italics. The 1995 edition used bold without italics, but the main print is slightly smaller, hence the words in bold are consequently far more explicitly highlighted. The 1992 NS posed some sub-headings in the form of questions, such as, 'Who are these NS for? What do NS achieve? What do NS require?' On the first page under the heading '1.1 Why National Standards?' there are four bullet points, written as incomplete sentences. The rest of the text examined is written as complete sentences. The 1995 NS, in comparison, is permeated with bullet points. Each highlighted area comprises definite assertive short statements. The text is thus written as a series of bullet points which are gathered into lists.

The discursive levels of NS 1992 and NS 1995

First, what will be uncovered is what is superficially apparent on the surface of the text, and we will then go beyond this stage. The key *lexical fields* will then be identified with a view to establishing what has been included in the text and what has been left out. A lexical field is a grouping of key words in the text which have a common denominator. In a sense the text sets out to undertake this task as it uses sub-headings and then it groups points beneath them. This is not necessarily completed accurately or logically, especially in NS 1995. It can be seen that many of the sub-headings in the text have been utilized unchanged if they are coherent, and others have been added as appropriate. In NS 1995 some of the lexical fields have been relabelled, more appropriately, in square brackets. There is a common lexical field in both editions of NS which has been entitled 'interest groups'.

The NS acts as a set of rules for probation officers (POs) to follow and for chief probation officers (CPOs) to monitor. It is intended to be used by probation management and staff and to be seen by other professionals in the criminal justice system. There is also an element designed for public consumption, namely that the standards are a public declaration of the government's attitudes towards offenders and victims. However, it is unlikely that members of the public ever saw either version of the NS. The official coat of arms on the cover gives the NS an official, indeed royal, seal of approval and adds to the solemnity of the document.

Lexical fields in NS 1992

I. Why NS?
(para. 1.1)
Response to crime
Challenging and skilful
Demanding and constructive
Strengthen supervision
Clear framework
Help offenders stay out of trouble

II. Status of NS?
(para. 1.2)
Issued by HO, DOH, Welsh Office (WO)
Services to follow standards
Inspectorates to regard attainment
Norms rather than requirements

III. Who are NS for?
[interest groups]
(para. 1.4)
POs and SWs
Probation/social services committees (employers)
Voluntary sector
Sentencers
Other criminal justice agencies/professions
Offenders/defendants other service users
General public
Central government

IV. What do NS achieve?
(para. 1.3)
Quality assurance
Accountability
Consistency
Equal opportunities
Good practice and management
Management of risk
Support to staff

V. Professionalism
(para. 1.4)
Challenging and skilful (para. 1.1)
Professional social work (para. 1.1)

VI. Assurance
Quality assurance
Use of resources

Build on *skill* of practitioners (para. 1.1.3)	Efficient, effective, accountable
Professional judgement (para. 1.1.3)	Monitoring standards
Imagination, initiative and innovation (para. 1.1.3)	Independent review
Develop good practice (para. 1.1.3)	
Fair, consistent and without discrimination (para. 1.1.3)	
Anti-discriminatory practice (1.4, equal opps)	

VII. Offenders

Restrict liberty (para. 1.1)
Mental and physical demands (para. 1.1)
Responsible members of community (para. 1.1)
Risk to public (para. 1.4)
Entitled to be treated fairly, courteously, without discrimination (para. 1.3)
Informed of their rights (para. 1.3)

It is interesting to note that 'the public' does not form a lexical field. They are recognized as having 'an important interest in the efficient use of resources, in protection from crime and in the effectiveness and results of supervision' (Home Office, 1992b, p. 3).

A number of oppositions can be postulated:

Offender	versus	Public
Good practice (p 25, lines 1–2)	versus	Unnecessary prescription
Expectations and requirements	versus	Expected norms

(this latter opposition refers to the status of NS)

Knowledge of the probation terrain reveals further oppositions:

Firm requirements	versus	Risk of breach
Conformity	versus	Breach
Discrimination	versus	Anti-discrimination

Turning to the NS 1995, the sub-headings have again been utilized from the text, some have relabelled them (more coherently) in square brackets. There is an attempt to reconstruct the lexical field 'professionalism', which was present in NS 1992 from the sub-headings, but it is difficult to show the designated tasks as professional activities.

Lexical Fields in NS 1995

I. Relevance (of NS) to:
[interest groups]
(P1–2,4)
General public
Victims of crime
Private/voluntary sector
Probation/social services committees (employers)
Sentencers and criminal justice professionals POs/SWs

II. Aims (of NS):
[sentencing outcomes]
(P2,5)
Effective punishment
Disciplined programme
Offenders to benefit others
Protect the public

Consider effect on victims

III. Role (PO and CPO):
[probation worker and service tasks]
(P2–3,6,7)
Supervise in accordance with NS
Meet the standards
Support staff
Make use of partnerships in voluntary sector
Collaboration/liaison between services
Effective complaints mechanism
Sharing information
Enforcement/breach

IV. Practice (guidelines):
[control mechanisms on POs]
(P3,8)
Clear statement of aims
Management risk/public protection
Provide for demands of courts
Specific targets/timescales
Monitoring/prioritizing workloads
Information identification
Keeping courts informed

V. Conformity (to NS)
[limits on discretion]
Exceptional circumstances (p1,3)
Professional judgement within accountability (p2,5)
Consider effect on victims (p2,5)
Punishment (p2,5)

Accordance with *each* NS (p2,6)
Basis for demonstrating accountability and achievement (p1,4)

VI. Professionalism
[PO injunctions]
Judgement within accountability (p2,5)
Framework for good practice (p1,4)

Good practice (p2,5)
Reintegrate offenders (partnership) (p3,7)
Offenders become responsible (p2,5)

VII. Partnership
(P3,7)
Use facilities/opportunities
Collaborate with other agencies
Share information (p3,8)
Private and voluntary sector partners

VIII. Punishment

Breach proceedings (p3,8:p1,4:p2,4)
Punishment (p2,5, twice in para.)
Disciplined programme (p2,4)
Action which will be taken if they [offenders] fail to comply (p2,4)

If the lexical field of probation professionalism is accepted then, from the above lexical fields, a number of oppositions can be observed:

Professional judgement	versus	Conformity
Professional	versus	Role
Professional (as a practitioner)	versus	Partnership

This author would argue that it is not possible, however, to construct a lexical field around the term 'professional'. The task does not require reflection, but adherence to procedures. The above oppositions are particularly interesting, with the reader being led to the 'common sense' viewpoint that punishment is important to give the public confidence. To this end, only in *exceptional circumstances* can NS be departed from, to be *authorized by the appropriate line manager*.

What has disappeared from the list of lexical fields, from the 1992 NS, is the one for 'offenders'. The author would argue that the attempt to recreate the field 'professionalism' fails, as NS 1995 does not engage with the skills needed to undertake the task. All links with a knowledge/skills base to complete the task have disappeared. A new lexical field, 'punishment', sets out the terrain for offenders in an explicit manner. Thus the offender and the practitioner do not have a voice in NS 1995. In addition, perhaps in consequence, the sub-heading *Practice guidelines* does not form a lexical field. They are not guidelines, rather a series of tasks for the probation service. Given that NS 1995 explicitly states that the aim of NS is 'to strengthen the supervision of offenders in the community, providing punishment and a disciplined programme for offenders…' (Home Office, 1995a, p. 2) and deviation from the rules is exceptional, there is no need for the first practice guideline which should 'include a clear statement of aims which set out the key objectives for work with offenders' (Home Office 1995a, p. 3). Clearly this is punishment!

Further oppositions can thus be postulated. The opposition attributed to public confidence can be found in NS 1995 on page 2 under the heading 'The Aims of the National Standards'. Here in the final bullet point it explicitly states that public confidence in supervision in the community will be possible if this is carried out as an 'effective punishment' (in bold in the original for emphasis). NS 1995 emphasizes the following two oppositions:

Effective punishment	versus	Rehabilitation
Work by probation service	versus	Use of voluntary sector

One interesting repositioning of names concerns the 'interest groups'. In NS 1992, under the heading 'Who are these NS for?' the list starts with 'probation staff and local authority social workers', the penultimate entry is 'general public' and it ends with 'central government', which was concerned with 'efficient, effective and accountable supervision'. In NS 1995 the list is reversed, beginning with 'the general public, including victims of crime' who should be 'offer[ed] good value for money' (Home Office, 1995a, p. 1) and *ends* with the practitioners (my emphasis). Thus the punishment ethic is being carried out on behalf of the public *including* victims of crime. The Home Office is freed from obligation to justify the shift to punishment, it is justified by 'public confidence'. In consequence any disagreement has the implied opposition:

The public versus The practitioner

The public is being influenced to believe that only by following National Standards will they be safeguarded. Probation officers and SWs must not deviate from the NS, without higher authority. The lack of mention of professional skills reduces practitioners to the level of operatives or technicians. There is no mention that other approaches might be at least as positive. Offenders are reduced to an amorphous mass. Compare this to the NS 1992 which stated, 'No two offenders are identical. It is essential that supervision takes adequate account of the individual needs and circumstances of each person' (NS 1992, p. 3). NS 1992 also stated: 'Supervision is *challenging and skilful* requiring *professional social work in the field of criminal justice*.' (NS 1992, p. 1) (emphasis in the original).

The original NS 1992 were written in a fairly chatty style, yet the official nature/formality was present in the shape of the Royal Coat of Arms, the signature of the Ministers, HO/DOH/WO logos, and the use of bold type. The NS 1995 is not chatty, but is more authoritarian. It is permeated by the auxiliary verb 'should' 'to indicate that an action is considered by the speaker to be obligatory' (Collins English Dictionary, 1991).

Textual Cohesion in NS 1992 and NS 1995

Having already considered the lexical fields within the text from 1992 and 1995 and considered oppositions, we will now consider the dominant lexical fields. In 1992 the dominant fields are 'Why NS?', which argues for the need for NS and 'professionalism'. There is a link between the two lexical fields, as the 'why' field includes much discussion on the need for a professional workforce and this theme, including reference to 'anti-discriminatory practice', recurs throughout the text. The dominant field is that the PO is a professional.

In 1995 the dominant fields are 'punishment' and 'conformity to NS'. In 1995 the field of professionalism has disappeared and the twin mandate of the lexical fields 'punishment' and 'conformity' change the PO's role to that of a technician. 'The public' does not form a lexical field, but in its name punishment is invoked, to be applied to the offender. This paradigm shift between 1992 and 1995 is neither explained nor justified.

Surface grammatical structure of NS 1992 and NS 1995

We will now examine the relationship between the reader of the text and the narrator. This will involve an examination of the communication or image created by the narrator. It follows from the premise that language is not neutral; rather, images are created by subtle manipulation, whether this is done consciously or not.

The use of the active/passive voice

The text creates an 'image' between the writer and the reader. NS 1992, as mentioned earlier, adopts a 'chatty' style. This is achieved by the posing of questions which implies a dialogue between reader and writer. The use of words like 'can' referring to restricting liberty acknowledges that NS will create demands on offenders, but it acknowledges the skills base of practitioners. In this sense the audience would appear to be the practitioners, rather than the general public. There was a charge on the book of £3, but all practitioners were given a copy. They were also trained to understand the demands that NS would make on their practice, such as time scales on seeing offenders, frequency that appointments had to be made, and so on.

The NS 1992 actively engaged with the practitioner and dealt with the public and offenders indirectly and passively. In direct contrast, NS 1995 is certainly not a dialogue. As mentioned, the use of 'should' is entirely directive. The practitioner becomes an operative. He must work with the voluntary sector, making sure this is to the benefit of others in the community. All must work to the Standards, which become the goal.

Enunciation or narrative voice

The use of pronouns

In NS 1992 there is little of a personal nature in the communication from the writer to the practitioner. Personal pronouns are not used at all. When discussing the voluntary sector it is seen as a partnership role, 'with whom' POs and SWs work. In NS 1995 the probation service '*should* make effective use of facilities and opportunities in the community' (Home Office, 1995a, p. 3) (my emphasis added). Probation services are thus commanded to work with the voluntary sector. National Standards 1995 is a list of 'should' commands and thus forms a quasi-legal document, although it has no legal backing. It seeks to be read as a legal document. It cannot be disputed by POs other than by approaching service management, but this is to be the exception, not the rule. 'The standards establish a clear and consistent framework, within which work can be viewed and decisions justified' (Home Office, 1995a, p. 3). This is the voice of authority *par excellence*.

Types of speech in NS 1992 and NS 1995

The public is not given a voice, but sanctions are invoked in its name in NS 1995. This is particularly true for victims. The public, it asserts, can (only) have confidence if 'supervision in the community is an *effective punishment* and a means to help offenders become responsible members of the community' (Home Office, 1995a, p. 2, emphasis in the original). The second half of the quotation is tautological, leaving the issue of punishment as a given fact. The text is devoid of quotations. NS 1995 utilizes the extensive use of bullet points, which affects the perception of the text. There is no temporal sense to the text but other devices are used, such as extensive amphora – the words 'by', 'should' and 'include' are used repeatedly in the bullet points in NS 1995. This device is used once in NS 1992, when discussing the 'objective of NS' (p. 1). Repetition is a useful device to highlight an issue or concern. In this case it reinforces the authoritarian nature of NS 1995.

Modality in NS 1992 and NS 1995

This refers to the commitment of the narrator to the text. In NS 1992, the narrator acknowledges the skills of the practitioners. There is therefore no attempt to force the Standards on the practitioner as a doctrine. 'It should be emphasized that the standards seek to encourage good practice but avoid unnecessary prescription' (NS 1992, p. 2). In contrast, the NS 1995 demonstrate *absolute* modality. There is no uncertainty, no deviation as a principle. It is an authoritarian piece of prose, '*professional judgement*' can be used but within the context of '*accountability*' (Home Office, 1995a, p. 2). It is a brave practitioner who would put himself out on a limb on behalf of the offender. This has implications for oppositions – is the supervisor on the side of the offender or the public? The practitioner is thus dominated by the narrator. The authoritarian nature of the text becomes clearer on repeated reading. The aims of NS *will* be carried out. The guidelines *will* achieve their purpose. In reality there are strategies for subverting these categorical modalities but these will not be considered here.

Fairclough commented that, 'Modality is to do with speaker or writer authority' (1989, p. 126). He distinguished between 'the authority of one participant in relation to others' (Fairclough, 1989, p. 126). As can be seen from the above, relational modality is strictly hierarchical in NS 1995, which is a major change from NS 1992, when authority was shared. The second area he called expressive modality which he described as 'the modality of the speaker/writer's evaluation of truth' (Fairclough, 1989, pp. 126–127). In the example of NS 1995 there is the categorical assertion that 'the public' wishes to see offenders punished. The reality is more complex than this and this view is not supported by research findings. The 'public' has been hijacked by the politicians.

The use of active/passive voice in NS 1992 and NS 1995

In NS 1992 the role of the PO is an active one, for example, 'supervision is challenging and skilful'. By NS 1995 this has changed to a passive voice, when 'in exceptional circumstances' the PO wishes to depart from NS 'this should be authorized by the appropriate line manager'. This passivity reflects the loss of power and autonomy. In general NS injunctions are active and the officials involved have a passive response which outlines how they will meet the NS. It is a device to disempower and depersonalize not just the practitioners but also Chief Officers and Probation and Social Services Committees, in essence the employers of POs and SWs.

In 1992 the '*general public*, including victims of crime', are attributed with the active 'interest in the efficient use of resources, in protection from crime and in the effectiveness and results of supervision.' (NS 1992, p. 3, emphasis in the original). In 1995 the '*general public, including the victims of crime*', are given a passive role: 'who should be protected from further offending by effective supervision which offers good value for money and given accurate information about what the supervision entails' (Home Office, 1995a, p. 1). Note that the emphasis in italics now includes the victims – an important political consideration is to be seen as being concerned with this group. It is interesting to note the fiction here. The public, including victims of crime, do *not* receive information about what supervision comprises, although some victims might be consulted before offenders are released on parole. In any case, information about supervision does not equate with power.

Cohesive markers in NS 1992 and NS 1995

For Halliday (1973), language was a system for understanding meaning. He distinguished between cohesion and coherence, where the former is concerned with the explicit links within the text and the latter with the implicit. Here readers will draw on their assumptions about what is written based on their existing knowledge of the subject of the text. Utilizing this concept of Halliday's, we will now consider how the sentences, clauses and paragraphs are linked together. In NS 1992 there is a causal rationality to the text which poses a number of questions about the *raison d'être* of NS. It utilizes questioning statements: what, who, why to ask basic questions (dialogue with the reader). The professionals in the system are foregrounded to give an impression of authority. It draws on managerial terms: 'efficient, effective and accountable; quality assurance, consistency, good management' to give a scientific or specialized foregrounding to the achievement of NS.

In NS 1995, causality is expressed categorically. The device of anaphora is employed to constantly refer back to the NS. The extensive use of bullet points leads to the conjunctions 'by', 'should' and 'include', reinforcing the dominance of NS. The managerialism of NS 1992 is replaced by management/accountancy terms: 'provide for level of demand, information to identify trends, quantify costs, order priorities, monitor outcomes, control expenditure'. This again reinforces the passivity of probation management. The 'ends' are given, the task is to utilize the 'means' as efficiently as possible to meet the laid down objectives.

The narrative level of NS 1992 and NS 1995

We will now progress from the discursive level and turn to the more general/abstract narrative level. According to the Paris School of Semiotics this underpins all discourse (Martin, 1995, p. 9).

The text can be viewed as a quest to achieve a goal or object. This supposes that there is a subject who will attempt to perform an action to achieve the object.

In NS 1992 the subject is the offender and the object is to stop the offender from reoffending. The helper is the PO/SW and the opponent could be perceived as, for example, the criminal subculture and/or addiction(s) or other elements which prevent the object from being achieved. The sender on the quest is the courts who issue the 'contract' injunction to change, by placing the offender on some form of court order. The offender becomes a receiver when he receives a court sentence that places him in formal contact with the helper. Pictorially this would look as follows:

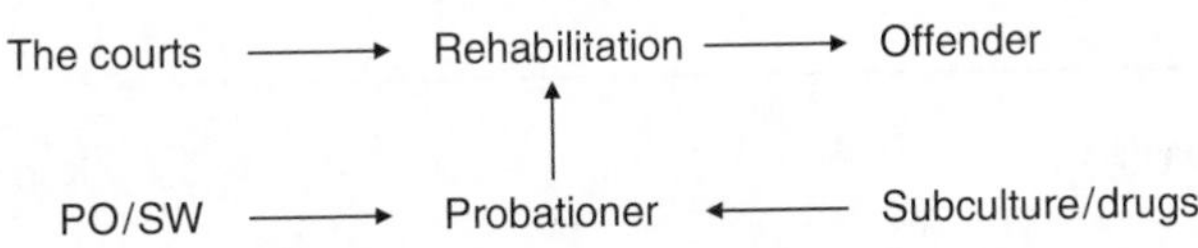

There could be 'anti-subjects' who actively try to prevent the probationer from achieving her quest. The 'qualifying test' is whether the offender stays out of trouble during the period of the court order ('stage of performance'), which involves dissonance between the subject and the anti-subject(s). Finally there is the 'glorifying test' where the outcome of the quest is decided – it may be the successful completion of the court order or failure either through reoffending or breach for failing to comply with the conditions of the court order.

In NS 1995, the actantial schema has changed dramatically, to the following:

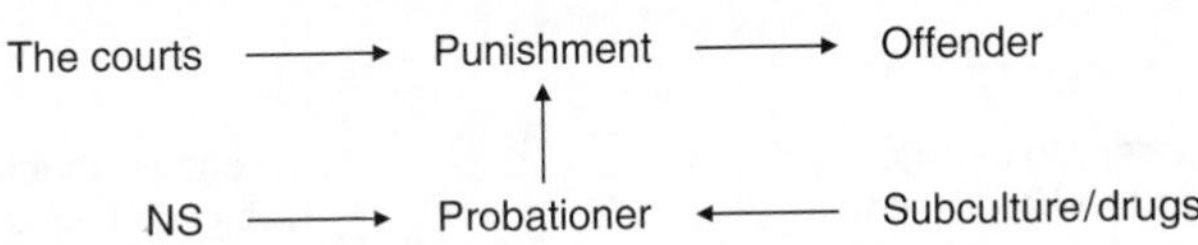

NS gives the task of ensuring that the probationer is punished. The opponent to this remains potentially the subculture/drugs as before, but may now include the PO/SW. The goal of the PO/SW from their training has been to rehabilitate the offender but not to punish per se. The PO/SW could be perceived as an anti-subject. This implies strategies to subvert punishment would be carried out while other quests are performed. Punishment (undefined) could be interpreted as the time taken to visit the PO in their office. Why should punishment and rehabilitation be synonymous?

The semiotic square of NS 1992 and NS 1995

The semiotic square is the elementary structure of meaning. It is the visible representation of the oppositions embedded in the text and represents the deep (third) level of the text postulated by the Paris School of Semiotics. Pictorially it is shown below:

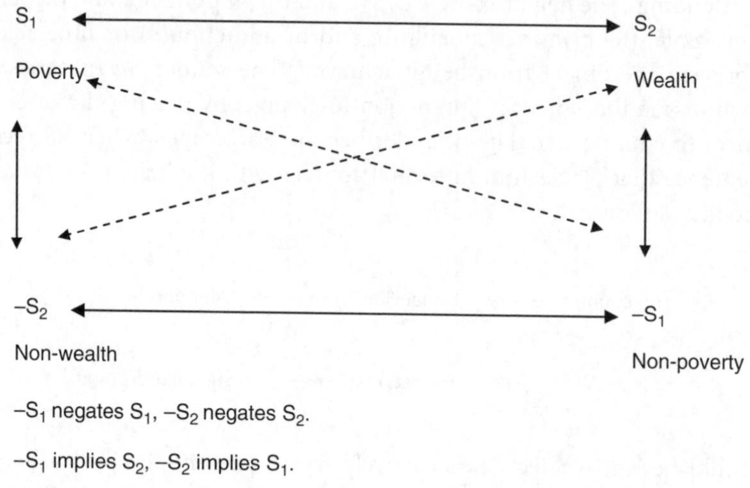

It can be seen that S_1 and S_2 are in a state of opposition. The existence of poverty assumes the reality of wealth.

Applying the above logic to NS 1992, my value judgement is that the principal opposition is between the public and the offender. This implies the risk to the public of reoffending and the desire to see the offender rehabilitated. This can be shown as:

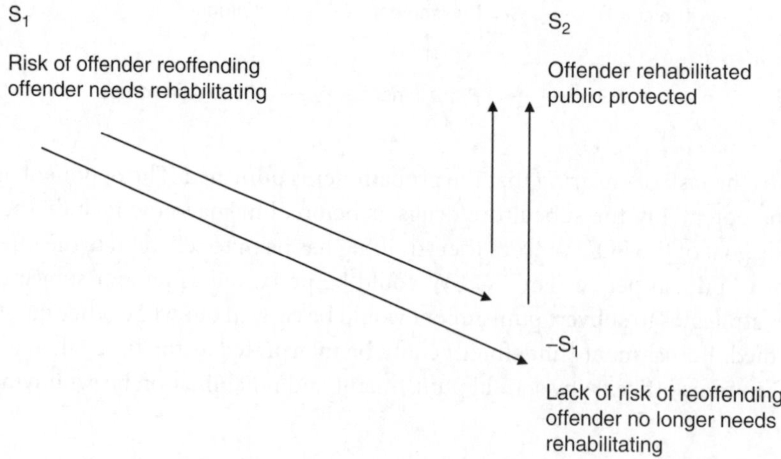

This equates with traditional notions of rehabilitation.

Moving to NS 1995, the semiotic square changes and the process of manipulation is revealed:

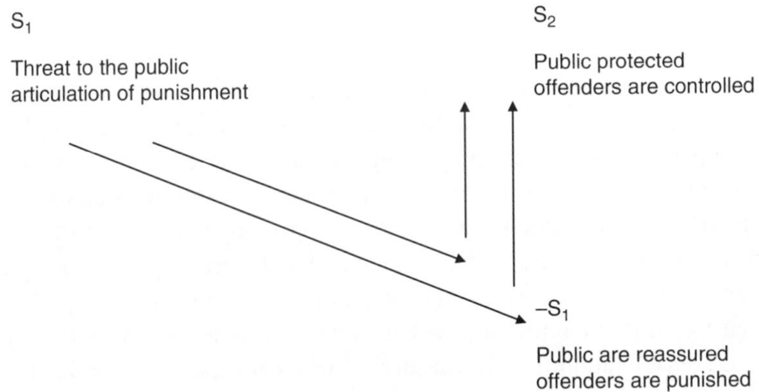

This equates with the need for NS to control POs to deliver punishment.

Commentary

Fairclough commented:

> 'Discourse technologies establish a close connection between knowledge and discourse, and power. They are designed and refined on the basis of the anticipated effects of even the finest details of linguistic choices in vocabulary, grammar, intonation, organisation of dialogue, and so forth...They bring about discursive change through conscious design.' (1992, p. 216)

There is evidence of a paradigm shift in the National Standards from 1992 to 1995. This shift is from reformation to punishment. There is also evidence that there has been a shift in power from the implementers of National Standards to the Home Office. A further target of the NS rhetoric is the public.

The debate about NS needs to be well informed. NS 1995 is one-dimensional and does not offer constructive advice to POs/SWs. It fails to acknowledge that work with offenders is challenging and requires more than just punishment. This was present in NS 1992. The move to NS 1995, according to the rhetoric, has turned POs/SWs into, at best, technicians and, at worst, into subversive operators as far as NS is concerned. If punishment really is meant to imply restriction of liberty, then the language should be adjusted to take account of this, otherwise the public as well as workers in the criminal justice system will be working on different paradigms. The message from the HAC (1998) report is depressing: POs to lose any discretion in interpreting NS, and the courts to be given even more sentencing options:

> '*We recommend that the Home Office introduce an increased range of options for sentencers to use where offenders breach community sentences to use where offenders breach community sentences and which, once imposed would allow the resumption of the community sentence*.' (Home Affairs Committee, 1998, xxviii, para. 97, italics in original)

Historically, alternatives to prison are used in place of other alternatives, not instead of prison. Offenders on community sentences have not committed an offence 'so serious' that only a prison sentence can be justified. The only weapon left in the noncustodial armoury, after probation and community service, is home curfew. The implication is probation supervision and electronic tagging, increasing the level of penal sanction and potential of failure, whatever the personal circumstances of the offender, who may well be striving to keep to the terms of supervision, with the approval of their PO. The irony is that the report rejected the possibility of increasing the prison population, placing its faith in probation, NS and the mantra of 'what works'. Recent research by Mair (2011) has indeed found that community sentences have become more punitive, with less emphasis on rehabilitation. This is considered further at the end of this chapter.

National Standards 2000

The third version of National Standards was produced to start on 1 April 2000. It is a (regal) purple-coloured A4 loose-leaf binder with the words 'Home Office', with its emblem, in the top left-hand corner. In the centre of the cover is written 'National Standards for the supervision of offenders in the community', with '2000' in large numbers in the background. Opening the cover reveals a quotation set out as follows:

> 'WE ARE A LAW ENFORCEMENT AGENCY.
> It's what we are. It's what we do.'
> Paul Boateng, Minister for Prisons and Probation

These Standards are not addressed to the public or victims, but are the means by which the Probation Inspectorate will evaluate services' performance. They are to be adhered to except in exceptional circumstances, when full reasons, endorsed by the PO's line manager, must be entered into the offender's file, by the manager, not the PO. On 30 March 2000, one day before implementation, 'Probation Circular 24/00 Guidance on Enforcement of Orders under National Standards 2000' (Probation Circular, 2005) was published. This did not give the services time to prepare for the changes. The Circular to the Standards contained a number of mixed messages. There was a new 'Yellow/Red Letter Warning System' – presumably the analogy with football referee cards was understandable to the Home Secretary and other (male) officials and viewed as understandable to all offenders. Warning letters to offenders had to be in yellow/red, or have yellow/red stickers on. The problem was that as the new Standards only allowed one missed appointment for community sentences (two for prison licences), the red sticker had to be used immediately (equivalent to the premeditated serious foul?). The Circular helpfully pointed out that 'services have the discretion as to whether this means letters printed in red ink, on red paper or with a red sticker or other red marking device' (Home Office, 2005d, p. 5).

Examples of the warning letters were attached to the Circular and they were unambiguous in their threat to breach the offender. The Circular referred to 'professional discretion and judgement taking in all circumstances of the case'. However, examples of 'acceptable absences' were given as medical appointments and *proven* absences due to *unscheduled* work or job interviews (my emphasis). Given that the Standards warn that 'Staff are accountable for the use of their judgement and in departing from the Standards (for example by reducing the frequency of contact or not taking breach action as required)' (Probation Circular, 2000, p. 2), it would be a brave PO who risked his job by condoning weak excuses for noncompliance. NS 2000 (Home Office, 2000) appeared to be even more punitive than the previous two versions.

Hedderman and Hearnden (2001) conducted a third national audit of enforcement following the implementation of NS 2000 supervision (all audits were commissioned by the Association of Chief Officers of Probation (ACOP)). They commented that each revision cut back on the level of discretion available to supervisors. In their opinion, this was a managerial concern by the government 'prompted by a desire to see the service toeing the line and recognizing that it was a law enforcement agency rather than a branch of social work' (p. 216).

As successive versions of NS toughened up on reporting, the level of compliance increased. Hedderman and Hearnden added that those most likely to complete were those least likely to be re-convicted. They added that there was a danger therefore that offenders who were breached had not had the opportunity to be 'changed', as they were quickly taken back to court and resentenced. Her Majesty's Inspectorate of Probation (HMIP) in a small scoping study (HM Inspectorate of Probation 2000b), cautiously suggested that tentative preliminary findings linked enforcement and lower re-conviction rates. Hedderman and Hearnden were scathing of this interpretation:

> 'Despite these cautions, HMI Probation goes on to say that the results are evidence of a link between tough enforcement and reducing re-conviction. In fact, we are a long way from being able to make such a claim. There are several other explanations for these results, including sampling error associated with unspecified but small sample sizes or the possibility that those who were breached were resentenced to prison and were thus out of circulation for some part of the re-conviction period.' (Hedderman and Hearnden, 2001, p. 222)

Ignoring the concerns voiced by Hedderman and Hearnden above, the NS was then revised in 2002. This will now be analysed.

National Standards 2002 (A Revised Version of NS 2000)

Discursive level

The key lexical fields for NS 2002 are not as easy to identify as in the 1992 and 1995 versions as the introduction is a set of bullet points under two headings:

A1 The National Standards, called 'the Standards'
A2 The National Standards.

After this, the NS is a codification of the probation tasks and responsibilities. It is possible to construct some from these two headings and later components, for example, the set of warning letters to be sent to non-regular attending offenders. At this point, working in partnership with the voluntary and private sector was not contentious and was a consistent feature of good practice, such as in the area of substance misuse or accommodation.

Lexical fields in NS 2002 (Home Office, 2002)

'The Standards': their purpose

Applies to all offenders;
Set the standards to which Local Probation Boards should ensure offenders are supervised and services are provided;
Managers and staff held to account;
More effective working with prison service;
One set of standards against which Her Majesty's Inspectorate of Probation will evaluate areas' performance;
Set pre-written letters warning offenders who fail to attend.

Professionalism: firmness and keep to procedure

Avoid inappropriate discrimination to offenders;
Inform offenders what is expected of them and the action that will be taken if they fail to comply;
Offenders supervised with principles of effective practice;
Areas work with other agencies.

The NS: Staff under surveillance

Areas to monitor their work;
Areas respond to HO requests for information and statistical returns;
Areas to draw up contracts for partnership projects;
Keep full and accurate records;
Keep to the Standards unless endorsed by line manager (with reasons recorded);
Ensure continuity of contact.

This leads to some interesting oppositions:

Individualized practice	versus	Conformity to Standards
Discretion	versus	Accountability
Effective practice	versus	Reducing reoffending

The semiotic square of NS 2002

Like NS 1995, this equates with the need for NS to control POs/SWs to deliver punishment, but the concern for the public is implicitly contained within punishment.

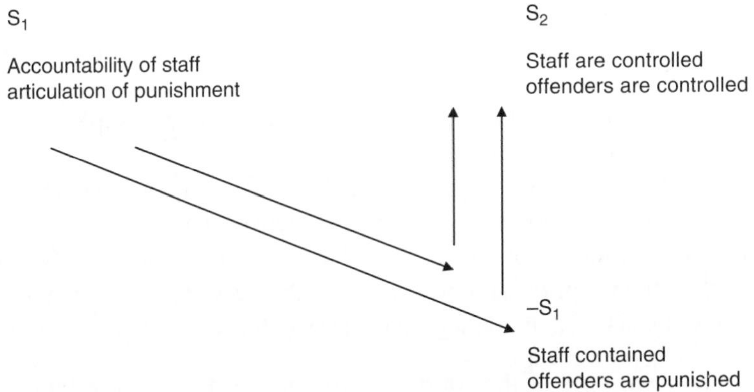

National Standards 2005

The Criminal Justice Act 2003 changed the sentencing structure and its impact on NS was highlighted in a Home Office document dated 4 March 2005 entitled *National Standards 2005* (Home Office, 2005b). It announced that: 'The new standards are based on the principles of offender management ... Reference is made throughout to the offender manager. This is not necessarily a probation officer' (p. 2).

In addition, it added: 'The language used in the new standards also reflects the importance placed on the restrictive, punitive and rehabilitative aspects of community sentencing' (p. 2). Thus probation intervention could be delegated to less well trained staff with the ethos predominantly being one of punishment.

National Standards 2005, which replaced the 2002 version, made the punishment element of probation supervision explicit, rendering discourse analysis unnecessary. Within its components, section GS6 states that 'The implementation of the punitive requirements of the sentence shall be prioritized'. GS7 states that 'The implementation of the restrictive requirements of the sentence shall be prioritized', while GS8 states 'The implementation of the rehabilitative requirements of the sentence shall commence as soon as possible following sentence, having regard to the need to integrate with the punitive and restrictive elements.' The last vestiges of welfarism had been removed from probation officers' work at this point. However, this was very much a transient time, as the probation service, just getting used to becoming a national service, was changed to the National Offender Management Service (NOMS).

The following analysis will compare and contrast NS 2002 and NS 2007 (Home Office, 2007) to investigate whether probation continued along this punitive trajectory.

National Standards 2007

The most recent edition of NS, published in 2007, is available on the internet, at www.warwickshireprobation.org.uk/assets/userfiles/warwickshire/OM_National_Standards_2007.pdf (accessed 6 April 2012) . It would be incomprehensible to the general public as after the cover page and a second page for the reader to write in their name, telephone and email address, there is an overview of supervision expectations depending on whether the offender is a tier 1, 2, 3 or 4 offender, and the reader is either expected to know what this means or they will have to explore this later in the NS. The public might indeed be horrified to discover how little supervision level 1 offenders are afforded over time.

Much of the text is technically complex and designed for professional staff to follow. Again, like earlier versions of NS, it assumes that there is a known public voice in relation to the implementation of sentences, and it incorporates the notion of commissioned work to the voluntary and private sector. By this stage probation has become part of the National Offender Management Service (NOMS), whose aim is to:

- implement sentences of the court in accordance with the expectations of the courts and the public
- protect the public
- punish offenders
- secure reform and rehabilitation
- effect reparation to those affected by offences. (Home Office, 2007, p. 3)

What is interesting is that NS continues: 'NOMS expects that this will be done with due regard to the human rights, dignity and safety of offenders, victims and partners, and that services will be respectful and responsive to the diverse needs and circumstances encountered in correctional work' (Home Office, 2007, p. 3).

National Standards here is affording offenders 'dignity', yet in the following year (on 1 December 2008, as a cheap popularity gesture) offenders on community payback were made to start wearing high-visibility orange jackets. The National Association of Probation Officers stated that there had been a number of incidents where offenders wearing the jackets had been abused. The Justice Minister commented, 'The public expects to see justice being done, and this is what the jackets achieve' (Travis, 2008). Zoe Williams, in a newspaper comment, likened this humiliation to the wearing of the 'Nazi yellow badge, a public degradation both emblematic and practical, as it dehumanized the wearers while laying down the administrative foundations for the horrors to come' (Williams, 2009).

Probation Circular 19/2008 issued on 13 November 2008 carried precise details for these jackets and is worth quoting at length for its precision:

> 'The distinctive clothing, which will also meet health and safety requirements, should be orange high visibility vests (to EN471 class 2 standard) with the Community Payback logo on the front and the words Community Payback on the back. The Community Payback logo must be in the standard colours of purple and green with the wording Community Payback in purple beneath (or the bilingual version for Welsh areas) and should not be less than 9 cm high. On the back, the wording should be in purple with the letters not less than 30 mm high. For Welsh areas, Community Payback should appear in both English and Welsh with the lettering not less than 25 mm high. The current practice for issuing clothing for supervisors varies around the country. Areas should ensure that members of the public can distinguish between offenders undertaking community payback and those supervising them.' (National Probation Service, 2008)

Thus supervising staff are to be spared the negative gaze of the public in order that humiliation is visited upon the offender. If NS 2007 have not been written for the general public to read, they are intended for organizations outside the probation service in line with the intention to tender parts of the work. What also occurred in the period between NS 2002 and 2007 was the slow realization that offenders could not be dealt with as passive entities and given programmes to complete without seeing them as individuals with particular needs. Simplistic punishment was too one-dimensional. Stewart-Ong *et al.* (2004) in an evaluation for the National Probation Directorate on the 'Think First' programme found that offenders who successfully completed the programme had a significantly lower re-conviction rate than those who didn't. However, 'there was a tendency for non-completers to have *higher* re-conviction rates than non-starters' (Stewart-Ong *et al.*, 2004, p. 1, my italics). Of course this result was inconvenient for a probation service being driven to process offenders in a manner as far removed from its social work origins as possible. This was exacerbated by a further comment:

> 'Good case management was associated with improved outcomes. Of greatest value were intense supervision around the start of Think First, supporting offenders with personal problems and frequent contact after completion of the programme, to assist offenders in using what they had learnt. (Stewart-Ong *et al.*, 2004, p. 2)

If this was to be represented within NS then there had to be a recognition that the relationship and quality of the contact between probation and offender counted for something. Could NS 2007 be less rigid in how offenders were to be supervised? Would there be some acknowledgement that the skills of practitioners were important? After its sixth incarnation, would NS return to the first version in terms of flexibility?

Lexical fields in NS 2007

Tiering allocation of cases
Basic level of intervention to deliver punishment
Routine information flow to monitor risk factors and review progress
Provision of information and advice
Offender management (dependent on level of risk)

Offender profile
Levels are a matter for professional and local judgement
Low risk, rehabilitation cases with less complex intervention plans
High likelihood of re-offending cases with multi-factor intervention plans
High and very high risk of serious harm cases – public protection priorities

The standards
Responsibility and accountability for the management of each offender
Assessment and assessment reports

Sentence planning: the offender manager ensures that the work to be done is set out in a sentence plan
Enforcing the sentence: prompt and appropriate enforcement action

The offenders' experience
The offender understands their obligations and sanctions
The offender understands their rights
The offender is encouraged to inform the offender manager of issues that help or hinder compliance

Relations with staff
Offenders experience their relationship with staff as being characterized by: courtesy, valuing diversity, enthusiasm and commitment, encouragement of compliance, recognition and reward for achievement and progress
Firm, fair and legitimate use of authority
Behaviour which models pro-social and anti-criminal attitudes
Teaching of problem-solving skills
Help to access community-based resources
Encouragement to take responsibility for behaviour and its consequences.

The oppositions from these lexical fields are somewhat reminiscent of NS 1992 as the skills of the practitioner are emphasized and public protection is still explicit. However offenders are still to be punished:

Professional judgement	versus	Accountability
Offenders to be punished	versus	Relationship with offender
Expectations and requirements	versus	Community support

The semiotic square of NS 2007

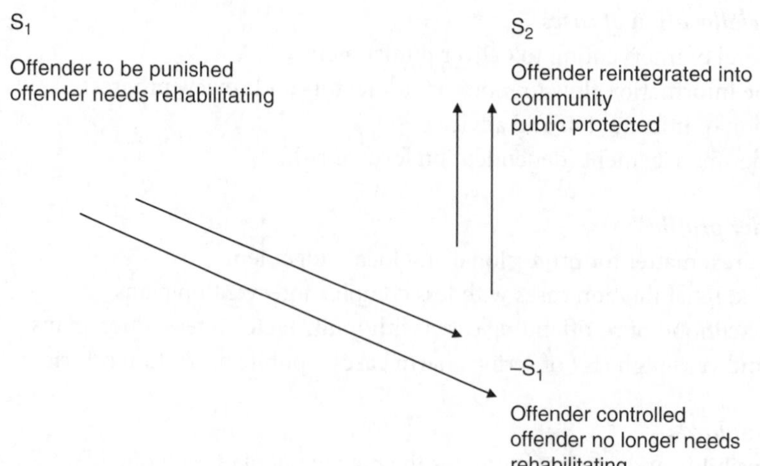

This equates with traditional notions of rehabilitation, mixed with responsibility.

Discrimination and the semiotic square

Thus far in this chapter, discourse analysis has been used at a macro-level, drawing on policy documents. On a micro-level, linking this to discrimination, in an important chapter in his book *Racism and Anti-Racism in Probation*, Denney (1992) commented on the 'power' of the language used by probation officers in their work with offenders. Drawing on the work of Pinder (1982, 1984), he commented:

> 'It has already been suggested that white probation officers tend to conceptualize black offenders within a correctional rather than an appreciative code … It would appear that in the discourse of the court an appreciative code can only be adopted when certain conventional requirements have been met: or put more precisely, both probation officer and sentencer can make it appear that they have been met.' (Denney, 1992, p. 132)

He postulated two possible probation/offender outcomes, which I have turned into semiotic squares:

'Offender worthy of clientization' (willing to become a client and conform to the rules)

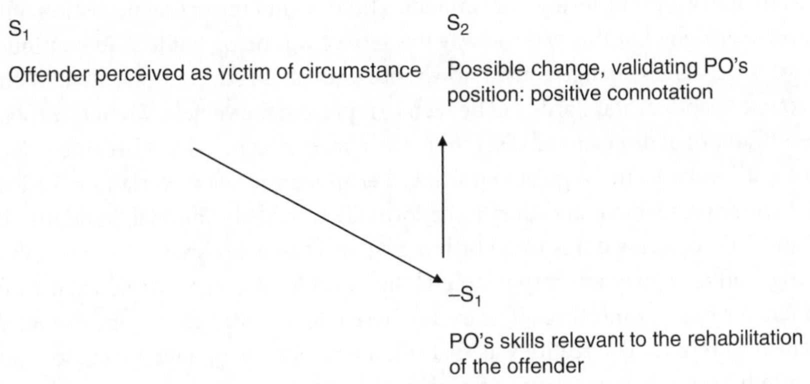

'Offender perceived as a threat'

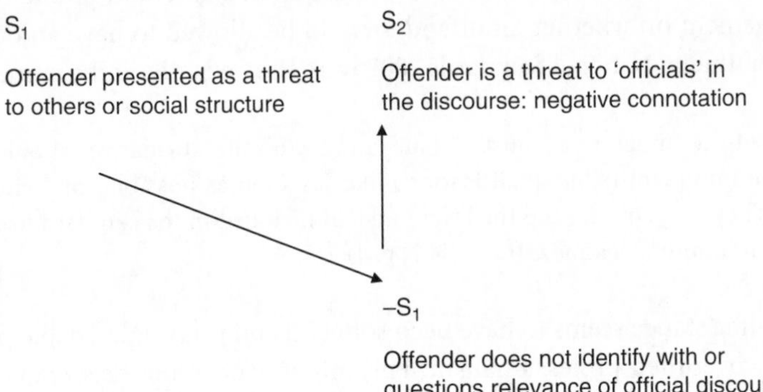

What the above figure shows is that the language used by POs can either process the offender into a positive frame or a negative one, with serious implications for the sentence in court, for example the work of Whitehouse (1982), which showed that POs 'wrote off' rastafarian offenders, drawing on stereotypes, but also how pre-sentence reports (then called social enquiry reports) reinforced stereotypes of black people and women offenders in the 1970s before 'gatekeeping' of reports was introduced. Gatekeeping refers to the practice whereby reports were read by others to ensure they were good enough. So a probation officer could not write a report that was damaging to its subject, and then send it off without it being checked first. It is of concern that services are dropping gatekeeping exercises, in the interests of economy, and so practice could return to its (occasional) stereotypical roots. Just because at one stage the service was aware of the dangers of discriminating, it does not follow that discrimination could not occur with a less aware, more rigidly operating workforce.

Summary

This chapter has shown that the language of National Standards changed between 1992 and 1995 as the probation service task formally moved from being a skilful social work activity to one of administering punishment. This does not mean that probation officers changed overnight, but this was the way the service was being guided. To continue the analogy, large vessels change course slowly, but once changed, continue along their the new course. National Standards can be seen to represent the vehicle, whereby probation officers' traditional professional discretion was reined in as managers became responsible for adherence to the regular reporting. Permission to allow variations had to be agreed with management and then to be formally recorded. National Standards 2000, 2002 and 2005 continued this trend by limiting unacceptable absences to one only, and warning staff that they are responsible if they decide to accept 'weak' excuses from offenders for missing meetings. The excuse here refers to the reason why the offender had failed to report. The reality was that offenders were being taken back to court in large numbers, not because they had reoffended, but because they had missed a couple of appointments during the period of their court order. In my experience, if college students were thrown off their courses for missing two classes, many educational establishments would be forced to close, yet probation staff could not be trusted to make a judgement on whether an offender could be allowed to have an occasional missed appointment. National Standards 2007 were less pedantic, and commented:

> 'They avoid the imperative "must", "shall" and "will", the normative "should" and "ought", and unquantifiable qualifications like "as soon as possible" or "whenever feasible". They also aim to keep the level of detail included in the standard itself to a necessary minimum.' (Home Office, 2007, p. 4)

The hard-line stance seems to have been softened and this might enable probation staff to rediscover their professionalism. This might depend on the size of caseloads which, if too heavy, can force staff to work to minimum standards. The case of Danno Sonnex, who murdered two French students, highlights the problems that can arise from a service that operates under too much pressure. The Chief Officer for the London Probation Service, David Scott, was forced to resign after this tragic event, and in his frank response he made two interesting observations. First, that the perpetrator, Sonnex had been 'wrongly classified by an inexperienced probation officer as being at only medium risk of reoffending, which meant he was not subjected to a more intensive level of inter-agency monitoring' (Scott, 2009).

Second, Scott commented on the need to recruit more high-calibre probation staff at a time when most probation areas were having to cut their costs. This was a particular problem in a large area like London:

> 'The inexperienced officer supervising Sonnex had a caseload of 127 offenders – compared with an average of 37.7 cases per probation officer across London … a probation officer's caseload can vary widely over a relatively short period of time … [London Probation] has to beware of "friendly fire" from those who seek to mask a very real lack of resources with charges of ineptitude.' (Scott, 2009)

The problem is that we lock up many people who are not a risk to the public. Relying on a mechanical approach to public protection does not protect the public more than allowing staff to have enough time to get to know their offenders and then making a professional judgement on whether they are safe to be released. In the Sonnex case, mistakes were made by staff who did not know the offender. His level of risk was under-assessed in prison, when there was more than sufficient information to get this right. Then he was allocated to an inexperienced officer who had a huge caseload. Relying on procedures instead of making accurate assessments based on real knowledge is going to give the public less protection.

The power of language should not be underestimated, and the interviews with informants demonstrate that adherence to the Standards, underpinned by the regular inspections of offender files, ensured that this message was translated into practice.

On a micro-level, the technique of discourse analysis is used to give an understanding of how POs can discriminate between offenders. It makes sense of Pinder's findings that at one stage POs wrote reports that examined the psychopathology and personal difficulties of white offenders and the attitudes towards authority of black offenders. The importance of 'gatekeeping' to prevent discrimination appearing in court reports was recognized in the past, and it needs to be reintroduced, although it is perceived to be unnecessary in a system geared towards actuarial justice. Finally, later iterations of National Standards were written explicitly to remove any vestiges of PO discretion. By this time the term 'offender manager' hid whether the supervisor was a fully trained probation officer or a less highly trained probation service officer (PSO). I am told that this latter group are increasingly being given higher-risk offenders to supervise, which is unfair on them, on the public and on the offender.

Chapter 4 highlighted Home Office research that showed how PSOs were taking on the work of POs, which is likely to endanger the public, as their knowledge and skills level will not be deep enough to understand the complexity of offenders' behaviour. Recent research by Mair (2011), who examined the implications of having a generic community sentence, the norm since 2005, found that the chosen cocktail of requirements was more punitive than hitherto, with less supervision as part of the order. This led Mair to conclude that traditional probation 'may be disappearing and this may have important implications for contestability' (Mair, 2011, p. 229). He was also concerned that 'with a fragmented sentence such as the community order whose various requirements may be different to hold together as a coherent single sentence, offender managers may lose contact with their offenders' (Mair, 2011, p. 230).

This might even make the brief of Janetta and Halberstadt (2011) from the USA seem less surreal in the UK context. They discussed a pilot project that took place in the District of Columbia where probationers and parolees reported to a kiosk, rather than 'in-person reporting'. Kiosks are automated machines where supervisees are able to log in using unique passwords and biometric technology. Offenders can answer questions about their circumstances and update their details, submit payments, and kiosks in New York City 'randomly select low-risk probationers for drug testing'. Janetta and Halberstadt added that using kiosks shifted supervision from low-risk toward moderate- and high-risk offenders, it was a quicker form of surveillance and, therefore, offenders towards the end of their supervision could be transferred on to kiosk supervision, which could be viewed as a reward. The report concluded that kiosks were a valuable tool. One might conclude that the use of kiosks was a logical conclusion to the downgrading of knowledge and skills in probation staff. National Standards requirements could be met without requiring any input from probation staff at all.

This would be an overly pessimistic conclusion at the present time, as the experience of the author in training experienced probation staff in public protection was that these staff were highly skilled and professional practitioners (discussed further in Chapter 9), but what might the future hold? Harry Fletcher, writing in *NAPO News* in October 2011 (Fletcher, 2011) commented that the Legal Aid, Sentencing and the Punishment of Offenders Bill, currently then at the Committee Stage, includes in Clause 59 the proposal that *any programme* can be imposed as a condition within a community court order, rather than an accredited programme. This opens the possibility for unproven ad hoc programmes to be delivered by the private sector. Thus the loosening of demands within the 2007 National Standards could be a vehicle that enables the private sector to take over offender supervision.

6

Views of Front-Line Staff

Setting the Context: The Opinion of Probation Service Professionals

I have collected interviews with probation personnel over many years for a variety of research projects. I refer to my interviewees here as PO13, SPO5, and so on, in order to protect their anonymity while showing their job title. What these interviews reveal is the state of the art of their time, but also concerns and thoughts about where the service was and is moving towards. Thus comments can be linked to distinct periods of time in terms of pressures and priorities within the service. Contemporary literature on probation practice will also be drawn on. Until the 1990s, probation officers (POs) might discuss social work practice and issues around prison resettlement, but attention then moved to the pressures of completing the bureaucratic tasks, especially electronic assessments. This period is given particular attention, as it marked an end of one long phase of practice and the painful gateway to another. As this book is being completed at the start of 2012, the wheel has turned full circle and social work issues are back on the agenda, alongside the threat of privatization and coping with high caseloads.

What Happens During a Period of Change? The Early 1990s

In 1994 I interviewed a number of staff about their practice with prisoners, with all staff stating that this was an important priority for them. The number of years that they had served in the job was impressive. It meant that their experience manifestly

Rehabilitating and Resettling Offenders in the Community, First Edition. Anthony H. Goodman.

informed their practice. One woman with 18 years' experience had been a senior probation officer (SPO) for five years. She was on the verge of leaving a non-specialist field team that worked a patch system (i.e., where each PO covered a discrete area for clients in the community), to manage a civil work unit. This work is no longer a probation task but is conducted by the Child and Family Consultation and Advice Service (CAFCAS). She succinctly described the changing nature of the probation service and the tensions resulting from this:

> 'I am a social worker. I am an SPO, but I am a social worker. People have said to me that now that I am leaving, that I hope that your successor will have a commitment to social work principles. I think that they are 100 per cent correct to have that fear, because my successor could adhere to social work principles or not ... They would not be made an SPO because of those virtues. If you want to become a senior, you don't say that I am a good social worker... You say I've grown up now – management speak – but within management speak you can adhere to social work and I will strive to do it. I know that it cannot be said of all SPOs.' (PO2)

She had a predominantly inexperienced team, with most POs in their first or second year of the job. She was the only woman among four SPOs in the borough. Most of the POs were women and were 'invariably replaced by women'. She felt that the management, at headquarters, had not taken sufficient notice of the high caseloads and numbers of pre-sentence reports being completed, the implication being that the office was under-resourced. The budget capping of services following the Criminal Justice Act 1991 had clearly had an effect. There was also an implication that pressure led to staff moving on after three years or so, leaving inexperienced staff to work in a stressful and deprived area.

This practitioner highlighted the changes that have taken place in probation. First, the many years of experience prior to becoming a senior. Currently, staff may be promoted to this level in as little as two years, which would not have been possible in the past. Second, in terms of identity the senior was trained on a social work course and this had had a profound influence throughout her career. The link with social work was severed in 1995, with the last trainees exiting programmes in 1997. Many of these failed to get posts in the service, due to financial constraints and there was an exodus of social-work-trained staff in later years as priorities changed.

One probation officer mentioned the evolution of through-care and after-care support for prisoners in her borough. The task had been through a number of incarnations, starting as a specialist team then merging into teams that had specialized in work with adult offenders before re-emerging as a specialism again when an extra senior post had been found. However: 'youth work was the flavour of the year – decade. We now have a youth team and a through-care team.' Thus it could be seen that management set the priorities.

There had been a further change in policy that the probation service would open a file on all defendants charged with murder. It had been decided that these (pre-trial) defendants should go to through-care specialists, which involved a considerable amount of work preparing reports (despite the statutory life sentence if found guilty of murder).

One probation officer commented that the bureaucratic (or paper-pushing) side of the job was increasing, with numerous home leave reports (the interview was before the Home Secretary announced a dramatic cutback in home leave), parole assessment reports (previously called home circumstances reports), and pre-discharge reports for prisoners who were to be released on automatic conditional release (ACR). There was a report to be sent back to the prison at the end of the ACR licence, and reports to the Home Office on lifers, pre- and post-discharge. A major change also was for POs to become more involved in 'sentence planning'. This was very much welcomed by this officer. Of course what this didn't include was the computerized risk assessments, which will be discussed later in this chapter.

At the end of the session with the probation officer, we were joined by a colleague who had been in the service for ten years. Two very interesting further themes emerged. The first was the imminent computerization of the probation records (then called CRAMS). The PO was concerned that this could result in the computer 'tripping' automatically to the fact that the offender was not keeping to National Standards for reporting, for example, weekly for the first three months. He saw computerization as a sinister development for the service that had serious civil liberty implications. This period was a difficult time for staff, as their ability to make decisions on reporting became more limited as acceptable reasons for non-attendance were progressively being removed.

The second PO I spoke to was far more overt than the first in their mistrust of the SPO, who was clearly not regarded as a support, rather as a bureaucrat who ensured that National Standards were being adhered to. Perhaps the tape recorder inhibited the first PO from being fully honest. The notes I made during the meeting recorded the fact that this PO appeared uncomfortable at the point in the meeting when the issue of support/supervision was discussed.

A third PO was very uneasy talking to me with the tape recorder running and very early on in the interview I made it clear that all matters discussed were confidential and they would not be identified to the service. Notwithstanding this, the interview was considerably shorter than other interviews. After my reassurance, this PO stated that they felt that the service was changing with the personnel department coming much more to the fore: 'People – both staff and clients – seem very [much] lower on the list.'

This PO felt that she could still offer what used to be described as casework, and although she could discuss this with her SPO, 'I'm not sure that the organization encourages it. It is far more important to count numbers and fill in forms [and] do the various sorts of monitoring that have to be done.'

In terms of National Standards she acknowledged that prisoners were to be seen on their day of release:

> 'In theory [subsequently] at home within five working days and then in five days at [the] office again. We operate a degree of flexibility – if on release they have seen a duty officer, then the next visit will be in the office [with their own PO]. If they are in a

hostel [the PO] may not visit there at all. We can confirm that [the] person is there without visiting an address. We see them weekly for a month and then fortnightly and then less if they are on a long sentence.' (PO5)

Another senior expected POs to write to prisoners within fourteen days of allocation and hoped that prisoners would be visited more frequently than quarterly. The senior acknowledged that there was considerable variation in probation practice. She had also been concerned about the feasibility of home-visiting new clients within five working days, but this did not seem to be an issue. She had not been given the message that this was a high priority, so she did not push it. Many of the clients resided in large estates that were best not visited, as they were 'risky'. With the squeeze on probation service budgets, brought about by cash limiting the probation services, following on from the CJA 1991, she thought that services could not afford to staff units which had a lower task priority. There was a squeeze on staffing levels at this time, as the number of new officers emerging from training courses were diminishing. Indeed, there was the prospect of redundancies within the existing workforce.

On the Cusp of Change: Life Before and After National Standards 1995

In 1995 the second version of National Standards was published and, as discussed in Chapter 5, the emphasis on punishment became much more explicit. In 1998 I interviewed a number of staff of different grades, experience, gender and ethnicity. In the intervening period it became almost impossible for staff to get either the time or the permission to conduct prison visits. The emphasis of my enquiry changed to the entire work of the service, its ethos, including enforcement and other priorities.

Changes in the bureaucratic tasks of the Probation Service

Informants described the implementation of National Standards (NS) as a watershed in how the bureaucratic tasks of the probation service had changed. As a consequence the service became more preoccupied with processing offenders so that the numerical aspects of National Standards could be monitored: for example, the number of appointments offered in the first three months, taking offenders back to court (breach action) after a certain number of missed appointments, and so on. Monitoring was concerned with keeping appointments, rather than what occurred during meetings between the probation officer and offender.

There was concern expressed by senior officers at the lack of evaluation of the *quality* of contact with the offender, as this was neither monitored nor evaluated. As one senior commented:

'In this service all clients on probation or combination orders [probation and community service] are expected to complete the same thirteen-week group programme, which

> covers a range of lesser criminogenic needs, whether or not the client has been identified as having needs in those areas. Clients can be assessed as being unsuitable for the group programme, but this is expected to be agreed by the SPOs, some of whom take quite a rigid stand on limiting the availability of such exclusions. When the group programme was introduced, staff were told that the delivery and impact would be evaluated, but this has not happened over two years later.' (SPO3)

In some offices in his service, it became expected practice that following the thirteen weeks, offenders were referred to a reporting centre, rather than have any other quality assessment or work undertaken. This appeared to be because some managers were viewing the first thirteen weeks of an order as being the *only* important part of the order, as that was what was monitored by the Home Office and the Inspectorate.

The time before NS was described as one with 'rough standards' when 'there was a lot of discretion and a lot of difference in practice' (PO16). Offenders could be given very different supervisory experiences, according to the whim of their PO, which was not seen as fair. National Standards 1995 did not require a major change from the 1992 version, but SPO1 thought that POs still felt deskilled as they were 'accountable for *not what they did with the person*, but for what they had *written down*.'

POs generally felt that the quality of their reports was decreasing, as they became simply an added pressure on their time, even if there had been improvements in setting priorities for work with offenders. PO15 liked the move towards helping offenders with employment, training and education, but this was not reflected in file inspections: 'I would rather they checked us on quality of work rather than baked beans and quantity.' SPO2 did not see that POs needed to acquire new skills to work under NS, but as mentioned there was a need to record more accurately. These changes had led to PO becoming case managers rather than caseworkers. This raised the question of working in partnership with outside agencies, which some SPOs did not feel was happening as much as was necessary. Newer POs were 'more geared to partnerships than older officers who are geared to saying what are your problems, what are your needs, how do I deal with them … [New POs are] more case managers than therapeutic worker' (SPO1).

Processing offenders

There was consensus by the senior officers that the service had become more preoccupied with *processing* clients so that the numerical, that is, measureable, aspects of National Standards could be monitored. This was to ensure that the correct number of appointments were offered in the first three months and that breach action was initiated after a certain number of missed appointments. Thus SPO3 concluded that 'there is a lack of concern over the *quality of contact with clients*' which was not monitored or evaluated. Earlier in his service seniors had to agree when offenders were assessed as not being suitable for a group work programme, and some seniors 'took a rigid stand' against excluding offenders from them. Access to these programmes was supposed to be determined by *criminogenic need, not administrative convenience.* Two years before, when the group programmes had been introduced, staff were told that the programmes would be evaluated, and this was still to happen. The changes in supervision were perceived to have given offenders an easier time and were less challenging than 'traditional' probation practice. This was mostly due to the shorter time offender and officer were together. Furthermore, partnership programmes, which had originally been 'sold to the service' as an addition to probation supervision, had become instead, an alternative to this. For many offenders, supervision might consist of an assessment meeting, six sessions in a group and then ticking in at a reporting centre. A PSO who worked in a reporting centre complained that the speed needed to 'throughput' offenders made sensitive and 'meaningful work' impossible. For staff, who he stressed were not lazy, there was a feeling that their work was a 'deception'. He also commented that the staff were leaving in two ways: established officers who had become disillusioned were leaving, but bright new staff were doing so also.

Main grade officers were concerned with the effect of NS which was seen as looking for the 'most common denominator' as opposed to the 'most important things' (PO11). What NS attempted to look for in offenders' lives was described as 'offensively basic' by this PO, who had a student training role, and she described the official expectation of practice as being pitched at student level. This type of supervision was seen as likely to produce 'a nice compliant client' but not deal with their personal problems. The result of NS was the development of a high turnover model with a fast throughput of people where POs tried to discharge orders on them as quickly as possible in order to take on more. This model was not completely controlled by main grade officers in all the informants' services. PSO2 described his role as being placed 'exactly in between the demands of the Home Office (via management) and the needs of my colleagues (with whom I had to work, and often socialized).' Probation officers might need to maintain good relationships with offenders and be flexible, but this was not the message from management. He eventually decided to toe the management line, not the main grade one. He cited a number of reasons for this: the positive support he received was from his manager, not the main grade manager, who did not regard him as 'one of them', and some were even rude to him. The exceptions to this tended to be younger officers 'who are not expected to abandon *decades* of social work values in favour of punishment.' He no longer regarded 'NS as a guide, but as a job description'. He admitted that even in the short period in the post he had become 'cynical and embittered' and had changed his views on offenders away from welfare towards punishment, for self-protection: 'Out of necessity I have erected protective barriers, as it hurts when you are disliked for the job you do, when you are personally judged for your professional conduct, and your profession is essentially negative.'

Some SPOs described their role as having become autocratic, with central allocation of tasks which might be shifted to meet NS requirements. A further consequence was that there was no longer 'meaningful discussion about cases' between the SPO *or between the POs themselves.* One PO mentioned that in her office POs would still meet to discuss the work they were undertaking with individual offenders, but this was now rare in her service. A service that had prided itself on working in a sensitive way with offenders had instead become process-oriented: this was difficult to reconcile with the notion of protection of the public. Main grade officers talked about the sheer pressure of coping with the paperwork, and not going under due to the stress. Files were removed and checked to ensure that NS were being met, sometimes without warning if there was a crisis, although usually a week's notice was given.

The other 'innovation' that was impacting on the way that offenders were supervised was the rise in use of the electronic tag. Main grade staff were predominantly negative about this and senior staff were more pragmatic. Originally the equipment was unreliable but this is no longer the case. When offenders realized this, they began to conform as the alternative was certain breach and prison:

> 'It seems to have worked best where there has been cooperation between the probation service and the tagging company, and where the offender is being provided with, well I suppose what we still call social work input alongside just being tagged. The tag on its own will work in enforcing the curfew because it does produce fairly high levels of compliance, but beyond that it is totally non-constructive.' (SM1)

The option of tagging was not cheap, and the general feeling was that it would only work, not as an alternative to probation, but to prison. It could not be un-invented, and PO refusal to engage with it could lead to it (at least partially) supplanting probation.

There could be an element of collusion between main grade and management, described to me as 'impression management'. In some offices it was left to the PO to decide whether the offender was to be breached. There was a downward pressure from management to breach more, with little emphasis on quality of work, which had led to some of the more experienced staff feeling alienated as the traditional value base of the job was ignored. One PO described himself as not being a breach enthusiast but he was prepared to take this action in the face of complete noncompliance. He mentioned a recent case of an offender who had a particularly chaotic drug pattern and health and housing problems, where the magistrate had commented: 'It's nice to hear of a probation officer who's not a slave to National Standards.'

The implementation of NS in 1992 had left many officers feeling deskilled and there had been a process of transition, for example POs questioned whether they could complete a risk assessment, were overburdened with making sure that they were seeing offenders often enough, and were not having to breach and take them back to court (SPO1).

Taking offenders back to court (breaching)

The notion that newer POs, who had not known the autonomy of working prior to NS, coped easier with the continuing changes was a perception shared by the newer

POs, more experienced POs and their managers. Probation officers who had worked in the service in the 1970s and 1980s found the change difficult as they felt that they had lost autonomy and independence. Conversely, new POs who had been trained under NS: '[New officers] … worry if they don't breach. I've developed a system if they are worried about [not] breach[ing] due to vulnerability etc., then I get them to put it on file and I take responsibility to postpone the breach. They get extremely worried about not being seen to be breaching' (SPO2).

Individual offices with a low breach rate were criticized by their service, especially if the service as a whole had been criticized by the Probation Inspectorate. This had resulted in the 'enforcement team' (officially called the legal proceedings team) going into one office to 'beef up' the breach rate: 'everyone got a bit anxious and started breaching. My breaching figures have gone up, I have to say, and this was highlighted in a couple of my appraisal reports. I was slow to breach, but in the last two years or so I began to breach a lot more' (PO8).

When an offender was breached, it was common for the order to be continued and the offender fined for failing to keep to the conditions, such as appointments. A first-time fine could be a sum of between £50–£100, but could be considerably more depending on circumstances. A probation service officer told me that it was standard practice to ask for this, thus offenders would be likely, eventually, to complete the number of visits to a probation office and/or the hours of community service, but in addition they would have both paid an additional fine *and* the Crown Prosecution Service (CPS) costs. The CPS automatically asked for this and the PSO was under pressure to do likewise. He was resisting this pressure as he saw the: 'fine as equivalent to, in many cases, a couple of weeks of dole money, survival money really'. With legal aid being cut back, there was no guarantee that an offender, in breach of their order, would get legal representation, especially if it was likely that the offender would be fined and the order continued.

Coping with the changes

This did not mean that this type of officer, with a pragmatic view of the job, was averse to the changes. Other POs could work within NS in 'imaginative ways' to avoid taking offenders back to court, if they were trying to cooperate with their PO. The notion of working in partnership was seen as positive, not least because the changing nature of the bureaucratic component of the job was becoming much more time-consuming and doing the breach itself was a very time-consuming affair in terms of the time it took to take out the warrant in court and do the paperwork. One PO described a situation where an offender was doing very well on the probation component of a combination order (probation plus community service), but had failed to keep to the community service requirements. It was the PO's responsibility to go to court and prosecute, although there was a good relationship between them, and the community supervision was working well. This was described as difficult. This had led to POs describing their culture as one of concern to check whether the appropriate forms had been completed, rather than had the intervention with the offender affected their life for the better. NAPO policy was to suspend National Standards and substitute a code of practice, based on the 'what works' initiatives.

In one area the work had become compartmentalized, with each piece of work given a token amount of time for its completion. Thus the average completion of 10 court reports per month was given a time allowance of one and a quarter days per week, leaving the rest of the time for direct work with offenders. New cases were considered active as they had to be seen weekly but as soon as they were transferred to reporting schemes they gained less time credit for the PO. Certainly it was not possible to hide cases at the back of a filing cabinet, as they all had to be logged into the 'time economy' and were liable to be inspected. Probation staff were given time to see offenders according to what National Standards allowed. After the first three months, offenders were not supposed to be seen as often as before. Thus if probation officers wanted to give them more time, this would have to be done on a voluntary basis as it was not seen as necessary: an example of a time-and-motion study being mechanically applied rather than related to human need. Probation officers working in services not operating this type of token economy also prioritized work. Pre-sentence reports were of the highest priority, followed by the paperwork on 'high risk' offenders. This was described as a 'cover your back' exercise:

> '[T]his risk assessment business … is a main priority in [her probation service], that everyone is assessed at risk level 1, 2 or 3 and I kind of feel as well like the sex offenders' registration … it's nonsense. Because filling out a form isn't going to stop someone doing what they're going to do, and we were assessing people's risk anyway beforehand, and notifying appropriate people and whatever, but you can't be responsible for somebody's behaviour for 24 hours a day, or at any time. I think that is a paper exercise as well. And like the sex offenders' registration, it creates a false illusion to the public that they'll be protected because we've got everyone registered.' (PO14)

Recording contact with offenders

Ironically, although there was a greater emphasis on paperwork, to demonstrate compliance, recordings of offender contact had become truncated, even trivialized. Thus a PO stated that routine recording of offenders on minimal contact would say something like: 'X reported today, pleased at continuing good progress and time used to discuss next appointment.' Workload measurement in some areas meant that processing offenders, *and* communications with them, had become uniform. Any communication, whether from the offender, prison or court, had to be responded to within two working days. The way of coping was using standard letters, 'a whole batch of them', which were not seen as 'human' letters. The date for the next appointment was entered on the computer and the letter was printed automatically.

The increased computerization of the Service meant that probation officers spent a greater proportion of their time sitting at computer terminals, lessening their availability to deal with offenders. In some services this meant a reduction in the level of administrative and support staff employed, while in others these staff were the ones seeing offenders when they came into the office.

A senior manager acknowledged that the administrative complement had 'been reduced to a mere shadow of what they were'. CRAMS, the computerized records scheme, was paid for by this reduction. It was stated by a senior staff member that it was well known within the service that it would not work. CRAMS had a pre-Windows operating system and was not up to the task. The consequence was that POs had to start typing court reports and other documents where accuracy was essential, as legal documents could influence the lives of both offenders and victims for many years to come. It would appear contradictory to train POs in the interpersonal skills they need to interview, assess and work with offenders, and then give them clerical tasks to complete, while at the same time giving the remaining, experienced clerical staff responsibility for face-to-face contact with offenders. This was particularly so when clerical staff could complete the administrative tasks in a fraction of the time it took some POs to do them. A further indirect consequence of CRAMS, I was told, was to make it impossible to operate on any sort of social work model as it was not designed to record detailed interviews:

> 'If you've got an unexcused absence on a CRAMS record, it takes away the discretion of the professional, it tells you – next step, drag on a letter and breach them. It triggers breaches … and it allows senior managers to monitor much [more] easily to make sure that breaches happen, if officers even try to disguise them.' (PSO1)

The implications for confidentiality of CRAMS, or the introduction of any computerization that was meant to link services up (not only to each other but also to other organizations in the Criminal Justice System), lay in the access all organizations would have to the information the service held on offenders. It also concerned the safeguards that were in place to protect access to those who needed to know. The Data Protection Act, and the authority to disclose information under the Crime and Disorder Act, would still apply to each separate organization within the Criminal Justice System. It should not be assumed that because probation may share the use of the same, or a similar, computer application, that the information kept on the application within each individual organization would, or should, be shared with the others. It was not clear whether this had been clearly thought through by the Home Office in its attempts to develop an information sharing system within the Criminal Justice System. Some POs thought that the sharing of information on offenders with other agencies was a price worth paying for the greater protection of the public.

Historically, POs admitted to falling far behind in their recording of offending contact, six months or more was not uncommon to some very experienced informants, but POs couldn't afford for this to happen now, I was told. This was avoided either by shortening interviews, or working very long days (PO18 said that his day was usually 10–11 hours, and he worked many Saturdays to keep up. He was still giving some offenders long in-depth interviews).

The effect of working through the changes, I was told by main grade officers and seniors, was a high level of sickness and stress among POs. Seniors hoped that reporting centres would take the pressure off main grade staff but staff still felt under pressure. Probation officers had found ways of controlling their workload pressure by not visiting offenders serving time in prison. The 'knock on' effect for seniors was that prisoners wrote to them complaining at the lack of PO contact. This was not a desired outcome for the POs who wanted to visit more often but could not due to work pressure. The fact that many prisoners had literacy problems made communication by letter difficult.

Main grade staff complained at the need to complete 'user-unfriendly' documents and 'meaningless statistics'. The flow of information was one way, from main grade staff to the Research and Information section. It was not seen to be of use in the task of supervising offenders. An example of this was a quarterly summary on the stability of each offender's housing. What constituted 'stable' housing for that particular offender, did it need to be kept for a week, or a month or three months? Sometimes a person might move regularly between different accommodations, so at the time the form was completed it might look stable and be so again in time for the next summary, but in between there might have been several moves. It was difficult to do justice to this in a simple yes/no tick box.

Some senior managers felt that the move to make POs type their own reports was a waste of their skills, while others felt that this was part of the process of change and the need for more flexibility. One, undertaking an MBA, with a number of private sector managers, thought that POs could be somewhat precious and needed to 'get real'. The intention was to speed up the administration of justice. Administrative staff, who were becoming a rare breed in the service, were acknowledged as being under great strain as POs failed to develop their administrative, typing and computer skills fast enough, and secretarial staff tried to deal with the backlog. One solution was to have peripatetic workers who could be 'parachuted' into problem offices to support teams in crisis. The office for PO8 had been criticized, for example, as reviews on their offenders were not being completed every three months (which was changed to a maximum time of every four months under NS 2000). Each time there was a change in procedure there was a 'confusion lag' until the changes bedded in, and this had been a particular problem when the sex offenders' register had first started, with the possible sanction for the offender of a fine or six months in prison.

All informants concerned with providing a direct service to offenders commented on the considerable increase in the number of forms POs were expected to complete in relation to each task they undertook. This, I was told, was explained to them as being important for monitoring the work the Service undertook. While there was an acknowledgement by some middle managers that some of the information gathered was useful, POs saw little benefit from it. However, it had meant that supervision of POs by SPOs has become focused on whether monitoring forms had been completed, rather than on the development of practice and work with clients. It seems ridiculous that the task of completing these forms could be completed by administrative and clerical staff from the case records and other information available in case files, thus allowing practice staff more time to develop quality work with clients. The erosion of the tasks between secretarial staff and PO was seen as a further aspect of the de-professionalization of the service. Probation officers talked to me about coming in to the office at weekends, working very long days and cancelling leave to try and keep on top of the paperwork.

On the computerization of probation records, CRAMS was declared unsatisfactory, and SPO3, while commenting that his service had not implemented it, added that its effect had been to significantly increase levels of stress and frustration among practice staff at the amount of time they had been expected to sit in front of a computer terminal rather than doing the job they were trained to do. CRAMS, and the system used by his service, was slow to use, confusing in the language it used, and in the way it operated, easy to make mistakes on (but it was difficult to rectify those mistakes), incompatible with other applications in use in the service, and also with the other parts of the Criminal Justice System that it was meant to link probation officers to. Because of the major faults within the application, it also increased the level of stress and frustration among administrative and clerical staff.

Some officers found the idea that actuarial feedback on the offender's likelihood of reoffending was given was a helpful addition to professional judgement or 'gut feeling'. However, this was not always the case, particularly as this percentage figure was shared with the offender. One PO mentioned that a colleague's 'client' was very upset as the risk figure for him computed was very high, and the offender stated strongly that he had *not* reoffended on the order.

Contact with prisoners

In through-care (or resettlement, as it has recently begun to be known) there was a decreasing emphasis on visiting prisoners regularly during their sentence. This was partly due to budget limitations, but was also due to the greater role prisons were playing in developing sentence planning and delivering programmes of work with prisoners during their sentence. A senior manager stated that regular prison through-care contact was really 'history' and furthermore:

> 'Even the sentencing planning demands upon us are something we can't deliver on regularly … the role of the PO is to supervise people in the community, to discharge our responsibilities to the court, to work collaboratively with people and the partnership agencies. Prison visits per se are increasingly less part of that equation.' (SM3)

However, while the emphasis within the Service was on less contact with the prisoner during sentence, prisons were expecting probation officers to visit more frequently, to attend reviews of work undertaken on group programmes within the prison, and were often dissatisfied with the response when probation officers said they were unable to do so. The lack of prison visiting was rationalized by some POs as logically following on from the change of emphasis away from relationship-building with offenders and the 'mystique' attached to this.

However, for most POs it was simply a question of work pressure preventing contact, especially visits, with people in prison. Report writing, that is, offering a service to the courts, was the primary task of a PO. There was absolutely no discretion in refusing to undertake the preparation of these reports and no control on their frequency, which depended entirely on judicial decision. A minority of POs had the principle of showing court reports to offenders in the probation office prior to the court date to explain its content, away from the anxiety and stress of the busy court. This was seen as being professional, but was yet another pressure on probation staff. This work was undertaken at the cost of not visiting offenders in prison. As mentioned earlier, prisoners complained at the lack of probation contact.

In one service, offenders serving less than one year, who did not therefore receive any probation supervision on discharge from prison, were seen by the Society of Voluntary Associates (SOVA). Probation officers would not be given any time allowance to see them at all. This was seen by senior managers as a possible area where POs would become involved again. The case for probation intervention with short-term prisoners had been made very strongly in the 1998 Prisons Probation review, but in the light of the budget cuts, and the need to maintain front-line staff, it had had to be sacrificed, alongside mileage allowances for prison visiting. There was an awareness that the probation service could be criticized for this policy. Prison probation staff numbers had also been greatly reduced, but the frustration for service managers was the inconsistency between prison governors. Policy appeared to be made on the hoof whereby the Treasury decided that bail information in prisons would be run by seconded probation service officers, yet probation services had not been asked to recruit them and, I was told, even the Chief Inspector of Prisons had not known of the innovation.

Understanding the World of the Offender

There was an increasing expectation that missed appointments inevitably led to breach action. The introduction of guidelines which limited the number of 'acceptable' reasons for missing appointments meant that a larger number of probation officers, especially those new in the service, were seeing their role as insisting that offenders attend appointments or face breach action, rather than explore the reasons for failing to keep appointments, and encouraging offenders to see the service as having something to offer them. The number of breaches has increased, as POs saw themselves as increasingly expected to take such a stance by senior and middle managers.

With the changes outlined above and less contact time between POs and offenders, they were less aware of the context of offenders' lives and thus were not in a knowledgeable enough position to make allowances for the realities of the day-to-day occurrences that affected offenders' ability to keep appointments regularly. Some chiefs were very keen on the growth of electronic tagging, and the changing political climate allowed a hostile, punitive approach towards offenders to develop. Traditionally probationers were referred to as 'clients' and many POs interviewed used this term. A PSO interviewee was explicit about this and the dehumanizing penal climate:

> 'We were told not to refer to our clients as clients any more, we can only refer to them as offenders and I just can't do that … you know, we tag yachts and cattle, and you know, property you don't want to go missing, you don't tag human beings. You deal with people in a proper sensitive, civilized, thoughtful way, which is a balance between care and control; at least that was what I was brought up to believe.' (PSO1)

The idea that most offenders led chaotic lives and many found conforming to NS difficult was echoed by main grade officers who felt that offenders wanted to work with their POs particularly when they had immediate problems. In particular when writing reports on unstable drug users, POs anticipated that they would not immediately be able to comply with the rigours of NS:

> 'What you try to achieve in the [probation] order is a change in their lifestyle, with change in the way they behave, when their whole day has been spent trying to think about how to get your next set of money for your next fix. These are not the people who comply immediately – if I breached all of those people I would not be out of court for most of the week.' (PO11)

Concern was expressed by experienced probation officers that offenders would eventually be seen behind glass barriers as staff became less skilled in dealing with face-to-face interactions. Older POs, who had worked with untrained direct entrants, likened them to newly qualified staff in terms of rigidity of approach. Conversely a newly trained PO contrasted her approach with that of older, established colleagues who did not breach offenders very often. One PO expressed a view that her training in NS had led to an 'obsession to breach'. She had been told at her interview for her permanent job that POs did not breach offenders very often and she had pointed out that this was not the case for her. She complained that the ability to take offenders back to court had become an attribute to put on a PO's CV. There was a tension between management and the Home Office, who put pressure on POs to take offenders back to court and the wishes of many main grade officers not to do so. The courts had an ambivalent reaction to these offenders being returned for resentencing, and might defer sentence to postpone making a decision. The police also often failed to execute breach of probation warrants so that the offender was left in limbo for a considerable amount of time (PO15). An experienced PO gave a different view of the earlier, less stringent, supervision:

> 'We modelled very badly for people who needed limit setting, I don't know if there is a shift in society, but in the past we let clients down as they were lacking a structure in their lives and we were the agency to provide such a structure, and because of the kind of ethos of limitless growth free association we failed to provide those limits.' (PO9)

Discrimination and Offenders

While a lot of effort went into attempting to ensure that certain categories of offenders were not discriminated against, and that all offenders were offered the same level of service, the impact of the more negative approach of the service towards offenders who were already experiencing discrimination had been largely forgotten. Thus the impact, for instance, of being black, and dealt with in such a negative manner by a predominantly white organization, being perceived and received as increasing the experience of discrimination, was being ignored. I was told the same could be said of gay/lesbian clients, and women offenders who were all, in the name of being dealt with equally, increasingly being dealt with on the basis of structures set up to deal with white, male, heterosexual, able-bodied offenders. One aspect I was told where there was a 'gaping void' was the issue of class. Many offenders were getting into trouble as they had experienced a life of unending poverty. In terms of access to decent accommodation, work and other basic civil rights, the position that they had occupied within society meant that their life opportunities had been poorer than others. This was related to their social class. While it did not excuse their behaviour, some POs believed that it helped to explain it. Society was unfair; while some people had advantages in life, others had little chance of a decent education or were not expected to achieve much in life. They were almost destined to fail. Structural issues were not on the probation agenda. In language reminiscent of Foucault, I was told: 'We've got the body and we are going through to the soul, and the fact they [the offender] had to adhere to weekly reporting, is almost touted as a kind of war cry of probation officers' (PO12).

An officer with a number of women on his caseload complained that resources for women were scarce. He had wanted a woman with an 'anger management' problem to attend a group to work on this. This was available to men but not to women. He had had to work hard to obtain the money from his service to pay for crèche facilities despite the fact that this should have been readily forthcoming. His experience, both as a PO and previously working in community service, was that court sentencing for women was sexist, with a reluctance to give community sentence orders to women (PO15).

The use of actuarial scales meant that offenders seen as being at low to medium risk of reoffending were sent to reporting centres, rather than being offered individual contact with a PO. The implication of this with regard to female offenders (who tended to commit less serious offences) was that they were rarely offered the opportunity to have one-to-one work with a PO, thus many women offenders lost the opportunity to be supervised which is at the centre of the difference between the old casework model and the actuarial 'risk to public' approach. One PO put this very well:

> 'When we teach students, we say you have got to get your theory into shape, so we make them do child development work, we make them understand human development processes … what we teach people on social work courses is that early life experiences

> will have a significant impact on later functioning. Now the reality is that we know the vast majority of probation clients have suffered either emotional or physical or sexual abuse. There are a good proportion of them from very, very broken damaged homes, so you are talking about issues around attachment theory [which] become very significant for them … you have people who may not have had a significant connection with another human being [and] whose expectations are low. If as an organization you start to repeat those cycles, you risk reinforcing their understanding, and I think it is very dangerous. If part and parcel of the risk assessment is that you don't understand the nature of the person's experience up until now, you lose the whole point that might assist towards a proper understanding … [that could lead to] change.' (PO11)

The change to an actuarial approach has also meant that the emphasis on monitoring equal opportunities in service delivery has moved from ensuring the differences in the various offender groups are taken account of, to focusing on ensuring every offender is dealt with in the same way. One example of this, according to SPO3, was the introduction of standard warning letters for missed appointments. To take account of the low level of literacy among some offenders, letters were written very simply, and in big type, in outlined boxes. For some offenders, however, this has meant that the letters received were seen as patronizing and/or threatening, and potentially modelling the type of aggressive approach that probation was meant to be encouraging offenders to reduce.

Changes in the language of National Standards in the 1995 edition emphasized the quantitative aspects rather than the qualitative aspects of client contact and work undertaken. I was told by a number of probation officers that the processes for gatekeeping, or quality assuring, reports written that came about as the result of services developing anti-discriminatory practice initiatives in the 1980s had been diluted by ACOP and the Inspectorate into a checklist of tick boxes to measure quantitative aspects of reports, rather than measure the quality of the content.

Discrimination and Staff

A report written by Dews and Watts (1994) upset a number of black staff and was perceived by them as a personal attack. More black staff were leaving the service than were joining, and very critical comments were made to me by black staff at how the service was failing them:

> '[I]f the services are saying that we're working in an anti-discriminatory practice way, we're looking at race issues, we're seeking to forward a career [for] our black staff, it doesn't show, because, it seems as though you get … to the glass ceiling and you don't get any further. Are you saying that black staff are not good enough to become chief officers? What are you saying? What message are you giving?' (PO8)

Black staff also experienced difficulties if they were placed in areas that were particularly racist. This might be because they ran a higher risk of being attacked when they went to and from the office or else on their visits. Some had had rubbish dumped on their cars. I was told that the local authority had been very unhelpful about this, and the probation service management had not wanted to get involved. The other aspect of discrimination which was described to me was the disciplining of black staff by the probation service. The issue of black staff having their literacy skills formally investigated was mentioned, including the use of external consultants in this process. One PO was investigated on more than one occasion and did not receive an apology when he was declared competent. Main-grade white staff were predominantly seen as supportive, and the problem was described as being at an institutional level.

'Advise, Assist and Befriend'

The old adage of 'advise, assist and befriend' was seen as a set of values mostly by the POs who had been in the service prior to NS. Protection of the public was seen as a key value by all POs and managers. However, anti-custodialism was *not* mentioned by any POs and it was questioned by some managers. Indeed, one SPO stated that POs would not argue against a custodial sentence if it was perceived as being 'deserved'. New adages included: 'advise, supervise, enforce' and certainly *not* befriend; 'protect the public', 'care and control'. The most extreme response mooted was: 'Deliver whatever you are asked to deliver, do it cheaper, do more for less, punish more'. Even when 'advise, assist and befriend' was seen as relevant, this way of working was not with the blessing of management:

> '[it] now it feels like a very administrative role, you know, they report, we tick 'em in, and that's fine. They don't turn up, we breach them. The bit in the middle, the kind of social work, addressing what the underlying causes of their offending behaviour seems to be, gets a bit lost, I think.' (PO14)

Senior managers did not have a problem with the maintenance of 'advise, assist and befriend', as long as the order was enforced, and they were concerned to point out that the job could not be reduced to 'some kind of mechanistic, form filling administrative type task'. It was pointed out that the national standards did not prevent the continuation of this old adage. Discussion of values with some POs had the potential to depress informants. On a positive note, one PO felt that the values that had brought her team into probation was still 'alive and well'. There was an incongruity between how some POs positioned their own value statements and how they saw the wider service values. Interviewee PO16 was positive about the values she operated to: 'help offenders take responsibility for their actions', 'reconcile the offender with the community', 'develop a victim awareness' and 'protect the public', but she did not ascribe these as the aims of her service. Largely staff interviewed could be described as demoralized, depressed by the sheer amount and pace of change. Respect for offenders was being eroded and the understanding of discrimination in society and how it impacted on certain groups was not reflected in how NS was being enacted.

Changes in the Skills Base of Probation Officers

Social work skills were seen as useful, in particular interpersonal and communication skills. The commitment to fight discrimination was not seen as the prerogative only of social work. It was not seen as helpful to try and 'rally round' these 'old values' but there was a worry by the majority of informants that the emphasis on process might deskill the probation staff. As one PO stated about his preferred way of working, which was psychodynamic rather than cognitive, it was important not to ignore feelings or anger from the past as these had implications for behaviour in the present and future. The uncertainty of the future was such that nobody could predict how the service would operate in years to come. Some saw this as a threat, some as an opportunity. What the future values of the service would be was unclear, but many aspired to new growth and development of skills which would place the probation service centrally within criminal justice, rather than in the past when probation was a marginal influence.

The member of the Central Probation Council I interviewd spoke in terms very reminiscent of social work values when discussing the role of the probation officer, which was seen as:

> 'to care for the offender … and to hold the offender to account and therefore to protect society … you achieve that by using your personality and your relationship with the offender to influence them … if you wanted just controlling punitive officers you might want to employ something similar to a community-base[d] prison service rather than a probation service, and the probation service has traditionally been about hav[ing] an understanding about why particular people act in different ways and I suppose, to put it another way, it is about recognizing that crime is expressing a societal ill which needs to be tackled.' (CPC1)

Seniors didn't think probation officers had had to learn new skills to operate under National Standards, but how to use new systems (apart from keyboard skills). The use of the Standards in a quantitative way had reduced the opportunity for staff to use their *existing* skills. The changes brought about by the Criminal Justice Act 1991, which preceded the introduction of National Standards, meant that the application of skills staff already possessed was more in relation to assessment: risk assessment, needs assessment, assessment of intervention needed to reduce the likelihood of further offending. All of these were involved in the role of the probation officer prior to the 1991 Act, but in a more diffuse way. Some POs felt that they had had to learn to be more businesslike in their practice, for example the sending of standard letters for appointments, like 'dentists and doctors'. In terms of traditional skills, these were important to make risk assessments (for the individual and to the public), but POs had to be more focused and had to learn where to concentrate their energies. The growth in the use of partnership agencies was uncomfortable for many POs who did not want to give up primary responsibility for contact with offenders. Some of this unease was about the *quality* of what the agencies were capable of giving to offenders.

The focus on developing programmes for offenders under the Effective Practice initiatives meant an increased focus on skills in delivering prepackaged programmes. This was perceived, on occasion, to be at the expense of the use of group work skills, as the package has come to be an end in itself, rather than a means to an end, and the content has become more important than the process. The recent ACOP Enforcement Audit showed there was no proper way of measuring whether the quality of work had improved since the introduction of National Standards. New effective-practice initiatives were described as 'new techniques based on old ones', but just called something else where the underpinning theories were essentially the same. Cognitive behavioural methods of working with offenders were taught on the old social work courses, but psychodynamic training was also offered, which was time-consuming and did not allow for the case management approach now demanded. Probation services were now using computer-driven programs to determine the risk of reoffending, the two most common packages being ACE and OGRS. Scores were entered, of between one and five, under various categories for example, sex, age, criminal history, accommodation (including type, degree of permanence), alcohol issues, and so on, and then the programme gave a percentage score of the degree of risk presented by the offender.

Having generated the score, the program (and not the PO) automatically generated the type of intervention the offender would receive; for example, low scores would mean low-level reporting (ticking in) at a reporting centre; high-level risk might mean twice-weekly attendance in a thirteen-week group programme. The process of quick assessments and then moving offenders on made some POs question their part in the process which was described as 'shuffling people about' and did not lead to much job satisfaction. The task was to move offenders on quickly, without getting to know them. Working with a large number of 'lower risk' offenders meant the pressure came from completing the large number of risk assessments that had to be completed regularly. Probation officers made the point that whatever the score said it still eventually meant the offender and the PO meeting together in a room, which required some skill. The main concern was for those offenders who were assessed as low-risk in terms of reoffending, but where there was a risk of self-harm. Interviewee PO17 was worried that these offenders could fall through the net and she hoped the person's needs would be picked up in the reporting centre. This new PO was sceptical about whether she was doing 'any good' with offenders and described her intervention as 'more of an enforcement'. She did not feel that enforcement, without building up a relationship with the offender, could be effective. Her responsibility was to pass on offenders quickly, once the assessment had been completed, but the resources were not there for the offenders to be picked up and worked with immediately. The responsibility to send out the warning letters and to enforce the orders lay with her. It was not a question of learning new skills, and the job was not giving her satisfaction. In the supervision centres, low-risk offenders would be required to sign in a book to confirm attendance. They would be seen by untrained probation service assistants and the process was rudimentary. However, it satisfied the demands of National Standards.

Senior managers were enthusiastic at the opportunities offered by the 'effective practice' initiatives, which had replaced the depression of the 'nothing works' scenario of Martinson, who had 'haunted' the probation service for many years (Martinson, 1974). The multi-agency public protection role had led to a positive sharing relationship with the police and acknowledgement of probation expertise. It was put to me that the probation service had to satisfy a number of stakeholders, which included the courts, as well as the Home Office. The latter, in a power position over the service, were fixated on national standards, but this was not always of interest to the courts who viewed this as part of the 'executive', not the judiciary. The judiciary and the Home Office did not always see eye to eye. Many magistrates still wanted to be able to offer welfare services to 'inadequate' offenders, and did not take kindly to being told that their (inadequate offender's) criminogenic need was too low to require probation intervention. These stakeholders wanted the traditional probation skills.

Probation Officers: Case Managers, not Case Workers?

Changes in the use of service spending, to ensure that a certain percentage of service budgets was spent on funding partner organizations to deliver services to clients, meant that probation officers have increasingly seen themselves as case managers rather than case workers. Interviewee SPO3 applauded the move to encourage clients to use more community-based facilities than was the case previously; however, he added: 'I am concerned about the quality of some of the services being provided. In some instances I am aware of probation officers being obliged to refer clients to services whose staff are less knowledgeable and skilled than the probation officers referring them. This is particularly true, in my experience, of drug and alcohol work.'

Another change was the increasing specialization of the service into functional roles, so that pre-sentence report (PSR) writing, community supervision, through-care and group work had all become specialisms in themselves, in the same way that prison and hostel work were seen as specialisms. A consequence of this for the offender, I was told, was that the offender would be seen by a number of different staff and, in consequence, would not know who was supervising his order. This could lead to an (anomic) lack of commitment to the order. Conversely, this had reduced the opportunity for new staff to experience the range of work that probation officers undertake to get adequate experience in order to feel confident about moving between the different areas of work; and a similar lack of investment in working on a one-off basis with the offender. While this was not a direct consequence of the 1991 Criminal Justice Act, it is a result of the continuing changes that have been introduced within the service since the 1991 Act came into force. Rather than bring together the various pieces of legislation that affected the work of the service into a consolidating Act, and allow a period of consolidation, as was stated as one of the aims of the 1991 Act, the introduction of the Act preceded an period of increasing change and further legislation that is still continuing, with the threat to cut offenders' state benefit if they fail to conform to community sentences and also the threat of automatic prison sentences for those who breach community orders.

Even before this, POs were very aware of the changing ethos in the job, which was now to help offenders complete the community sentence, rather than primarily achieve personal change:

> 'I think the first thing that we've learned is to accept that we are not a social work agency, but rather a criminal justice agency, to manage the sentences that are imposed by the courts, I think that's one thing. But then, I think the new skills have something to do with talking to our clients in a way that is not frightening, but at the same time, is very open and frank whereas hitherto they'd be looking at growth in the long term…' (PO10)

Some POs were happy to describe themselves as case managers and the possibility of organizing 'packages' was seen as potentially useful to 'sell' non-custodial options to magistrates. Instead of 'advising, assisting and befriending', PO5 described herself as a 'referrer', but admitted to feeling low in terms of morale and said she would leave the service if she could. Other POs were more positive about the changes, but linked the changing nature of the offender profile to serious offences, to increasing stress for staff. PO7, who was probably the most enthusiastic exponent for the changes, felt that managers were not actually managing the changes very well. This was because she thought that senior staff either did not understand what was meant by 'effective practice' or else they were stuck in the befriending role and were leaving the main grade officers to cope as best they could. Thus there was a 'crisis management' model which she saw as being at variance with the Home Office model. She did not see that there was a problem in ticking offenders in to fulfil their obligation to report to a probation officer under NS, as long as a full risk assessment had been undertaken. There was no need to think in terms of befriending, which she saw as confusing to offenders, as POs were not meant to be offenders' 'friends'. Contact now was to undertake 'specific tasks' and the job was now less 'fuzzy'.

The difference between being a case manager and a case worker was very important to some POs as they wanted to be 'hands on'. The former role was described by some as being a 'paper shuffling' exercise, not requiring people-centred skills. Many older POs took earlier retirement as they did not like the amendments to the changes and POs adopted different strategies to cope. Some experienced POs were described as 'paperwork professionals' who could 'churn out reports'. It was stated that POs could not both keep up with all the paperwork and maintain the previous level of contact with offenders, and this upset many of the staff.

As part of the case management role, POs liaised with other community agencies, making new alliances. In particular, probation now worked much more closely with the police. This was seen as important by senior managers. The police were now called on to manage and keep surveillance on high-risk and dangerous offenders and they saw that the probation service as one of the few organizations that had the skills to assist them in this task.

Engaging with a Different Type of Offender

I was told that the offenders' probation had engaged with over the last eight years, since the introduction of the 1991 Act, had become increasingly more serious. They presented greater risks to the community than before. These people were in the system and in the community previously, but the service had little to do with them as they were those not considered for, or not granted, parole until the 1991 Act had changed the parole system. With all offenders sentenced to imprisonment for a period of 12 months or more now being released on some type of licence, a group of offenders that the service previously had had little to do with now became a considerable proportion of the probation caseload. A senior manger commented that, although offenders were less likely to have had any say in whether they were to be supervised by the probation service, this did not mean that there was less reason to try to engage with them. Her concern was that newer POs were quick to instigate the breach process, but they had not attempted to find out *why* the person had not attended a meeting. The unanswered question was whether the new officers had developed the knowledge, inclination and ability to engage with (at least the) reluctant offenders:

> 'I found myself, with some experienced officers, saying you must breach this person now and with some new officers saying, don't breach them, go and put some effort in … some of the new officers are so keen … that they no longer see it that they have to use *social work skills* trying to get someone back. I think my view would be that enforcement does not mean that you do not try to engage somebody and keep them coming, and enforcement on its own actually fails.' (SM2) (my italics)

'Advise, assist and befriend' was still appropriate in delivering service to offenders according to many staff. However, risk assessments and working 'effectively' had become the central priority. The new 'buzz phrase' that appeared to have developed was 'protection of the public', although 'enforcement action after two missed appointments' ran it a close second on occasion. What was less certain was whether it was the role of probation officers to deliver direct work with offenders. The increased emphasis on the use of partnership organizations in providing services in the community meant that the delivery of some services had become the responsibility of others, and this created mixed reactions in main grade staff. Many did not want to lose their interpersonal skills, but recognized that working in partnership required different skills.

The effective-practice initiatives presumed a knowledge of cognitive skills and the delivery of agreed programmes in areas like anger management, sex offenders, substance abuse, and so on. Some senior managers were concerned that with the speed of change, POs had not yet learned how to understand and implement an approach that drew predominantly on cognitive skills. Probation staff would be trained to do this and it was not clear to informants at the time of interview how much personal discretion they would be allowed. The traditional role of befriending and working long term on problems from the offender's past was very much out of favour and was not seen, at least at senior level, as being as effective as the cognitive approach. This view was not shared by all at main grade level, many of whom talked fondly of their 'social work knowledge and skills'. There was a fear that a 'checklist' mentality was developing.

Much of the above analysis focused on the effect that NS has had on the probation service, with its central thrust of compliance. The emphasis on ensuring this compliance has become a central tenet of the service. This was difficult because there was not a simple causal relationship between compliance to court orders and ensuring that the risk to the public was kept as low as possible. Extreme examples were given to underline this point: mentally disordered offenders who had become completely disassociated and cut off, and who were unable to keep appointments, or sex offenders, who were usually the epitome of compliance, but this did not mean that they were not intending to abuse, as their offending included a measure of pre-planning, cunning and plausibility. The Home Office Inspector felt that there was still 'an enormous scope to work with offenders and not just be doing, and monitoring, a tick box sort of basis … it is the job of probation service managers and indeed us lot, to make that sort of government expectation'.

One probation officer was very involved in the training of new staff for the new qualification of Diploma in Probation Studies, the successor to the social work-based Diploma in Social Work. It appeared that a different ethos was being inculcated into the trainees by the service:

> 'They are much stricter and also much clearer about the role of probation, and they are not coming from so much of a social work angle, which is quite interesting. They seem to be quite clear about why the person is there, about the harm that that person has caused in the community and the victims of society. They are quite on the ball in terms of enforcement if people do not turn up and what they would do.' (PO7)

I was told by other staff that the new recruits were 'an incredibly bright bunch'; many were graduates, chosen because they had clear minds, had no preconceptions of what they were coming into, were capable of working at a frenetic level, and could operate more as case managers than case workers. For experienced POs, the changes in practice were uncomfortable. The computerization of records meant that records were becoming much more concise and it was not possible to record the quality of the work undertaken. This was put eloquently by one PO:

> 'I can fill out forms and rattle off reports til the cows come home, but in terms of actually sitting down one-to-one face contact with clients, that is what's having to go. I feel very sad about that, also quite angry about it because the reason I came into this work is to do social work with clients. It wasn't to fill out endless forms and appease governments and whatever.' (PO14)

The decision to work in ways that did not emphasize traditional 'casework' skills was seen as 'not very intelligent', as ultimately it would result in a less skilled and effective workforce. Newer officers could adapt to the changes, but as mentioned above, there was a schism, exemplified by an observation from a very experienced PO on what was perceived as acceptable quality of work under NS:

> 'an officer … qualified two or three years, sent a file over to our office on some work she had done with a prisoner, with a list of questions, and the first question was: "Are you addressing your offending behaviour? If not, why not?" The officers here were quite horrified that this had been done … what it actually meant and how it would be received and how it was going to enhance our work with that person or reduce the risk of offending, [or the] protection of the public on release; and the fact that [it] was held as an excellent file, because the records were up-to-date and written in the style of National Standards. But there seemed to be no interest in or concern about the quality of the input, other than that that officer was doing what she was meant to be doing.' (PO16)

The Organizational Response

One reason for the implementation of the changes, put to me by seniors and main grade officers, had been the inadequacy of the main service organizations to present a united approach to government proposals. Middle managers and main grade officers complained that the members of both the Association of Chief Officers of Probation (ACOP) and Central Probation Council (CPC) were so disparate in their views that neither organization had been able to take a lead in defending the Service's work coherently. In fact, one senior commented somewhat cynically that the main way the two organizations seemed to have found of presenting a united approach was to agree with all the changes that had been suggested. The united approach of the above to organizations, together with the probation officer's union NAPO, to defending the status, and to a large extent the content, of probation officer qualifying training, had not been matched in protecting the Service from other changes that had occurred. The CPC person interviewed described chief officers as pragmatists who had not forgotten that offenders were human beings. The problem was that the public elected the government who then decided on policy. The author was reminded that CPC, ACOP, NAPO and other organizations had resisted the strictures of the last Conservative government to abolish the need for a professional qualification to practice as a probation officer.

NAPO was seen by some informants as being on its own in arguing against the more major changes in direction that have been imposed on it by the Home Office under both Conservative and Labour governments. Other informants, at all levels, saw NAPO as being ineffective in opposing some of the changes. The disparate views of all these organizations were seen as responsible for creating the move towards a national Probation Service. This view did not include a consideration of where the power to create change lay. In many ways the successful rearguard action to hold on to a professional Probation Service in the last year of the Conservative government was an impressive achievement. The NAPO representative was concerned that probation services were locating all problems within the offender. The influential

Underdown Report (1998) typified this as housing, poverty and other social problems not addressed as 'offending behaviour' became the narrow focus for probation intervention. This was linked to an overconcentration on risk assessment and risk management. Early assessment tools like OGRS and LSIR were used on the premise that computers could tell the probation officer how criminal the offender was likely to be. The computer assessment tool only considered 'static' factors, such as offending history, sex, age and so on. The latter included 'dynamic', that is, changeable factors, but according to the NAPO person, it ignored whether or not the offender was homeless, being more concerned with the number of times he had moved in the last three years and whether he lived in a 'high crime' area. Homelessness *per se* was not seen as relevant in the consideration of the risk of reoffending. It did not address issues of changing behaviour and what might help in working with the offender. The (then) latest assessment tool, called ACE, at least asked a range of questions, which included detailed questions on finance and personal circumstances, and it asked the offender to comment on how they saw her situation, what they saw as her problem(s), and how hard it would be to avoid these problems in the future. A cynical experienced probation officer might suggest that this was the line of reasoning they used in the past, without the need of a computer-driven set of prompts. What gave the NAPO person cause for optimism was the belief that New Labour would put rehabilitation back on the agenda. Jack Straw was seen as being different to Michael Howard, although he was still more authoritarian than the service is currently. This implied that NAPO expected the service to become more authoritarian, without necessarily putting more people in prison.

Some probation officers felt that their chiefs were worried about the direction in which the probation service was moving, and that the pressure for change from the Home Office had caused services to respond in a reactive way. There had been an effective guerrilla war fought against Michael Howard but after Labour had come to power the resistance had ceased and chiefs followed the prescriptive rules from the Home Office, as they wanted to keep their jobs, as probation became a national organization. A typical comment was that senior managers wanted to stay in the 'good books of the Home Office'. There appeared to be an autocratic edge to how decisions were made, without reference to practitioner staff. One service had tested four different practice models in their area but had failed to indicate how they were going to choose which model would become the main one for the area.

A PSO with responsibility for taking offenders back to court told me that he was being told to prosecute breaches, even if there were only a couple of days left on the order. This was because these cases would be picked up by Home Office internal monitoring and the Service wanted to be seen to have delivered punishment.

There was considerable difference between the way senior managers and employers saw the changes, and the way they were viewed by main grade staff. The emphasis on quantity rather than quality that had been imposed by senior managers and employers seemed to be representative of a value base which was not concerned with the quality of work, or the recognition of difference in developing anti-discriminatory practice. This was in opposition to the values of the majority of workers in the Service who wanted to focus on providing quality services to offenders, but were increasingly limited in their opportunities to do so. The probation service was described by some main grade as more of a 'business organization' being concerned with performance, statistics and budget. National Standards, working in the most cost-effective way, and low reconviction rates during the sentence were the central priority. One of the more enthusiastic POs, who worked in an office where anti-discriminatory practice (ensuring that all offenders received as fair an opportunity and access to probation resources as possible) was a high priority, mentioned the high stress and sickness rate and unhappiness among POs. She felt that management were:

> 'so enthused about their effective practice and what we are going to do in the future – which in a way is good and positive – but the other side of the coin is that I am not sure whether they really had an understanding of the strength of feeling and therefore they are not terribly responsive to it, but I also believe that is the same everywhere … the Service is under pressure to respond to meet governments' changes and expectations. I am just not convinced that they have gone about it in the most intelligent way.' (PO16)

Probation officers wanted to practice in an anti-discriminatory way but the criminal justice system was still operating in a racist way. This was not perceived as a central priority of the probation service, which had to respond to outside performance targets. Senior managers spoke of a commitment to anti-discriminatory practice but there was a danger in forcing all black offenders, for example, to attend empowerment groups. Voluntary attendance was likely to lead to low attendance. The problem appeared to be lack of dialogue as the different strata faced up to their particular pressures and strains. This was referred to by one senior manager as 'part of our cultural problem' (SM2). Main grade officers felt the financial pressures as offices closed, secretarial staff were laid off and there was an attitude that they should be grateful for having a job. Middle managers felt there was a gulf between them and the next rung in the hierarchy. One critical comment from an SPO was that they 'had to make the operation work … there is a lot of management currently, I am not sure whether there is a lot of leadership.'

In contrast, a senior manager expressed some exasperation with some main grade staff where 'it had become part of the culture' to resist changes, including National Standards, and saw the rift at the next level of responsibility:

> 'The practitioners don't focus and blame their seniors, because they have a bit of loyalty and they know them. I think we have an increasing gap between the management and the senior managers … What higher middle managers have done is to try to protect their staff, but what that has done has allowed them a kind of false illusion and some complacency ... if you don't want to work and deliver this then you had better start looking elsewhere because there is not going to be an option.' (SM2)

The poor record on enforcement was seen by another senior manager as a reason why the new Labour government was not 'trumpeting more loudly the success of the probation service'. Because of this, the probation service was innovating ways of increasing the rate of enforcement (and breach) by piloting the use of a specialist breach officer.

Morale and Issues of Control

The change to a Labour government had led to a hope by some main grade officers that the service would regain a feeling of professionalism after a period of low morale. However, Jack Straw was described as being as punitive in outlook, and anti-probation, as Michael Howard had been, despite the resurrection of professional training. A senior manager described morale as 'very, very low', although he hoped to be able to engage with the government agenda in the future. There was an acknowledgement that to be seen to be engaging too closely with probation was 'political suicide'; however, they knew that the service was needed and it fulfilled a vital role. The service, as a very small component in the criminal justice system, had been forced to see itself as a cog in a bigger wheel, and hope was expressed that this might lead to its influence expanding as it worked in partnership and its knowledge and skills were acknowledged. Some POs adopted a conciliatory approach to management, while acknowledging that there was a strong anti-management bias by main of the main grade, associated with the contract culture, electronic tagging and other changes. For senior managers, the new culture held a danger that practice was viewed simplistically by politicians and the Home Office. It was pointed out to me that at a time when many of the controls on the public sector were being removed by the creation of 'Next Steps' agencies, the Home Office was moving in the opposite direction to greater centralization and central control. An example of this was a naive Home Office survey on practical projects, which found them to be ineffective, and was followed by a letter to the different probation services saying stop supporting these projects. (Practical projects were used to teach offenders skills for future work and other life choices. The one referred to above was a motor project, which entailed teaching offenders car maintenance. It was supposed to help them to legalize how they viewed car ownership by encouraging them to understand how a car worked, and how to drive and maintain a car legally. This was seen as more likely to make them law-abiding than fining and banning young offenders who were drawn to cars and repeatedly offending.)

The service's own research, written up in the *British Journal of Criminology*, contradicted this, and there was evidence that it reduced offending and was cost-effective. They were able to keep the project going.

It was the sheer intensity of the change that was problematic, and the way the offender was considered. There was clearly a high level of stress within the service, which had in turn produced a high level of staff sickness. The impression was given that the SPOs were pragmatists seeking to contain a difficult pressurized situation of rising demand for services and diminishing resources. The probation world had moved on from 'advise, assist and befriend', especially the 'befriend' part. It was questioned whether 'anti-custodialism' was a common value, particularly of the main grade. The new values of the profession were still to be articulated, but it was clear that there was a vacuum to be filled. This might become clearer in years to come, as qualified staff from the new Diploma in Probation Studies emerge and begin to take influential positions within the service. They will not have known social work values, but what will be put in their place? They were being trained to be case managers, but would they be able to make relationships and hold on to difficult offenders, especially if they were trained to breach quickly those offenders who did not comply with probation conditions? If values are not articulated clearly, then the void is likely to be filled with procedures which do not recognize difference in terms of race, class, life opportunities and experiences and gender, and which treat each offender as fully responsible for their (premeditated) action(s), and therefore fully entitled to receive the same punishment and justice.

Where did this Leave the Probation Service?

Bureaucratic tasks

Graphic detail was given on how this was becoming ever more of a burden, and POs complained of being under huge work pressure, not least because of the sheer number of new forms they had to complete. The implementation of National Standards had resulted in a break from what had occurred before, and a common complaint was that the supervision and inspection of probation work was concerned with ensuring compliance to the standards and not with the quality of the work undertaken with offenders. Many officers complained that they felt 'deskilled' as they became more concerned with 'processing' offenders rather than working therapeutically with them. 'Meaningless statistics' were being generated, along with computer-generated assessments of reoffending risk.

Control, therapeutic work and the value base

There was an increasing expectation that missed appointments inevitably led to breach action. It was clear that POs wanted to work in a therapeutic way, but were prepared to exercise their authority and breach offenders for noncompliance to National Standards. There were clear differences between pre- and post-NS trained POs in this respect, although experienced POs had been pushed into increasing their breach rate and felt that they had no choice but to do so. It was easier for post-NS POs to adapt to changing requirements, but this group was feeling more stressed as the inflexibilities of NS become manifest. They were adopting strategies to keep chaotic offenders away from the courts which, they explained, did not want to deal with breach. 'Social work values', as mentioned by Mair (1997a, b) earlier in the text as being an area of some mystique, was important to POs.

Probation officers had been instructed to stop using the word 'client' when talking about offenders but most, of all levels of seniority, used this term in conversation. It was felt by many main grade officers that the more rigid system of reporting and the increasing use of standardized letters and procedures did not allow for the problems experienced by chaotic offenders. This was seen as discriminatory. The need for anti-discriminatory practice (ADP) was essential: probation officers should work in a way that did not disadvantage offenders due to their race, gender, sex, sexuality or any other basis. Cultural sensitivity may sound like a form of political correctness, but it was a very important professional objective. Many offenders had suffered a lifetime of discrimination, and so it was vital that they experienced no prejudice, inadvertent or otherwise, from probation staff. Tentatively, it would appear that more black POs were cynical that senior management were not interested in promoting these values, but more interviews with black and white POs are needed to substantiate this.

The old adage of 'assist, advise and befriend' was a convenient metaphor for the old service ethos and values. Staff at all levels had a mixed response as to whether this was still appropriate. The argument on one side was that POs had to have the skills to engage with and gain the trust of offenders, while others felt that this was harking back to a bygone era, and was unnecessary and confusing to offenders who did not regard POs as their 'friends'. Other phrases put forward included terms like, 'protect the public', 'supervise and enforce', 'care and control'. More cynical alternatives were also extended, focusing on cheapness and punishment. This part of the interview brought out feelings of demoralization from many POs and there was an acknowledgement at all levels of the service that morale was low.

Alongside more frequent but briefer contact with offenders had gone the computerization of probation offices and a dramatic decline in the number of administrative and secretarial staff. Probation officers were then expected to input their records into the computer and to type their own reports. Had the system worked, there would have been important implications for confidentiality, as hitherto confidential information was shared between different criminal justice agencies. Instead, it was an expensive incompetent fiasco. The computerization of the records made it easier for senior staff to monitor case records from their officers, without main grade staff knowing which files were being viewed by management, as they could then read all records online without having to physically inspect files in the probation officers' rooms. The brevity of the records de-professionalized them, as they simply became descriptive accounts of offenders' attendance at meetings with POs.

There was a shift away from working with offenders during their time in prison for both time and financial reasons. Senior managers were more ready to accept the move away from undertaking welfare-oriented work to the new ways of working, which included spending more time on completing structured computerized risk assessments, but many main grade probation officers regretted and resented their inability to work with offenders during their time in prison.

Changes in probation practice, and its skills base

Traditionally offenders had always been seen by POs, not a 'pool' of POs, where they would not know who they were reporting to. It would appear that many offenders received what can only be described as a very superficial service. Probation officers had lost their flexibility to decide when offenders needed to be seen, as National Standards decided the frequency rates. Thus some offenders would be seen when there was not a need to do so and contact was usually for a shorter time. There was limited opportunity for more in-depth work to be completed. Some offenders might still receive a 'traditional' interview, but time pressures largely precluded this.

National Standards was a major preoccupation with newer POs but was also talked about a lot by their more experienced colleagues. Its impact forced POs to manage their time in a different way. However, one interesting observation that was made in my interviews was that newer POs trained in NS enjoyed working in a traditional way and adapted to it very happily when offered the opportunity. Senior probation officers would have liked to offer the type of meaningful supervision deemed by Kemshall (1997, 1998) to be necessary in the supervision of dangerous offenders. It was clear that they did not have time to do this and POs confirmed that this was the case.

Other noteworthy points arising from my interviews were as follows:

- Newer POs experienced role confusion when they did not have to follow as strict a NS model than the one they had been trained in.
- Newer POs appeared to have the same value base as their more experienced colleagues.
- Senior POs referred to newer POs as case managers rather than caseworkers.
- All POs were prepared to engage with partnerships; experience did not seem to be a factor in this.
- The more recent emphasis on risk assessments was approved of by all POs, although some complained that *every* offender had to have an assessment, which was time-consuming.
- POs stated that magistrates recognized the need to give some offenders time, more than did the senior managers and the Home Office, who insisted on adherence to NS inspections, derided by some informants as a waste of time and money.
- Senior managers were the ones who had to implement the orders of the Home Office, and some expressed irritation that the main grade officers and their immediate managers had been protected from the realities and pressures of being forced to implement budget cuts and new procedures.

Responses to the Changing Offender Profile and 'Effective Practice' Initiatives

This must be considered in two parts. First, in terms of considering 'risk to the public' posed by offenders, a term still needing a rigorous definition (reoffending, dangerousness, etc.), offenders were not seen generally as becoming more dangerous. The nature of the offence was different; according to POs interviewed, there were fewer burglars and car thieves, more drunk driving and drugs-related crimes. Second, different areas generated different problems, so that in one area there might be a higher proportion of asylum seekers, and offenders needed the services of an interpreter as they struggled to survive in a strange, unfriendly environment. Notwithstanding this, all offenders had to be seen in the same way. The main difference was that *all offenders* sentenced to terms of imprisonment for one year or more were seen on statutory licence on discharge. These were involuntary 'clients' of the service, and who many were predominantly low-risk were given only a rudimentary level of supervision. These tended to be the offenders who had been given short periods on automatic conditional release. However, long-term offenders who would previously have been considered bad risks for parole would still be given periods of probation supervision. Sex offenders were unlikely to get parole but now could receive extended probation supervision and have their names on the sex offenders' register, so they would have to report future changes in address and circumstances to the police. Where in earlier terms there was antipathy and suspicion between POs and the police, there was now closer liaison, as they were charged with the responsibility of overseeing and keeping checks on these offenders.

In terms of probation practice, new cognitive skills programmes were being implemented, possibly at the cost of spending time getting to know offenders personally and gaining their trust. The programmes were likely to be implemented during 2001/02 but it was likely, for the sake of programme integrity, that POs would have to stick to a taught script. There appeared to be some concern that new officers were too ready to breach and take offenders back to court without trying to find out why they had missed appointments and whether they could be worked with to encourage compliance. Could this be the cost of putting compliance as the goal of probation, rather than befriending and understanding the world of the offender?

Why Staff Believed the Changes were Taking Place

Who had generated the changes, and had this led to changes in values/perceptions within the service? The old value system which placed emphasis on respect for the 'client' (now a taboo word) and on 'difference' was gone, as the offender became an object to be worked with. His or her permission was no longer necessary; they could no longer give consent to be made the subject of a probation order; it became an order of the court in the Criminal Justice Act 1991. The growth in compulsory prison post-release supervision also increased the involuntary nature of probation contact. Ironically, the new priorities of risk assessment, protection of the public, structured assessment, working in partnership and interdisciplinary cooperation have gained precedence in social work at the same time as in probation practice. These changes have not occurred in a vacuum but at a time when there has been dissatisfaction with traditional social work. There was a general acknowledgement that traditional probation practice had been idiosyncratic and contact with offenders had been unspecific and unstructured. A move towards change would therefore have been supported.

It was the sheer intensity of the change that was problematic, and the way the offender was considered. There was clearly a high level of stress within the service, which had in turn produced a high level of staff sickness. The impression was given that SPOs were pragmatists seeking to contain a difficult situation of rising demand for services and diminishing resources. The probation world had moved on from 'advise, assist and befriend', especially the 'befriend' part. It was questioned whether 'anti-custodialism' was a common value, particularly of the main grade. 'Anti-custodialism' means trying not to send offenders to prison, by recommending (in pre-sentence reports) constructive sentencing options to the judiciary that did not result in a prison sentence. The new values of the profession were still to be articulated, but it was clear that there was a vacuum here to be filled.

This may become clearer in years to come as qualified staff from the new Diploma in Probation Studies emerge and begin to take influential positions within the service. They will not have known the old social work values, but what will be put in their place? They were trained to be case managers, but would they be able to make relationships and deal with difficult offenders, especially if they were trained to breach quickly those offenders who did not comply with probation conditions?

Transitions and Change in Probation Practice

Leach (2003), a Deputy Chief Probation Officer, wrote about his 30 years in the service and the changes he had experienced. He was particularly concerned at how accredited ('what works?') group work programmes were being implemented, which he described as 'over-centralized and, in my view, over-bureaucratic' (2003, p. 21). He also cited the 'abject failure of the Home Office to [provide a high quality information system] … with CRAMS … as a warning of the perils of providing support services in a centralized way' (2003, p. 27). He could have predicted the C-NOMIS fiasco for similar reasons. At this point the probation service was adjusting to becoming a national organization and he concluded his book with a plea that it was 'crucial … for the probation service to control its own destiny'.

Farrow (2004) conducted research in two probation service areas examining how much experienced POs (with over 10 years' service) still felt committed to the service. She found that those she interviewed were demoralized, alienated and while, remaining committed to their work and colleagues, were not so loyal to the service as an organization, not least because they did not feel valued. In 2005, I interviewed two probation staff about their practice. The first was an experienced probation officer with six years' experience, who had started five years before that as a social worker specializing in child protection. She felt that she had had the skills that had been wanted in the service and was happy to transfer to probation. Thus all of her career had taken place under National Standards, but she had had experience of the move from the first to the second edition. Her experience echoed comments made to me by other staff, and so forms an interesting case study. She commented on the staff who had joined her office and the exodus of others, resulting in a new balance of knowledge and skills. New staff did not have the knowledge of the 'welfare side' and the balance that had to be struck between this and enforcement. 'I still call the people I supervise "clients" quite a lot and I am corrected to call them "offenders" by the new officers straight away … I think one of the things that's very telling is the phone, because it's an open plan office and you often hear the new officers being very strict and being very boundaried in how they are talking to the people they supervise, whereas I think the previous officers were bit more befriending … although there were boundaries, you tended to be a bit more flexible about how you spoke to [offenders]. It sounded very robotic with the new [staff], that's my experience.' She has now left probation.

My second interviewee concentrated on what was called an 'enforcement uplift' as his service had not performed well in the national league table in terms of returning offenders to court quickly when they failed to keep to National Standards. There was a tightening up of the system of sending warning letters to offenders to ensure compliance. There was a feeling that staff were being 'bulldozed by above into passivity' to concentrate on meeting the required contact time with offenders. The random nature of reporting centres was also commented upon.

Personal reflections on probation practice appeared in the *Probation* journal, such as Annison *et al.* (2008) and Matthews (2009), a newly qualified probation officer, reinforced the findings recorded above. He commented that he had joined the service perceiving it to be a 'people-centred' job. However, like the findings of Annison *et al.*, who had examined newly trained POs' perceptions of their job, he had experienced a 'high level of frustration' with the bureaucratic demands of the job. He cited research that emphasized the importance of relationships, and commented that high caseloads meant that relationships could not be formed to any great extent. Annison *et al.* recorded that their informants had entered the job for humanist reasons and were able to articulate both positive and negative experiences. While they felt that they could change the lives of their offenders in a positive way, they also mentioned the lack of direct work with offenders, lack of resources, high workloads and repetitive form-filling. Their article ended on a plea that practitioners' voices needed to be heard if the service was to continue to protect the public.

Given the high turnover in probation staff and the earlier comments expressing concern about the changes, it is important to gain an idea of whether new recruits have the same motivation as the earlier social-work-trained staff. Deering (2010) looked at the views and values of two cohorts of students, a total of 103 informants. He found that 'some of the attitudes, values and beliefs expressed … might not be seen as too far removed from those seen as more traditional and akin to social work' (Deering, 2010, p. 19). His concern was that given the government agenda that prioritized 'offender management and control, punishment and the protection of the public' (p. 23) there was 'potential for a degree of organizational and personal strain' (p. 23). Ledger (2010), a career probation officer who became NAPO General

Secretary, commented on the contempt felt by the previous Chief Executive of NOMS, Phil Wheatley, for the calibre of probation management, and said that NAPO had waged a campaign for the end of NOMS. He cited the evidence of Oldfield and Grimshaw (2008) which showed that although expenditure on probation had increased by 50 per cent in real terms between 2000 and 2008, with a 65 per cent increase in front-line staff, workloads had risen by 39 per cent between 1999 and 2009 and in the last three years front-line staff numbers had dropped by 17 per cent. Only 24 per cent of practitioners' time was spent on face-to-face work and the rest was spent on record keeping and on the computer. He was cautiously optimistic about the future of probation, but concerned about the loss of staff, threats to training, and the lack of clarity between NOMS, probation trusts and Directors of Offender Management (DOMs) who would have a commissioning role. David Scott, who was the Chief of London Probation before he resigned in the aftermath of the murder of two French students by Danno Sonnex, who was under probation supervision at the time, did not mince his words:

> 'The emasculation of the probation service over the past ten years has been accomplished by political apathy and public indifference. [In 2000] there was much talk of giving probation a national voice and a strengthened role in the criminal justice system. [By 2010], probation has been pushed from pillar to post. Far from having a national voice, the organization, which at any time supervises [over] 200 000 offenders in the community, is not even represented in its own right in key national decision-making fora, but subsumed within a vast Prison Service-dominated bureaucracy. A national asset is being squandered.' (Scott, 2009, pp. 291–295)

In his article he acknowledged the tragedy of cases that had led to murders by offenders under probation supervision, for example Sonnex, of whom he commented that probation resourcing was trivialized by the Justice Secretary (I return to the question of blame in Chapter 9; see Fitzgibbon, 2011). Staff mentioned two major initiatives with their service, 'Going for Green' and 'Going for Gold'. After the Sonnex case, ILPS set up the first initiative 'Going for Green', to meet the targets set by Her Majesty's Inspectorate of Probation on public protection work. 'Going for Gold' was a second initiative to meet targets in four key areas: public protection would be a shared task by staff at all levels and a priority for the probation service area; staff at all levels should have the necessary skills and support in risk assessment and management; the probation area should work with partner and other agencies to maximize the protection of the public; and the probation area will maximize its experiences of effective risk management in order to continuously improve its work with offenders.

Both required daily office briefings and total adherence to National Standards. I was told by a senior manager this had been necessary for the survival of his probation service. For staff, working towards these initiatives had precluded much direct contact with the client group, but everyone had realized that there was a survival element involved – there was a danger that the service would not survive in its current form and could have been taken over by either a different public sector organisation or one in the private sector. The second initiative had been more positive and had focused on professional issues, such as improving assessments and risk management.

Most recently I have been privileged to work with many experienced probation staff completing a Master's degree in Public Protection that I set up in collaboration with the London Probation Trust. The commitment of the staff to protecting the public was strong and their motivation was high. They had large caseloads and were burdened with many bureaucratic tasks, but still they were positive at the opportunity to have some time out to reflect and discuss their work. Their philosophy was mostly sympathetic to social work values but morale was a major issue for many of them. The sessions highlighted the variation in how multi-agency public protection worked (see more on this in Chapter 9) but essentially POs were committed to working creatively with offenders in much more than a rigid and risk-focused way. Risk was still a major factor, given the serious offending history of the client group, but it would be unfair to characterize these experienced professionals as being besotted with managing risk. This would be an unfair caricature of people under pressure. In the words of one PO I worked with:

> 'As an experienced probation officer I have benefited with the organization supporting me in developing my learning in working with offending behaviour. Sadly, I feel that I am witnessing the tragedy of its demise, with its core values being eradicated despite the upper echelons of management highlighting "offender engagement", a relaxation of National Standards and a rehabilitative approach rhetoric. In today's climate the service's key focus is a "business approach", with its client group defined as customers. This is a conflict for me as a business represents money, hence the money ideal … There is a significant gap between front-line staff and managers, possibly due to different agendas, with stress and pressure affiliated to all roles. Nevertheless, front-line experienced staff are overlooked … copious spreadsheets with an abundance of names, numbers and dates are seen to be more important than the consideration of lower caseloads, significant reduction of targets, and an increased awareness that society has created a more demanding, damaged and discriminated offender group.' (Quote from an experienced probation officer on the post-graduate Public Protection programme)

The strain this PO is working under can be seen in his final comment to me:

> 'Probation has been and can still be an intelligent, thought-provoking service that, despite my negative views, actually allows me to be proud to be part of it. The frustration is with de-professionalizing the Service, in particular the role of the probation officers, many of whom work long hours, engaging in intense work with complex individuals who require a welfare approach, as well as trying to maintain the public protection mandate.' (PO19)

Similarly, another PO commented on the uncertainty surrounding the future of the service, with talk of privatization, new National Standards and a return to generic caseloads in the context of spending cuts: 'staff are feeling frustrated and despondent about not only the future of the Probation Trust but [also about] where their own future lies in terms of employment and career.'

Finally, I have spoken to a number of staff at different stages in their careers and at both PO and PSO grades. I was surprised at the complex level of cases held by PSOs who had picked up the change to a more humanistic approach, described as 'old fashioned'. The service was described as being in a 'testing phase', which could be creative in places with more personal autonomy. One PO had become disillusioned and had left for a while, as the lack of opportunity to work in a non-rigid way had been too frustrating. The current high caseload of, on average, 60–70 meant that the opportunity for creative work was still limited.

These personal testimonies from staff over a period of time demonstrate their commitment to working with offenders in a humane and constructive way, but highlight the high level of interference from central government that has been evident in earlier chapters. Ironically, staff were just as committed as the government to changing offending behaviour, but the recent changes to the infrastructure of probation and the removal of much of the inflexibility from successive waves of National Standards were seen as heralding a period of uncertainty and danger for the future as a professional organization. From the first to the last version of National Standards, there was a move to more and more rigidity in how offenders were to be supervised and less flexibility for POs to exercise their professional judgement and discretion. There are indications from the current government in their Green Paper (Ministry of Justice, 2010a) that this will be relaxed. Instead, the greater involvement of the private and not-for-profit sectors is being encouraged, while 'payments by results' is trialled. Less control, and conditions over the way that offenders are supervised, may enable other organizations to join in this task without them having to work to any defined standards. This theme will be picked up again in Chapter 9.

7

After-Care and Resettlement in the Inner London Probation Service (1965–1990)

This chapter focuses on the history of the specialist probation after-care unit (ACU) at 289 Borough High Street in London, the function of which was to resettle the homeless and rootless, particularly on their release from prison. This case study serves as an illustration for the changes that took place in the wider service at the time, as it became less welfare-minded and ultimately dropped its commitment to resettling prisoners in the community. I worked in this unit from 1984 to 1989 and was able to access material from its inception. I was involved in researching changes in its function and organization and interviewed an Assistant Chief probation officer (ACPO) from the early days of the unit.

This 'rich' history illustrates the changes that occurred in the wider service, from the time when individual officers were autonomous. In terms of the ACU, this included setting up hostels, running volunteers and controlling their work. Senior staff worked alongside main grade officers and offered casework supervision. They were not managers in the modern sense of concentrating on quality control and accountability. The managers of the unit became the senior managers of the service as a whole, including the late Sir Graham Smith, who became Chief Probation Officer for Inner London and later Chief Probation Inspector. Initiatives from key staff within the unit led to specialist programmes being rolled out in the wider service. Material I have quoted here is from unpublished archive documents. It is unusual to be able to chronicle the work of a particular probation unit as it thrived and declined, to see it as a microcosm of the wider probation world.

The ACU was conceived of on 1 January 1965, the product of a union between officers from the National Association of Discharged Prisoners' Aid Societies (NADPAS), who were already present working in the building, workers with the

Rehabilitating and Resettling Offenders in the Community, First Edition. Anthony H. Goodman.

men's division of the Central After-Care Association (CACA), who had also been working there, and a number of probation officers who moved into the building. NADPAS changed function to become the National Association for the Care and Resettlement of Offenders (NACRO), a voluntary penal campaign organization and provider of hostels and many other services. Initially there was an Assistant Principal Officer and two senior officers. In February 1966 a further senior officer arrived, who was responsible for training.

This senior officer, Georgina Stafford, wrote an article a year later which described her experience in settling into the unit. She had assumed that her knowledge of 'human problems' would be relevant in her new task of after-care work, but she commented: 'Now at the end of a year I know only too well how little I really understand of the problems of after-care prisoners' (Stafford, 1968, p. 429). The Assistant Principal Probation Officer, in a report dated 9 May 1968, commented on the service's inexperience in the after-care field: 'This is an area … which in the past has received only limited consideration; with continued support there is no reason why Borough High Street should not make a significant contribution in the field. We are becoming increasingly sure that far from after-care being an "easy option", an activity suitable for lesser qualified staff, it in fact demands from officers all the skill and expertise which is at the Service's disposal' (Pratt, 1968, unpubl. data).

Stafford gave a description of the building that accurately reflected its character throughout the life of the unit: 'a dreary building near the Elephant and Castle. It has five floors with five long corridors with rooms opening on either side and a rather antiquated lift; we have no ground floor. Two large rooms house the Central Registry for (Inner) London. We … deal only with the homeless. Clients walk up to the first floor and are seen by a receptionist, and then go into a quite pleasant waiting room' (Stafford, 1968, p. 429).

The factual account described above of how the ACU came into being does not describe the tensions of assimilating the different working groups into one building, and this is not commented on in Stafford's article, which concentrates instead on the client group seen at the ACU, who had major personal difficulties in terms of mental health, drink, drug and other social problems.

In 1968 the Assistant Principal Probation Officer, based in the ACU, circulated a paper around all the probation officers that detailed the changes that had occurred in the unit after it had been taken over by the Inner London Probation and After-Care Service (ILPACS). He mentioned that ILPACS did not finally take over the entire building until December 1967, when responsibility for maintaining it passed to the Receiver of the Metropolitan Police from the Ministry of Public Buildings and Works. On a purely practical level, a new telephone system that allowed internal communication was installed, along with internal security doors on each floor to close off officers' rooms from callers. An automatic lift was also installed. However, he mentioned a much more difficult issue, namely how to raise the status of the ACU, both to external probation colleagues and to signal to clients that there had been a change in management and personnel. 'We were well aware of the fact that in continuing to use these premises we were likely to carry over existing feelings which ex-prisoners had about the help which had been available from those sources … One of our most important considerations has been to raise the status of after-care in the Service and particularly to enable officers generally to see the value of the work being done at the Borough High Street (ACU)' (Pratt, 1968, paper, unpubl. data).

In order to achieve this objective, Pratt mentioned that Dr Hyatt Williams, consultant psychiatrist to the Tavistock Clinic and at Her Majesty's Prisons (HMP) Wormwood Scrubs and Maidstone, had been engaged to give a fortnightly seminar to officers at the ACU. These seminars were also available for prison welfare (probation) officers. They continued until the late 1980s (with consultancy from eminent psychiatrists such as Professor John Gunn from the Institute of Psychiatry and Dr Pamela Taylor, consultant forensic psychiatrist at the Maudsley Hospital and the Bethlem Interim Secure Unit, both in London.

In a report on the Unit by the three senior officers, dated May 1970, it was stated that, 'At the end of 1964 the Inner London Service was instructed to take over part of the building … The London Service was given floors one and three and this meant that officers had to work under very cramped conditions' (ILPS ACU Report, May 1970, unpubl. data).

The report also mentioned that in addition to workers from NADPAS, and the men's and women's division of CACA, four officers came from the Royal London Discharged Prisoners' Aid Society and two from the Holloway Society. The Prisoners Wives' Service was based in the ACU but it operated autonomously. There was a part-time probation officer at the ACU responsible for liaising with prisoners' wives, who would organize a visitor within 24 to 48 hours of receiving a referral to help the family of a man sent to prison. A very high percentage of the ACU clients would have lost their family support a long time ago.

The ACU report stated that the unit inherited the work patterns established by the hitherto separate groups, namely that NADPAS had encouraged people to call without appointments, while CACA worked by appointment with clients they had known for longer. Thus from the outset the unit catered for two different client groups, the casual caller and the known client. These two groups had very different problems, and a systematic way to deal with them was not decided on until late 1984 when the Unit again split into separate functions.

The 1970 report detailed the fact that NADPAS clients would visit the office between 8.30 a.m. and 5.30 p.m. The common denominator was that the client was an ex-prisoner, but he would not currently be on any form of statutory supervision: 'A policy had been formed that nobody should be turned away and it was customary for these people to be given a small handout of money or perhaps some second-hand clothing or bed vouchers and food tickets' (ILPS ACU Report, May 1970 unpubl. data).

The effect of this policy was that the ACU was a very popular establishment for the itinerant population, and as many as 80 clients a day called at the office. The report commented that this number of casual callers 'imposed great burden on those who were trying to formulate a new policy and method of approaching the whole question of after-care' (ILPS ACU Report, May 1970 unpubl. data).

The CACA worked with clients who were either on statutory licence, preventative detention or corrective training, or else were voluntary but had been known to the supervisor for at least five years in the case of males, or four years for females. Thus after-care arrangements would have been made long before their release. The 1970 Report commented that the two women members of CACA were reluctant to change their working practices to cover the tasks of the entire unit. In addition to the above tasks of NADPAS and CACA, after 1 January 1965 the Inner London Probation Service (ILPS) became responsible for the supervision of homeless young men released from detention centres. In 1967/8 the ACU became responsible for homeless borstal boys who wished to come to inner London on discharge.

When the unit opened, the 1970 Report commented that all staff, together with the assistant principal probation officer who had an office in the building, 'had only a hazy idea of what was expected of them. Consequently considerable burden was placed on the senior officers ... to try to form a cohesive policy towards which everybody could work' (ILPS ACU Report, May 1970, unpubl. data).

The distinctions between NADPAS, CACA and the London Probation Service ceased at the end of 1966 when the probation service absorbed these separate organizations. Over the next two years a number of the (younger) officers left the unit to receive training in the wider aspects of probation work, and they did not return to the unit. Their places were taken by probation officers from the London Service and by officers directly from courses. At the end of the first year the establishment held three senior officers, 14 full-time officers and one part-timer, who was responsible for liaising with the prisoners' wives, a voluntary service. At the end of five years the complement had risen to three senior officers and 19 probation officers, and a part-time ex-probation officer who worked for the Southwark Diocese.

The report in 1970 contained harsh words for fellow workers in the inner London Service, as it stated: 'While we have welcomed a number of officers direct from training, we deplore the constant turnover of staff and the unwillingness of experienced colleagues within the service to move to this more specialized kind of work. It should be remembered that this unit has been in operation now for over five years, and while we are grateful for an ever increasing measure of stability, this aspect needs even more and urgent attention' (ILPS ACU Report, May 1970, unpubl. data).

Thus it can be seen that work with homeless and rootless offenders was not popular with the majority of probation officers in the inner London area as a work specialism. The 1970 Report commented that after the amalgamation into the ACU there was a 'considerable change in the work performed in the unit'. This was characterized by a 'marked decrease' in the number of casual callers seen and a 'corresponding increase' in the numbers seen who were on statutory licence, or who were described as 'ongoing' cases. This shift in emphasis 'necessitated considerable increases of staff over the last five years'.

What the Report failed to comment on was why this change had occurred. Was it because the change of workers at the ACU (the moving out of ex-NADPAS workers to be replaced by ILPS probation officers who had been on a training course)? An implication of this was that providing a 'hand to mouth' service of handouts to casual callers was less professional and therefore not to be encouraged. Cook, while commenting that the probation service was seen by vagrants as a source of providing money, or a bed voucher, mentioned that a refusal was seen by the alcoholic as offensive. He gave an example about the ACU that could not have occurred under the old NADPAS regime:

> 'The officer at Borough High Street refused to give me any money because he said that I would drink it. They never give anything there – they know you'll spend it on drink. Mind you, they'll give money to a boy out of borstal. But once you've got a name for yourself – once they know you're an alcoholic – that's it, you're stigmatized. Everywhere they treat you the same.' (Cook, 1975, p. 122)

In Cook's experience, the probation service was viewed by many alcoholics as a source of 'nothing but handouts' and this was not restricted to the ACU:

> 'I asked another dosser where the probation officers were? But I only managed to get two bob off them. I thought that I might get ten bob – the woman who gave it to me asked if I drank, and then tried to smell my breath. She made me sign for the money, bought five woodies, but it wasn't worth the bother. Being skint is a problem – I think that I'll give Borough High Street a try tomorrow – maybe I'll have better luck there.' (Cook, 1975, p. 122)

The Professionalization of the ACU

Records

When the unit was taken over by the London Service in 1965, it inherited a number of files maintained by NADPAS and by CACA. An original idea was for the building to house all the files of after-care cases in London but this was rejected. The Service as a whole was investigating the possibility of setting up a central index, which later occurred at the headquarters building. The Unit started its own registry on the first of January 1965 and after five years this had grown to 35 000 records. The NADPAS records were seen as having little value and were duly 'sent away for pulping'. The CACA records were kept but not incorporated into the new records, and the Royal London and the Holloway Society records were never sent for.

Finances

The previous accountant from CACA was appointed as accountant and bookkeeper to the unit with an imprest account from 1 January 1965 of £1500, provided by the Receiver of the Metropolitan Police. Having a finance officer on the premises was a resource not found in ordinary probation offices, where accounting was the responsibility of the senior probation officer. The money was provided for clients and was called the befriending fund. In addition, there was a voluntary donations account, a memorial fund and a sub-imprest account of £600 to give officers advances on their expenses. This represented an acknowledgement that officers at the ACU incurred larger expenses than field unit colleagues, as they visited far-off institutions on a regular basis.

Clothing – WRVS

Historically the ACU had a room for second-hand clothing to donate to clients, but this was used haphazardly, and individual officers were responsible for bringing in articles of clothing. When this room was empty, clients were given a voucher to use in a second-hand clothing store at the Elephant and Castle. However, it was noted that vouchers had been exchanged for cash, not clothing. In 1967 the Women's Royal Voluntary Service (WRVS) opened a large clothing store on the fourth floor which was open from 10 a.m. to 4 p.m. Monday to Friday. This clothing had been collected by the WRVS and was cleaned and pressed at the probation service's expense. In addition, the store had a stock of new clothing that was cheap and could be paid for from the befriending fund (a fund available to all offenders). Clients could also be given extra items like soap, towels, razors and alarm clocks. All clients had to be referred to the WRVS by a probation officer; the WRVS did not have the discretion to provide new articles of clothing and so on. This facility for new items and the provision of a WRVS store on probation premises was unique to the ACU and could not be used by clients from other field offices.

Community Service Volunteers (CSVs)

In 1966 the ACU obtained the services of a CSV recruit, typically a school-leaver who stayed for approximately a year. This post anticipated the later introduction of untrained ancillary workers, and later probation service officers, into the probation service. This post was used to support clients when they were vulnerable, such as when moving into accommodation or sorting out problems with the National Assistance Board (NAB). The role was much clearer than those of the later ancillary workers, which could be viewed either as an untrained helper's post, or as a source of obtaining pre-training experience.

The Beginning: the Operation of the ACU

Stafford (1968) stated that all the prisons in England and Wales were divided between all the probation officers, which included the senior probation officers, and she had responsibility for more than one institution. These officers were responsible for all enquiries and correspondence with their institutions; there was no central mechanism for monitoring individual referrals. Some institutions rarely received a probation visit, while Goudhurst Detention Centre in Kent had two officers and was visited weekly to see all the homeless boys about to be discharged to the London area. Officers visited the London prisons weekly. This aspect of the probation task resembled the work of the old CACA organization, and the NADPAS casual caller was also catered for. Stafford stated that a minimum of four officers were on duty each day. Although the front door was shut at 3.30 p.m., there was a duty officer available until 7 p.m. each evening. There was also a Saturday morning office duty session. Clients were defined by the service as being eligible for voluntary after-care support in the first year after discharge. Stafford defined the ACU casual caller as: 'people who say that they have been in prison some time between that morning and the previous 20 years, who come of their own volition with some presenting problem' (Stafford, 1968, p. 430). The numbers of clients seen reflect this liberal policy of entitlement to seek help and also what was offered to them, in practical terms. Apart from Saturdays a minimum of 15 callers were seen in one day, while the maximum was a staggering 79. The average was between 30 and 60 a day.

Analysis of casual callers in 1966

Stafford gave the following figures (Stafford, 1968), from 1966, when 2575 male and 42 female casual callers were seen in inner London. The ACU saw all but 192 men and 13 women of this total, which was further broken down into age brackets and previous sentences, as follows:

33 were under 20
395 were between 25 and 29
736 were between 30 and 39
633 were between 40 and 49
363 were aged 50 and over.

The Early Years of the ACU

The early years of the ACU were characterized by striving to define the task of the work of the unit, and the article by Stafford typified this. The unit closed down on Fridays between 2 p.m. and 4.30 p.m. for a staff meeting, attempting to knit the unit into a cohesive group. A vast number of papers were written on the different client groups and the perceived deficiencies in service provision. A roll call of the officers who staffed the unit demonstrated that a number of them went on to run key units along the lines of the perceived deficiencies, for example, the Hostels Department, Sherborne House Day Centre, and so on.

On 2 February 1971 one of the officers from the unit, John Croft, wrote a paper entitled *A New Bottle from Old Wine*. This paper commented that the traditional way of working with ex-offenders was not suitable for the 'grossly deprived, rejected, under-privileged and damaged'. He believed that the probation service was at the end of its sphere of influence with this client group, as the offenders saw their criminality as fully justified. In order to overcome this, he proposed that with the necessary finance, a centre should be set up 'where ex-offenders could be stimulated physically, emotionally, and intellectually'. He wanted the client group to be involved in the planning and construction from the outset and he believed that this would not only have an appeal to the client group, but it would also appeal to the workers in the centre and it would 'give meaning to the knowledge that has been accumulated at this unit over the years and to be an inspiration to others in the service and the wider community'.

Croft did not see this as a pipe dream, and he commented that 'His Honour Judge Hines has indicated that he has resources [access] to substantial funds if a practical scheme could be put forward'. Croft envisaged a place where the ex-offender 'could identify and feel at ease and where after an initial brief interview he could bathe to wash off his feelings of contamination that imprisonment has engendered'. Croft envisaged food, medical services, DHSS, employment and recreational facilities being available, as well as emergency hostel accommodation. The description of the 'stately pleasure dome', as he described it, pre-dated the philosophy of the Day Training Centre, as it would allow the ex-offender to 'play and act out his fantasies in a secure, tolerant, understanding atmosphere and where his creative, intellectual and spiritual capacity can be appealed to and stimulated through developmental activities such as music, art and drama'. Croft wrote a further paper, 'The Stately Pleasure Dome', dated 29 April 1971, which provided more detail of what he described as 'an intensive care unit for recidivist offenders'. He envisaged a residential complex that was an extension of the ACU with a senior probation officer being responsible for the development and use of the unit. The complex would have three main components, namely:

1. An assessment unit with probation support on the premises.
2. A self-contained hostel for eight men and one emergency place.
3. A community centre with creative and workshop facilities. Further accommodation for four men who were less independent, with a housekeeper's flat.

In May 1971, David Hancock wrote a paper that attempted to synthesize the opinions of the 'project group' that had been set up in the unit. He commented that in notes from March 1971 the project group listed four priorities, one of which was accommodation and facilities for borstal girls. He stated that this was being pursued adequately through other channels and focused on the need to improve residential facilities for rootless recidivists, 'especially for very damaged and unmotivated clients who are presently unacceptable to all specialist hostels in London'. The ethos of the hostel he saw as being needed was not to be based on 'success' but rather would endeavour to meet the residential needs of the client group. He felt that the 'accommodation [should be] set up and administered by the probation service itself. If this aim is lost we fear that we would not retain sufficient control over the facilities to enable us to fulfil the aim for which they were designed' (Hancock, 1971, unpubl. data).

The project for ex-borstal girls referred to here was written up in a paper dated 27 May 1971 by Miss Bickerdike, the ACU officer for homeless borstal girls. This paper was the result of discussions between the assistant principal probation officer (APPO), SPOs and Miss Bickerdike. It recommended that inner London needed a pre-release hostel for when girls first left Bullwood Hall (secure) borstal. This hostel was intended to provide support and 'preparation for working and living in the community' (Bickerdike, 1971, unpubl. data). The young women could then move on to a post-release hostel, which would let them live more independently, before obtaining an eventual bedsit. Thus release from borstal could be carried out in easy stages. However, the paper warned that 'Drug taking, refusal to work, stealing from other girls – might best be dealt with in many cases by the girl being demoted from a single room to the "emergency room"' (Bickerdike, 1971, unpubl. data). The emergency room was planned to be inferior to the single rooms, and this was seen as a way of encouraging girls to find employment. The paper, read many years later, could be described as 'parental' in outlook, with its description of the warden who 'might well be a married woman who would need to be kindly, firm and understanding … Her husband would go out to work and to some extent he would be seen as a father figure by the girls' (Bickerdike, 1971, unpubl. data). The paper was written at a time when female officers supervised women and men, and male officers supervised only men. The paper pointed out the current lack of provision, and made a plea for after-care residential facilities. It clearly stated that the writers didn't care whether the hostel was run by either the probation service or by the voluntary sector. It saw probation support at liaison level, probably by a SPO.

The following year, three probation officers at the ACU wrote a paper entitled (*Short Term Hostel Project*, 1972, unpubl. data). This paper was an attempt to convey the feelings of the Unit, as it stated that all officers' opinions had been canvassed for the paper. The proposal was to set up a hostel with a very short-term facility for prisoners at the point of discharge from prison and in times of crisis, that is, for those immediately out of prison and for those most in danger of returning. The residence was envisaged to be used by the same person for a period of not more than four weeks, and for a maximum of ten to twelve men aged 21 upwards. Young offenders were already catered for, it commented, but there was no mention of a need for emergency accommodation for women. It was not thought necessary for this hostel to have a resident social worker, but for somebody to live on the premises to be responsible for 'security, cleanliness and physical management of the house but with minimal involvement with the residents themselves … possibly an ex-offender' (ACU, 1972). The above paper was at variance with another anonymous paper written at approximately the same time signed by the four senior officers which, although it argued in a similar way for residential/day care facilities, also stated that they should be under the Unit's control with its director/SPO belonging to the ACU.

A Hostel Run by a Probation Officer

The concern that traditional ways of working and the usual levels of community support were not sufficient for the average ACU client was also being expressed by the main grade officers in the office. Mark Rankin, in an internal ACU paper dated 16 December 1977, described why he set up a self-help organization called Special Housing for Ex-Prisoners (or SHOP), for prisoners who were not accepted by any hostels apart from Salvation Army ones. He commented that the 'main aim is the creation of a sanctuary in which severely disturbed men and women are encouraged to support each other, with minimum interference from either a statutory service or an external group of volunteers.' He contended that the client group could support each other without needing to be dependent on a probation officer. When Rankin joined the ACU in 1970, he wrote that he found that the probation officers had specialized in the type of institution that they visited, with an emphasis in areas such as young offenders, lifers, problem drinkers who were serving comparatively short sentences, and so on. He had three dispersal prisons and was faced with the problem of resettling men with no fixed abode who had served long sentences. Rankin said that 'prison after-care is largely meaningless unless it has been preceded by a major investment in through-care while the offender served his sentence'. He also felt that 'a strongly personal relationship with people in trouble was not enough'.

He had a caseload of approximately 70 serving and released prisoners, and he concluded that with this number he was unable to develop relationships beyond a superficial level (interestingly, a current PO with the same size of caseload made the same point about only being able to work superficially with these numbers). He decided to link the majority of his clients to volunteers while they were still serving their sentences, a manageable task as he already had an active group of volunteers at his disposal (the ACU was unusual in this respect). After a period of approximately two and a half years of intensive use of volunteers, Rankin discovered that he still had a number of problems, although these were different to his initial ones. First there was the problem of client dependence; clients were dependent on him even after he felt that they could cope with their problems. Second, clients became dependent on their volunteers, and the converse of this was also likely. Rankin's caseload continued to rise into the eighties and this made the level of his involvement with clients 'increasingly patchy and diluted'. As the referrals came directly to him from the prison probation departments, his attempts to establish boundaries by reducing the number of new referrals succeeded in straining his previously good relationship with the prison welfare officers. The moral pressure he felt to accept more and more referrals was compounded by the problem that he had a hard core of clients who were so difficult that volunteers did not want to become involved with them. These clients, mostly drawn from the psychiatric wing of one of his dispersal prisons, were also impossibly difficult to place, as they could exhibit bizarre and dangerous forms of behaviour.

In spring 1973, Rankin floated the idea to his group of volunteers of establishing a house for eight or nine people who would otherwise only be accepted in Salvation Army accommodation. The aim was to make the group mutually self-supportive, although one volunteer was to live on the premises with a mandate to collect the rent, liaise with the DHSS and deal with any severe crises. Rankin was very much on his own in starting SHOP: 'My paid colleagues were unwilling to become involved in such an entrepreneurial method of working, and I was unable to obtain hierarchical support. I was only too aware that I required support from somewhere ... I was therefore determined to draw upon the volunteers, as the only group readily available to me, for support' (Rankin, 1977, unpubl. data). He admitted to an immediate conflict with his volunteer group, as they wanted a mix of a few disturbed clients to mostly reasonably stable ones, while Rankin wanted a predominance of disturbed clients in the house.

The first SHOP house opened in October 1973 after Rankin had succeeded in raising £500, and a rent-free property was obtained in North London by a volunteer from a property company. He listed the problems that followed the opening with a client group that included a schizophrenic who believed that he was an opera singer, a chronic heroin addict, and a withdrawn man who had just served fifteen years in prison. Rankin admitted that he made no attempt to involve the probation service in the house, and the distance from the ACU to the house meant that he was too far away 'to defuse the rising level of anxiety experienced by the community leader'. The result of this was that: 'the rent was rarely paid. Violence and drunkenness coupled with deep depression comprised the normal pattern of the residents' behaviour at that time. Far from providing each other with mutual support, residents had to lock their possessions away because internal thieving was common. Sexual and drug abuse was also prevalent. There was also no effective liaison with the local DHSS office, and local people became increasingly hostile towards the house' (Rankin, internal report on SHOP, 1974, unpubl. data).

Clearly, a fraction of these problems should have been sufficient to sink the project for good. That this did not happen presumably meant that the unit at some stage recognized that SHOP filled a gap in service provision. This may not have occurred until after Rankin left the ACU. Although SHOP did not receive official management backing above senior level, the management committee included a number of the ACU staff and in 1984 the four houses in SHOP received weekly support from approximately ten ACU probation and ancillary workers. In the same year, a full-time project worker was employed. In 1987 two further workers were appointed. The ILPS senior management investigated the level of ACU input into SHOP and the result was a decision to cut back on probation officer involvement. It was a great pity that no records existed to explain why the project became a central part of the unit, but one explanation could be that the ACU senior probation officers' plans for hostel provision developed into the ILPS Hostels Department, which serviced the whole of ILPS and, ironically, refused to accept the more 'damaged' ACU client, the inspiration for this innovation. After this, the unit as a whole had the problem that hitherto had perplexed Rankin – where to put offenders whom no other hostel would accept. Rankin felt that the strains imposed by SHOP had ruined the relationship that he had enjoyed with the volunteers. By 1976 there were three houses and the chair had been taken over by a senior probation officer from one of the London prisons. The structure became more formalized and residents were given rent books. However, the principle that SHOP would take residents rejected by other hostels remained, as did the commitment to have volunteers on the management committee.

It is interesting to note the number of hostels that the ACU liaised with, and it had representatives on the management committee of all of these. After joint consultation between the ACU and NACRO, the 134 Project was set up at the Oval, and this hostel traditionally received nearly all its residents from the ACU (NACRO was the successor to the old National Association for Discharged Prisoners' Aid Society, or NADPAS). In addition, a probation officer from the ACU was the chair of Penrose Charity hostel accommodation and this resource was largely filled by ACU clients. The need for the ACU to initiate and maintain extra resources over and above those available to most field units was a reflection of the different client group, that is, the homeless and rootless, typically short-term recidivist or petty persistent offender, and long-term prisoners who wished to start afresh in a new area where the anonymity of London could overcome the stigma of a serious offence that may have achieved national prominence, or which would make resettlement in a small community impossible. In this respect, the ACU was therefore a nationwide resource.

The Maintenance of the Voluntary Tradition in Probation

The theme, that the ACU was different from other units in ILPS, was investigated by Ms Raya Levin, an ACU PO, in a long paper written in 1974 entitled *The After-Care Officer*. She commented that voluntary involvement with the disadvantaged was a tradition in England. She believed that the tradition bequeathed by the voluntary organizations to the probation service after the takeover of voluntary after-care in 1966 left a positive legacy, despite the condescension some probation officers felt towards the previous system of 'handouts and a non-professional approach' (Levin, 1974 unpubl. data). She also saw it as significant that there was a move back to community involvement in the field of care for offenders. She believed that the old voluntary agencies 'contributed a very important tradition to the probation service, mainly in the unknown areas such as the understanding of institutions and their staff, greater flexibility in dealing with and generally personnel being more readily available to the client, even though on a more superficial level … Another contribution of the voluntary societies was to introduce a new class of clients to probation officers who until then were concentrating on statutory supervision only' (Levin, 1974, p. 1, unpubl. data).

Whether Levin had more than anecdotal evidence of her belief that the probation service started with a condescending attitude to voluntary work is unclear. She believed that this air of condescension extended to the probation officers who worked at the ACU. Certainly a management review in the North East Division of the ILPS in 1979 found that the majority of officers dealing with casual callers to field offices wanted to get rid of the caller quickly to get back to their 'real work'. I have already commented that the senior officers had complained in a report of officers' reluctance to come and work at the ACU (ILPS ACU Report, 1970, unpubl. data).

Levin described the 'distance' between field probation officers and casual callers to probation offices as 'a professional coldness'. She felt that the legacy of NADPAS and CACA was still present in the ACU, in that the unit did not subscribe to the traditional probation values, which she listed as follows:

1. Tradition of selecting clients one feels able to help (by the preparation of a Social Enquiry Report (SER)).
2. Tradition of using the authority of a statutory relationship.
3. Tradition that change is possible.
4. Tradition of attempting change through the examination of the psychopathology of the individual.
5. Tradition of not using material aid.
6. Tradition that tasks can be confined to a particular timescale.

Levin was adamant that the ACU was not a specialist unit, in the same tradition as other units in the probation service which did not do mainstream work, including court duty, preparation of social enquiry reports for the Courts, (civil court) custody and access reports, and so on. Rather, its concentration on resettling ex-prisoners, visiting clients in prison and seeing casual callers forced the ACU officers 'to stick their necks out more – almost anything goes, because they have not got the answers' (Levin, 1974, p. 2, unpubl. data).

Levin commented that officers arriving at the ACU typically felt deskilled, because of the set-up and the irrelevance of traditional casework methods. Her paper, written nine years after the absorption of CACA and NADPAS into IPLS, commented that the ex-voluntary sector 'personnel [were] still identifiable but rather as individuals than as a style of work' (Levin, 1974, p. 3, unpubl. data). Individual personality was seen by Levin as a significant and dynamic variable in the unit, testing out new methods of working. When Levin considered the particular problems of the homeless and rootless offender, she concentrated on the theme of rejection. She looked at the common perception of the problems encountered by the client group, as viewed by the client and the probation officer, and she saw a gulf between the expectations of the two groups.

> 'What the officer may regard as rootless may not appear so to the client at all, because he may have roots which to him are meaningful whereas to the rest of society they appear as unacceptable ... an increasing number of people are driven either by necessity or choice to live away from the traditional family and there is no official housing provision made at all for single people ... Rootlessness can also be described as an alienation from all norms that keep people going ... sometimes this rejection of roots might hide deeper painful feelings which are protected by this attitude.' (Levin, 1974, pp. 5–6)

Rejection was not just a problem for casual callers to the office. A former ACU probation officer, now back in a field unit, explained to me the problems in seeing prisoners in the segregation wing in HMP Maidstone. This wing was for 'rule-43 s' – rule 43 allowed that prisoners convicted of crimes such as sexual offences should be separated from other prisoners for their own safety. Prisoners can be put on rule 43 to stop them hurting others or being disruptive. Here, I am referring to prisoners who have to be separated from others for their own safety.

His client group were people with very serious criminal records who would probably have qualified, he thought, as personality disorders in early assessments, and who had been pretty well beyond help at the age of 19 or 20. Many had left or been thrown out by their families; they had been deserted by earlier probation officers. However, he felt that a number of them had reached a point in their lives where they wanted to do some work on themselves. He could not tell what it meant in terms of results, but he felt that it now would be possible to help them. The wing also contained sex offenders who had to be separated from other inmates for their own safety. These men were unable to return to their family homes because their families had rejected them, or else Social Services would not allow them back into the family, or it was unsafe for them to return to the area. They might be incarcerated for the first time in their lives and would require time to talk about the offence and the strain of resettlement and being on their own for the first time in many years. These problems have not changed.

Levin differentiated between those clients who had the ability to change and those who were incapable of change. The former group required physical care and involvement in their subculture. The latter required liaison with the institutions while they were in prison and the investigation of their feelings and background. This era of probation practice was one where probation officers would explore offenders' pasts to see how early experiences had affected their behaviour and emotional well-being. Thus, for Levin, it was a deeper level of contact than merely ensuring that prisoners' basic welfare needs were met. In these relationships, the PO's aim was to get the offender to open up and discuss her past and how it had affected her. The responsibility of helping the client to survive was an essential task, and Levin believed that the client should be aware of how much they were entitled to from the befriending fund. 'Without completely abdicating the officer's discretion, the client should have some say in the manner in which this amount is spent towards the satisfaction of his needs' (Levin, 1974, p. 9 unpubl. data). (In Levin's time the client had a *lifetime* allowance of £100. This amount became an annual allowance, with the same proviso that the probation officer could decide how to spend £25; the sum could be made up to £50 with the permission of the SPO, and up to £100 with the permission of the ACPO.) This emphasis on money was due to Levin's hypothesis that clients needed to be 'fed' and then 'weaned'. Paternalism or client manipulation were other forces that she described as being potentially involved in financial transactions within the unit. The material emphasis for Levin served one important task, namely that the probation officer was seen as a 'person', not as a 'therapist'. Levin commented that working at the ACU 'makes one particularly aware of the injustices of society as a whole and sometimes makes individual officers feel guilty at being part of the system' (Levin, 1974, p. 20, unpubl. data).

Regular prisoner contact meant that a more accurate picture of the offender could be presented to the prison, and the client could be helped to express his feelings about his circumstances within the prison. Whether the ACU officer should act as a safety valve for the prisoner, allowing him to vent his emotions in safe surroundings, was debatable. Levin saw this as a valid role for the officer, but absorbing the prisoner's stress was draining. Her solution to this was for 'anxiety groups' for officers.

Finally, Levin considered the question of 'success'. She had generally low expectations of what the clients would achieve. At the minimum she saw it as the responsibility of the probation officer to ensure the physical survival of the client. 'This responsibility should not be relegated to other agencies; the very fact that the client's capacity to survive has been undermined by imprisonment makes him the responsibility of the probation service' (Levin, 1974, p. 12, unpubl. data). She realized that some officers found it hard to adopt a controlling attitude with the prisoner, as they needed 'to see some change or at least some signs of [their] work bearing fruit' (Levin, 1974, p. 13, unpubl. data). This laissez-faire attitude was acceptable in the 1960s and even in the 1970s, but was no longer appropriate in the 1980s when cost-effectiveness became a key priority in the probation service, and many other arenas in the public sector.

An Evaluation of the ACU by the Home Office Research Unit

If Levin saw POs arriving at the ACU going through a form of 'culture shock', it could be hypothesized that similar units in other probation areas had similar problems. In 1971 the Home Office Research Unit (HORU) report *Explorations in After-Care* was published, which looked at the ACUs' set-ups in London, Liverpool and Manchester. The report, the result of fieldwork undertaken in 1967, was essentially exploratory in nature, and it attempted to answer the following four points:

(i) 'What were the declared aims and objectives of the ACUs studied?
(ii) How did after-care actually operate in them?
(iii) Was there a gap between their declared aims and their concrete achievements?
(iv) If so, is it possible to identify structural elements which obstructed the achievement of the declared objectives?' (Home Office Research Unit, 1971, p. 1)

The research worker assigned to the London ACU was an ex-member of the Royal London Discharged Prisoners Aid Society (RLDPAS) and he analysed 200 case records from the registry by looking at every tenth file 'to see how far they revealed the problems of clients, and the measures adopted to deal with them. He also talked to various probation officers employed at the office, and so gained a more general perspective of the problems and tasks involved in their work' (Home Office Research Unit, 1971, p. 3). The report conceded that the fieldwork research was undertaken in London within 18 months of the ILPS taking over responsibility for the ACU, and in Liverpool and Manchester it was undertaken less than a year after they opened. Manchester, unlike London and Liverpool, did not take over an already functioning unit.

The HORS report found that there were differences between the three units. Borough High Street, in London, had an older client group than the two northern ACUs. It postulated that this might be for the following four reasons:

(i) The London ACU had a longer tradition than the other two units.
(ii) The London ACU had more 'old lags' who attended on a casual caller basis.
(iii) The London ACU gave out more clothing, and this might have attracted older people.
(iv) Older people might have migrated to London. (Home Office Research Unit, 1971, pp. 32–43)

One major difference was in the client group that the units catered for. All three units worked with single men, but in Liverpool the majority of clients were married. This could be accounted for by the fact that in London and Manchester men with homes were dealt with by other probation offices, whereas they were considered to be legitimate clients of the Liverpool ACU.

The HORU report detailed the problems that had been listed by clients, post-discharge, which were as follows:

(i) Immediate practical needs, such as money and clothing.
(ii) Accommodation requirements.
(iii) Employment problems.
(iv) Legal problems, non-payment of debts and domestic problems.
(v) Other problems, such as inadequacy, ill-health, mental illness and emotional problems.' (Home Office Research Unit (9), 1971, p. 20)

The HORU report commented that discharged prisoners frequently were not able to manage on their social security allowances. Although the clients were told that the probation service was not there to subsidize them, when they had used up their social security allowance, this was in fact a major task of the ACUs. Cash grants were typically given for the following items: accommodation, clothing, collection of property, fares, food, household debts, rent and tools. Vouchers were also sometimes used for accommodation, fares, clothing, food and tools.

The HORU report devoted an entire chapter to the London ACU and ended with the depressing conclusion that: 'As a casework agency the unit would have liked to help its clients by concentrating effort on the underlying problems and the provision of the material means required for their treatment or amelioration, whereas in fact the treatment of basic problems was left more or less in abeyance while much effort was spent in deciding on the allocation of inadequate means for day to day ends. Insofar as his basic problems were concerned, the client of after-care remained unsupported' (Home Office Research Unit (9), 1971, p. 42). This statement would appear to negate any benefits of the takeover of CACA and NADPAS by the ILPS and After-Care Service, for if the ACU was replicating the 'hand to mouth feeding' syndrome of

NADPAS it was not maintaining the longer-term through-care contact of CACA. The research failed to analyse the frequency and content of pre-discharge work with prisoners and whether this contact led to successful after-care. This pre-discharge contact might have been different in nature depending on whether the prisoner was serving a short or a long sentence, where there was more time to form a 'meaningful' relationship with the prisoner. (This latter group was the province of the defunct CACA, an organization that had operated out of the ACU building, working with men sentenced to over five years, and women sentenced to over four years, in prison.)

One paragraph commented that the 'regulars' were seen as having better prospects for rehabilitation, and these clients were given regular appointments 'by the same probation officer who may also have had pre-release contact with them' (Home Office Research Unit (9), 1971, p. 37). However, the researcher concentrated on the financial side of the unit, and he commented that these clients were assumed to be not merely interested in material assistance (as it was the duty of the service to provide it), but also that they 'warranted a greater expenditure of time and attention; their chances of receiving material help in a form which took greater account of their sensitivity may also have been somewhat better than those of casuals' (Home Office Research Unit, 1971, p. 37). The report commented that clients were divided into 'casuals' and 'regulars', although this latter group could have been attending the unit from the time of NADPAS. The author commented that many of the casuals were suffering from long-term alcohol problems and years of neglect. By specifically commenting that probation officers were more prepared 'to make allowances for their conduct' (Home Office Research Unit, 1971, p. 37), the researcher was making some qualification to the general principle quoted by one probation officer that 'the casuals had their asking price' (Home Office Research Unit, 1971, p. 37) – some just wanted money and had no intention of changing their way of life.

Files in the ACU were described as having inadequate information in them and this could be explained by the fact that the old records from NADPAS, CACA and RLPAS were not incorporated into the ILPACS records. The author of the survey on the London ACU was an ex-RLPAS worker, and he would have been aware that the old records were not seen as high enough quality for ILPACS. It is difficult to read the report and know quite how the researcher reached his conclusions. The researcher examined the records 'to see how far they revealed the problems of clients, and the measures adopted to deal with them' (Home Office Research Unit, 1971, p. 3). He also talked to various probation officers employed in the unit, and so gained a more general perspective of the problems and tasks involved in their work. However, the researcher drew on his previous experience of the work of the Discharged Prisoners' Aid Societies. What is conspicuously absent is any participant observation of interviews or direct client interviews by the researcher. Yet the researcher was able to say with confidence: 'Clients often asserted that they were ready to make a fresh start in life, yet many case papers contained notes of disillusionment on the part of probation officers' (p. 39).

This lack of direct evidence led Silberman, one of the section authors of the above paper, to speculate on how the client operated: 'One gained the impression that they [the clients] opened their interviews with a gambit of some kind or another, presumably in an attempt to represent their current situation as one that entitled them to receive the assistance asked for' (Home Office Research Unit, 1971, p. 40). That case records on occasion failed to mention what type of help had been requested by the client forcing the reader to guess from the result of the transaction, which was almost always recorded.

Having established to his satisfaction the adversarial nature of the contract between probation officer and client, the researcher could then comment that the client was sophisticated enough that: 'The client's need for material help may have discouraged them from mentioning problems of great concern to them, if they thought that to do so would have prejudiced their chances of obtaining help' (Home Office Research Unit, 1971, p. 40). It could be hypothesized that the client would 'invent' personal problems, if necessary, to hook the probation officer's professional desire to offer more than material help, but the researcher ignores this possibility to postulate whether the 'social welfare function' obscured rather than clarified the cause of the clients' problem(s). If clients saw meetings with probation officers as 'contests' where questions were 'parried' and evasive answers were given, with the intention of obtaining the assistance asked for, the question could be asked whether there was a role for the unit at all. This question was not posed; instead, the researcher commented that the level of funding available was too low for anything other than 'relatively small fringe benefits' to supplement social security grants. Thus the performance of the unit by and large 'depended entirely on the cooperation of other administrations' (p. 43).

In the summary and conclusions to the first part of the HORU study on the three ACUs, the researchers attempted to answer four questions, namely:

1. What were the after-care units trying to do? [Aim of the ACUs.]
2. How were they trying to do it? [Operation of the units related to their aims.]
3. Did their methods match their aims? [Structural problems.]
4. If not, could one identify anything in the way the units were organized which may have prevented this matching? (Home Office Research Unit, 1971, pp. 44–46)

The conclusions to the reports on the three separate ACUs were applied generally and were therefore applicable, according to the researchers, to each ACU. In answer to the first question, it was postulated that clients and probation officers had different views of immediate material needs and long-term solutions. The ACUs could be evaluated either as immediate 'welfare agencies' or as 'social casework agencies', or as a mixture of the two. In addition, there was the need to distinguish, according to the report's authors, the aims of the 'community at large', from the aims of the probation officers in the units and the aims of the clients themselves.

From the statistical tabulations, acknowledging the limitations of the research methods, the authors commented that the general trends were that the units functioned mainly as 'welfare agencies', handing out money and clothing. This had profound implications in how the ACUs operated. The clients called at the ACUs mostly when they wanted this immediate service. Probation officers had little pre-discharge contact with prisoners and, perhaps as a consequence of this, the quality of information on the clients was often inadequate. The sample clients' files considered in the research did not remain in contact with the probation officers for very long (approximately 75 per cent for three months or less, and 'very few' for longer than six months). It would thus appear that the majority of the client group examined in the survey were from the old NADPAS rather than from CACA. Why this should be to the extent shown in the survey is unclear, although numerically 'casuals' would vastly outnumber the 'regulars'. For at least the 1980s, probation officers kept their 'live' files in their own offices. It was not clear how the filing system was organized when the survey took place. It was possible that 'live' files were kept in officers' rooms and consequently the results might under-represent the number of long-term clients being seen in the unit.

In conclusion, the report commented that administrative control could not affect the 'unreliability of clients', or the 'urgency of clients' immediate material needs'. However, 'lack of material and treatment resources', 'lack of pre-release visiting' and 'lack of information on clients' could be positively changed. It questioned whether after-care would have an impact until more resources were forthcoming (such as hostels, more training and employment facilities). The final paragraph of the report demonstrated the psycho-analytic bias of the authors when, after contrasting the 'discrepancy' between 'concern and goodwill' and the 'lack of fundamental knowledge as to how best help discharged prisoners', it argued that if casework was to have a chance to work in the field of after-care then the 'means-test-oriented service' had to be replaced by one that focused on the 'assessment and treatment of the conditions preventing the clients of after-care from becoming productive and law-abiding members of society' (Home Office Research Unit, 1971, p. 46).

The HORU report varied considerably from the 1970 report by the senior group, which had described the changes in the unit after the takeover by ILPACS. The fact that by 1970 the London ACU had increased its number of clients on statutory after-care and decreased the numbers of casuals calling at the unit would imply that the findings of the survey rapidly went out of date. After the 1971 HORU report, no more surveys were undertaken of the unit's work by the Home Office, although the ILPS carried out two divisional reviews on how through-care and after-care were being implemented by the service

The ACU from the 1970s Until its Closure

In 1976 ILPS published *A Report to Commemorate the Centenary of Probation in London* (ILPS, 1976). In the period between 1963 and 1975, in the inner London area, chief officer numbers had increased from 7 to 16, senior officers from 27 to 65 and main grade officers from 155 to 281. In the same period, the number of people on probation orders had declined from 6336 to 3935, but those on after-care from prison (including pre-release contact with prisoners) increased from 1233 to 4527. It can thus be seen that work with prisoners and ex-prisoners was a more onerous task than work with probationers. In fact only 855 were on prison licence or parole,

504 in/released from detention centres, and 1438 from borstals. Inner London was different to the rest of England and Wales, as after-care cases comprised 44 per cent of the POs' caseload compared to an average of 32 per cent in the rest of England and Wales. Voluntary contact with ex-prisoners was insignificant in 1963 but grew rapidly and in 1973, 1847 (or 43 per cent) of the after-care caseload were voluntary clients.

The ILPS report commented that the Day Training Centre (for adults and legislated for in the 1972 Criminal Justice Act), like Sherbourne House (for young offenders) 'grew… from the idea of dealing with a man's problems – particularly his work problem – by engaging his creative potential in some purposeful and satisfying activity' (ILPS, 1976, p. 38). The compulsory and voluntary nature of the ACU was described in detail in the report, as clients were described as being on some form of licence or else voluntarily seeking assistance. 'In addition, the staff see people who call casually without appointments. These come once or many times; they may come every day, weekly or occasionally; they continue to come for whatever period of time they choose, from a few weeks to many years' (ILPS, 1976, p. 83).

The report did not shirk from the incongruity of providing aid with casework methods:

> 'Officers trained in the idea that material aid equalled "do-gooding" were forced by the experience of reality to re-think their basic assumptions and re-learn what the original missionaries knew at the turn of the century – that while each was a whole person, with an infinite variety of physical, emotional, spiritual and material needs, to the deprived person discharged from a penal institution, homeless and friendless, it is often the material need which appears most pressing.' (ILPS, 1976, p. 84)

It concluded the section on the ACU with a strong statement of basic humanity: '… it is hard to see how any man can be expected to survive long without a change of underclothes, socks and shirt, a razor, soap and towel. He may not unreasonably feel … [that] no one, in prison or outside, cares enough to accept the responsibility for meeting his needs' (ILPS, 1976, p. 84). This feeling endured almost until the time of the SNOP document. However, an ACU meeting in 1984 had begun to show a difference in opinion between newer officers and their older colleagues. The client-led giving of clothes and money was about to be challenged.

The ACU at the Time of the Home Office's SNOP Document

When I joined the ACU in August 1984 it was just before the Home Office's Statement of National Objectives and Priorities (SNOP) document was received in the unit (Home Office, 1984). This was the first time that the Home Office had stated the priorities of the probation service, when resettlement of prisoners became the third of five priorities. There was already a move to change the way that casual callers were dealt with in the office, to move it from a welfare-oriented operation. This was the part of the probation task that did not provide much job satisfaction, as there was a lack of continuity in client contact. Individual probation practice varied in terms of what practical (typically financial), and/or long-term help was offered to casual callers. I was told by my senior officer that new members of the unit offered casual callers follow-up appointments but, as the demand built up from the probation officer's prisons, work with casual callers became squeezed and was given a lower priority. In 1984 a total of 3572 casual callers attended the office. Of these, under 1 per cent were women, and half of the women had accommodation problems.

The work with institutions remained the primary task at the ACU and followed what was euphemistically described as the 'enthusiasm model' of social work. This rather cynical label invented by a probation officer in the unit described how responsibility for particular institutions changed hands. Typically when an officer left the unit their institutions were 'put up for grabs' and there was then an internal reshuffle. This meant that the last person in received either HMP Pentonville in London, the home of persistent short-term recidivists, or HMP Armley, which had a similar function in Leeds but was obviously much further away. Two other unpopular prisons were HMPs Coldingly and Blundeston. The former, as an industrial prison, could not be visited before 5.15 p.m., and the latter was at the end of a long slow journey into Suffolk and where relations with the prison were not good. It was my fate to receive Armley, Coldingley and Blundeston. Preference for other institutions was dependent on individual choice, with some officers preferring long-term institutions, and others perhaps institutions near friends or relatives. The allocation of prisons was not decided by considerations of category of prisoner, geographical location or any other kind of professional decision. Prisoners were still visited conscientiously (at least every three months) and the unit enjoyed the support of monthly meetings with a consultant psychiatrist from the Maudesley Hospital. There was a concern about working with 'lifers' as there were a number on the unit's caseload. An officer from the unit had been seconded to the Institute of Psychiatry for a research project on 'lifers'. There were no proposals to specialize the work with client groups or to develop different ways of working. Despite the negative comments mentioned, prisoners were visited regularly and often the PO was the prisoner's only link with the outside world.

Work with casual callers

The ethos of the unit, as far as casual callers were concerned, had not changed from its 1966 remit, which was as part of the 'circuit' for the itinerant casual caller population. Dissatisfaction with not helping callers to break away from their hand to mouth existence led to the desire for change, and for the unit to offer a more systematic approach. This process began with some probation officers on office duty refusing to give out cash or food vouchers to casual callers before they had shown some commitment to changing from their homeless and rootless way of life. This move was resisted by some of the long-serving officers, but the effect was dramatic in terms of the money that was given out from the befriending fund. One practice that did continue was giving out second-hand clothing from the WRVS store in the building. Each caller was allowed a change of clothing every six months, whether or not he had been seen in the office in the intervening period. The date of his last offence was not a significant consideration. The right to obtain clothing was therefore not assessed and remained a major casual caller task, alongside providing identification for the DHSS and requests for immediate practical assistance. The women from the WRVS who staffed the clothing store were the original group who had begun the store in the building. (In fact, they never did drop out and were the only WRVS workers for the unit.)

Before I joined the ACU, there had recently been a review day which had formally brought these conflicts into the open. Some of the traditional probation officers resented what they saw as a poorer service to casual callers. However, some other officers talked about casual callers as 'spongers' or a 'waste of time'. The discussion also centred on what could be achieved with itinerant casual callers: was the ACU a resource to stabilize clients so that they could be encouraged to join a day centre, or was it encouraging callers to remain dependent on handouts? One central concern of the unit was its survival within the service, as caseloads were lower than in field units. I was immediately struck by the fact that there was a desire by probation officers to analyse what they were doing and to try to make their intervention as effective as possible. Some officers, by the nature of the institutions they visited, had the problem of resettling short-term repeat offenders, while others worked almost exclusively with long-sentenced prisoners. The common link was that they all worked with casual callers and attended meetings in the unit. There was a contradiction in that casual callers might be called 'scroungers', but POs worked with them carefully and sympathetically. It appeared to me that the language used was a defence mechanism to cope with the stress of dealing with this group in a piecemeal and 'one-off' way.

In February 1985, there was a second review of the unit attended by all probation officers and ancillaries, as well as the ACPO. This implied that at this stage, higher management 'owned' what was going on in the unit. The group that I was involved in had to gather facts and figures for 1983 and 1984: the numbers of casual callers to the unit monthly, the numbers of ongoing clients to the unit, a survey of presenting problems of casual callers in a four-week period from 20 February 1984 (excluding ongoing cases), an analysis of the befriending fund expenditure, which demonstrated that money given to clients at the ACU had indeed dropped, a write-up of a questionnaire I had carried out on all officers in the unit, and an analysis of all casual callers to the ACU over a four-month period. My interviews revealed very negative feelings towards the casual callers, yet the review figures showed that casual callers reported a cluster of problems: nearly 50 per cent had accommodation problems, 45 per cent had financial problems, 40 per cent had clothing problems. The decision of the review was to bring more consistency to work with casual callers and to specialize in through-care work with petty persistent offenders serving short sentences and the longer-term work with more serious offenders, who generally were new to the London area. There would be one team specializing in work with the casual callers and with short-sentenced prisoners, for example from Pentonville Prison and other local prisons such as Armley; two teams were to undertake the longer-term resettlement work.

1986: the ACU After the Division into Specialisms

After the division into the two through- and after-care teams (TACs) and the Community Rehabilitation Team (CRT) working with casual callers was achieved, the ACU entered into a new phase of consolidation. The teams were conscious that they had to present what they were doing in a way that higher management would see as relevant. The homeless and rootless client received a poor to nonexistent service from field units, as the field unit staff wanted to get back to the 'real' work.

The Inner London Probation Service was divided into four quadrants or Divisions. One of these, the South East (which included the ACU) carried out an unpublished internal review in 1984.

This review found that field offices carried out less voluntary after-care than the ACU. Certainly offenders receiving a custodial sentence too short to be considered for parole were unlikely to be allocated to a probation officer in a field office, and longer-sentenced prisoners might not be allocated contact until some time into their sentence, when parole eligibility was being considered.

Thus the ACU was something of a luxury in terms of its resource allocation. It could offer regular through-care support from the time of sentence, not at the time of consideration for parole. It could also offer through-care to those clients who were serving sentences too short to be considered for parole. The Government Green Paper on *Supervision and Punishment in the Community* (Home Office, 1990b) argued that more resources needed to be put into work with young offenders. The implication for ILPS was that as more resources had to come from a finite source, special projects were vulnerable and the ACU would have to shed labour for the task. It was hoped that the reorganization at the end of 1986 would enable the ACU to demonstrate a more efficient way of working. This ethos was not limited to mainstream work. The SHOP hostels, set up within the ACU over a decade earlier, required a great deal of probation officer and probation service assistant time. These three hostels each had two ACU workers visiting weekly, and an SPO was the chair of the organization. Any problems had to be resolved by the client's probation officer. Given the unstable and volatile nature of the resident population (resulting from the SHOP policy of not vetting applications), there were regular problems to sort out. On the positive side, many residents, whose stories looked horrific on paper, would not have been accepted anywhere else, including statutory probation hostels. The reason for this was simple: statutory hostels took clients on statutory orders, including parole, but not voluntary after-care.

At the ACU, officers had the responsibility of resettling serious offenders, including arsonists and sex offenders. Most of these offenders were released at their expected date of release (EDR) with no time on parole. Officers in the unit had the difficult task of placing these offenders or else losing them. Clients like these had no statutory duty to remain in contact with the probation service and, given the nature of the client group, were unlikely to receive any time on parole. The unit had always worked with these clients on a purely voluntary basis, which was not reflected in the official statistics. It should have been seen as valuable both to the serious offending group and to the public. The SHOP hostels thus cost the unit a great deal in terms of officer time, but this was not reflected in the official workload figures. The unit therefore held on to high-risk offenders because these offenders recognized that they were receiving something useful from the service.

In March 1986 there was a review of how SHOP was managed from an organization where all the tasks had been carried out by probation officers and volunteers to one due to expand and employ three workers as it took on extra properties. This additional labour force would lessen the burden on the probation service, although considerable resources were still expended to keep the organization running. The ethos of SHOP remained the same, to accept residents that other hostels, including statutory probation ones, would not touch. The review day recommended the setting up of a staff and training subcommittee and a development subcommittee. In many ways the growth of the organization, while very worthwhile in terms of the accommodation provision it yielded, could be seen by higher management as a time-consuming excursion into an area (hostel places) covered by the voluntary sector. While this could be described as vertical integration of resources, probation management, with its concern to be seen as overtly managing all probation resources, was not prepared to allow staff to diversify from its (ILPS management) main priorities. SHOP was an independent concern, not part of ILPS.

Changes to the work with casual callers

In March 1986 the senior officers in the ACU approved a draft paper, which had been circulated around the unit, on what the CRT would be offering to casual callers. The main change was that the unit would restrict its service to casual callers to mornings only, unless it was an emergency. The notion of what comprised an emergency was defined and consisted of people released that day from either prison or hospital, and who were not known to the unit. Clients who were injured or emotionally distressed would be seen straight away. Immediate referrals from court or the DHSS would also be seen. Clients who could have attended in the morning, but did not, would not be seen until the following morning. Clients visiting the office might be offered follow-up appointments, which would be recorded in the registry book, and records would be kept on whether follow-ups were adhered to. These follow-up interviews would be made in the afternoons, the duty officer normally taking responsibility for the case. The records were to be formalized, and requests for identification were to go on to the client's record as a permanent record of attendance. There was a general tightening up of financial provision: 'Cash or vouchers would not be issued where they were clearly supplementary to established DHSS provision, unless the caller's record exceptionally suggests such provision, or was assessed as deemed to be appropriate in an emergency. The expectation would be, and should be followed up, that callers repay, by instalments as necessary, any such disbursements, when considered to be feasible. The ability to pay money was only seen to be appropriate in the above circumstances. It was specifically mentioned 'not as a means of disposing of persistent or troublesome attenders'.

The paper also signalled the end of the practice of giving second-hand clothing, on a six-monthly basis, to any casual caller who requested this help. The new policy became one whereby: 'Issues of clothing will normally be limited to callers known to this office, or where an assessment of the caller's circumstances otherwise discretionary suggests its appropriateness.' There were members of CRT who wanted the removal of the WRVS clothing store completely, it being seen as consistent with a policy of removing any vestige of creating dependency on casual callers on the unit. The demarcation line between the CRT and the through-care teams was that, apart from those discharged from HMP Pentonville, any caller previously known to the unit would be referred to the through-care teams within three months of release. Otherwise (usually following on from a breakdown in contact), the case would become the responsibility of the CRT. On the same day in March 1986 that the senior group agreed this paper, a member of the CRT group circulated a paper that postulated the adoption of specialist subgroups in accommodation, addictions, psychiatric facilities/therapeutic communities, day centres, employment, training, education, welfare rights and resettlement (housing). These subgroups would be staffed by CRT members, with volunteers from the through-care team. In the event, no sharing with through-care members occurred and, further to this, no formal sharing of expertise occurred between CRT and through-care members within the unit, apart from work with young offenders where the interest in the client group predated the move to specializing within the unit.

The Pressure on Staff to Move from Resettlement to Mainstream Work

The first year of the specialisms saw an exodus of officers from the CRT group either into other ILPS units, such as specialist civil work, or out of London completely. In consequence, the CRT became staffed with officers who had not had experience of undertaking through-care liaison work, and who did not sympathize with this ethos. Simultaneously with these changes, ILPS published a policy proposal, *Assignment and Reassignment of Probation Officers* (ILPS, 1986). The gist of this was that there was a crisis in staffing certain specialist posts in ILPS, namely in hostels, prisons and community service: '[This] crisis has only been avoided by carrying vacancies and recruiting experienced officers from other services. Because we have recruited experienced officers from other services, there is a danger that these units become increasingly 'disowned' by the rest of the service and an unhealthy tendency towards an increased sense of separation results' (ILPS, 1986). The analysis of officers' working patterns showed that they did not stay unduly long in field posts, but they did in specialist units. ILPS management decided on a policy that new officers would start in a field unit but would have to move after three years into a specialism, such as community service. The new job contract would enable management to direct officers. However, for officers on old-style contracts (prior to 1986), this could not be achieved (as an officer from 1975, I had never been issued with a contract; not an uncommon experience). This policy obviously would not have a 'pay-off' for three years, until new officers had completed their first field post.

The paper stated, 'Since the problem is with us today, it is necessary for existing probation officers of all grades to accept the principles outlined so that constructive movement can take place in the near future. Seniors and ACPOs will be expected to discuss service needs with all officers' (ILPS, 1986). The paper concluded that the proposals represented 'a fairer, more responsible and responsive approach to the problems identified and will go some way to establishing equality of status between different specific tasks at the same time providing a more professionally coordinated method of appraisal and career development'. As mentioned earlier, the CRT team quickly lost its long-serving officers, but this did not happen within the through-care teams. Other teams, other SPOs and ACPOs, contacted individual officers trying to persuade them to leave. This was frowned upon within the service, but there was no way out of the specialism. This was because officers were committed to the resettlement work. Their values were out of step with the management's needs to farm out experienced officers around ILPS, thus there was a conflict between ILPS management and the ACU main grade officers. Most officers in the through-care teams had more years of experience than the combined years of the average field team. This again marked out the unit as being different to field teams. The long-serving SPO at the ACU was out of step with his field colleagues and ILPS management in the degree of client contact he enjoyed. Most seniors did not supervise offenders but were full-time managers.

The three teams at the ACU met monthly in a combined staff meeting where areas of common concern could be raised. This typically would be concerned with practical, rather than philosophical, concerns. Thus the appropriateness of using a particular hostel would be raised, or issues to do with SHOP, which was an interest across team boundaries, rather than questions of policy on the giving of money, or the frequency with which prisoners should be visited. The probation service ancillaries had worked under the old system, and were accepted by all officers. They had built up a good knowledge of hostel provision and of short-term emergency accommodation. One of their main tasks was to staff the duty room, to see casual callers and arrange for clients to go into bed and breakfast accommodation or hostels. They also visited hostels and cemented good working contacts with them. The unit had negotiated for a number of local authority flats to be available for clients who had achieved stability in their lives. Given the nature of the unit's clients this was a very useful resource indeed, not available to any other unit in the service. It raised the question, was this a resource wanted or needed by the service as a whole?

The ACU was unique in ILPS, in terms of rehousing ex-offenders, in that it had its own direct allocation of ex-Greater London Council (GLC) flats each year for its clients. (SHOP also received some flats each year from the GLC.) The flats were offered by the London Area Mobility Scheme (LAMS). The responsibility for coordinating LAMS places was given to an ancillary. The ancillaries at this stage represented a further bridge between the different teams in the unit. The CRT team began to concentrate on its outreach work, seeing casual callers in the day centres, such as North Lambeth. The ancillaries were very involved with this changing ethos, not seeing the inhospitable first floor of the unit with its interviewing rooms as the most appropriate forum for dealing with the homeless and rootless. The through-care teams were also beginning to change their working patterns and to formalize procedures.

In June 1986, SHOP advertised for a full-time coordinator. It was agreed that this worker would be in charge of two other project workers. A close link with the ACU was to be maintained as the worker would be located within the office. The worker would inherit two hostels catering for ten residents, but plans were in hand to acquire at least two further properties, including one that had recently undergone major refurbishment. No client from the ACU would have experienced such comparatively spacious and luxurious living conditions in another hostel in London. By August, the new worker was in post and plans were underway to set up a further house for young clients.

The unit undertook major liaison work with a number of hostels around the London area. Professor Gunn, from the Institute of Psychiatry, a former consultant to the unit, had set up Effra House, and a liaison officer from the unit visited and supported the staff there on a very regular basis. Regular management committee work and/or liaison support work was extended to Penrose Hostel, 134 Project, Blackfriars Settlement (Salvation Army), Bondway (an emergency centre for those with severe drink problems) and day centres. In July there was a review, and short-term commitments were made to more establishments, such as Carrington House, Camberwell Circle Club (a residential resource) and the Tooley Street hotel ('hotel' being a rather flattering term for what was on offer). The ACU had a philosophy that since the client group, on paper, was difficult to rehouse, and hostel staff were typically untrained and operating under stressful conditions, that any problems with ACU residents would be resolved quickly and jointly. Many hostels and day centres recognized that the ACU honoured their commitment and obligations to their clients and were prepared to take on greater-risk residents. Clients were seen regularly, and when problems arose the unit officers would not evade their responsibility to the hostel.

The Senior Management View of the ACU

Later in November 1986 a management report for the South of Thames Division of ILPS was produced (ILPS, 1986a). In the introduction the Deputy Chief PO (DCPO) began by reminding staff that the South of Thames Division had been created in September 1985. The divisional management team had the task of implementing the service's aims and objectives as set out in ILPS's Statement of Local Objectives and Priorities (SLOP) written in response to the Home Office Statement of National Objectives and Priorities (SNOP) (Home Office, 1984). The SLOP document (ILPS, 1985) was the starting point for creating a framework of divisional, borough and team statements (cascading managerialism within the service). The ILPS November 1986 report represented the first set of draft borough statements and comprised *A Framework for Action*, borough statements for Greenwich, Lambeth, Lewisham, Southwark and Wandsworth (written by their ACPOs), and a borough statement for the ACU from the ACPO who was also responsible for Southwark. The DCPO commented that the Statements 'establish[ed] the basis for agendas for borough management groups for 1987'. The work of each member of staff would be related to ILPS's aims and objectives and the divisional/borough objectives and priorities. Units were to produce team statements of objectives and priorities to be submitted to the ACPO by February each year for approval, the final version to be ready for the March.

The ACPO, writing about the ACU, stated that he had taken over responsibility for the unit in September 1985. His starting point was the review day in October 1985, which he had attended, that had resulted in the split into the CRT and the through-care teams. He 'considered the changes to be appropriate' but continued:

> 'I was made very aware of the traditions of the ACU and, in particular, the feeling that ownership of the services was with individual officers and not ILPS or the unit management team. I was also conscious of the enormous folklore about the work of the ACU and its staff which, I believe, has served to blur the effectiveness of objective or measured assessment of the overall work of the unit … For me, as ACPO responsible, it is … a question of the place of the unit and the work it undertakes in the overall provision of services by ILPS. After all, it is a heavily resourced unit, costly to run, and without an appropriate place in the organization the likelihood is for those resources to be concentrated on clients without accountability to management.' (Internal report by the ACPO, 1988, to the Review of Through-Care in South London, 1988.)

After commenting that the CRT team was staffed largely by 'younger staff, some of whom are new to the unit', the ACPO continued by stating that the CRT SPO was 'clear about the tasks of the team and as they establish their interpretation of its role questioning some of the traditional methods of work is starting to take place'. Clearly, the ACPO approved of these changes. He also commented that the through- and after-care teams were also reviewing their approach to their work.

The ACPO did not hide his view of where the ACU stood in terms of the management structure of ILPS as a whole: 'The thrust is therefore towards management taking responsibility for the work of the unit which, to quote a recent paper from the Seniors, "had been shaped by history and practice" rather than the needs of the organization.' The needs of the organization meant the needs of the ILPS, certainly not of the client group serviced by the unit, who were the most vulnerable and isolated clients supervised by probation officers in ILPS. Finally the ACPO considered the future of the unit, again in terms of ILPS's needs. He quoted from SLOP, which had been prepared by ILPS as a response to the 1984 Home Office's SNOP (Home Office, 1984):

(i) 'It is essential for the Service to examine carefully the relation between through- and after-care and other areas of its work.
(ii) Further work will be done to disseminate more widely the specialist skills and information available there (the ACU).'

He did not mince his words when he continued: '*Both statements appear to place the ACU in a position of a "wallflower" at a dance. I do not believe that the unit can wait to be picked up*. After all, it is the equivalent of three field teams and I am not sure that we can afford to neglect such a large slice of Service resources … It need[s] to be examined against the other areas of work as does the question of where the specialist unit fits into overall service provision' (italics in original; ACPO internal report, 1988). The South of Thames Divisional Report generated much anger in the unit and increased the feeling of vulnerability. A clear message had been given on two fronts: management had to manage (and to be seen to manage) the priorities within the unit, and the future of the unit would be decided within the context of ILPS as a whole. On 17 December 1986 the review arranged for the through-care teams took place, in an angry atmosphere. The place of the ACU in ILPS was discussed, and meetings to discuss new referrals would start in the New Year.

1987: The Year of Consolidation

As agreed at the last review meeting, which had been held on 17 December 1986, the two through-care teams began 1987 with a weekly referral/assessment meeting. This had regular agenda items of client allocation, referral assessments and prison allocation. This was an attempt to make officers accountable to their through-care colleagues about when clients were assessed as being appropriate to the unit's remit. The review had also agreed to set up a working party to look at short-term prisoners, eligible for section 33 parole (who had been given sentences of between eighteen months and three years), which comprised approximately a quarter of the unit's caseload. One item of concern between the through-care SPOs and the community team SPO had focused on the role of the unit's untrained ancillary workers. In particular, were they sympathetic to the work of the through-care officers? The minutes of the review day revealed a certain amount of paranoia: 'There was quite a bit of discontent from officers saying that [new] ancillaries had not been formally introduced to them, and they hadn't known they were in the building until they bumped into them. There were other factors which created cause for concern, where CRT was undertaking different tasks without asking TAC to join in or indeed keep them informed' (internal ACU memo). Despite this unease between TAC and CRT it was decided at the review that the two groups would not meet until the TAC teams had 'completed their discussions on their own work and were ready to report back'. This did not happen until March 1987, and the delay did not help relations between the different groups.

The year began with the departure of one of the through-care SPOs, who had been at the unit for less than a year. The old pattern of very long service at the unit had been broken. The new senior officer was instructed by senior management not to take on responsibilities within SHOP, and the decision was taken that SHOP should separate from the ACU. In March 1988 the headquarters' Central Resources Department was asked to undertake a review of through-care. This was a major reassessment of how much resource to put into preparing prisoners for release. Its brief was:

(a) To undertake an analysis of present through-care provision in inner London with particular reference to the statement of Aims and Objectives and the impact of legislative changes.
(b) To complete a review of recent reports on through-care practice prepared within inner London, including a summary of research findings.
(c) To assess different models of through-care practice with an examination of resource implications.
(d) To assess the contribution which can be made to through-care work in inner London by specialist provision. (ILPS, 1988)

The final report was published on 20 July 1988. Three full-day workshops had been arranged to canvass opinion, involving more than 100 probation staff. It had also received ten written submissions, eight of which had been from the ACU. The report commented that 'the ACU has a proud history, and arguably, represents one of ILPS' best examples of upholding the Service's traditional values. Its role has been to care for those offenders least attractive to society and, as clients, to officers. It has a high reputation for professionalism and it is not surprising that many of our experienced staff served an apprenticeship there … It has sought to maintain the status of through-care when, increasingly over the years, this aspect of our work has been threatened.' This appeared a positive affirmation of the ACU and the report commented that practice with prisoners throughout the rest of ILPS was variable: '[there] is a lack of clarity about through-care objectives and the absence of clear guidelines about practice for the achievement of objectives' (ILPS, 1988). Work with prisoners was not focused on 'risk of future offending' and in many cases contact was a 'ritual response'. I had found this variation from my research from 1986, but this was not cited in the review. I had used a phrase given to me by one senior officer that through-care was 'whimsical and not planned', and this still appeared to be the case in ILPS. The review stated that 'wide variations in practice exist, and this cannot be justified when seen from the client's point of view, especially in the context of developing equality of opportunity policies for service delivery' (ILPS, 1988). It appeared that when an offender was known, he would continue to receive a through-care service, even if he was not eligible for parole for a long time. Similar clients not on a caseload would not receive this service.

The report did not advocate the demise of the ACU but looked at the CRT and the through-care teams separately. It advised that the CRT should make its resources and knowledge available to the whole of ILPS, for example, its knowledge of hostels and accommodation in general, its work in day centres and links to rehabilitation centres. For the through-care teams, the report did not make for hopeful reading. The report questioned whether homeless referrals were truly rootless. The work with life-sentenced prisoners was commented upon positively, but the report commented that 'there is no reason in principle why such practice cannot be produced from field offices' (ILPS, 1988). Pre-discharge work with rootless offenders was ignored and the report continued:

> 'But there are of course people who are truly rootless, who genuinely want to come to London *when they leave prison with little or no previous knowledge, and who will probably come anyway*. If, on their own volition, they arrive in London *and turn up at any probation office, we feel that office should take responsibility* for assessing their need and using the information base at the ACU for deciding how to help them. They should not be referred to another office.' (ILPS, 1988, p. 28)

The ACU was to remain as a referral centre for the rootless, with one team of officers to develop a release plan, including accommodation, and then refer them on to a new officer.

The report took the trouble to point out to other staff that this would not involve the transfer of many cases to them. In the event, the report signalled the death of the ACU. Staff did not like the change, voted with their feet and transferred. The last four officers took what was left of their ACU caseload into field units, and the CRT officers also moved on to other posts. I spoke to the person in the service who had responsibility for accommodation at this time and discovered that field units did the best they could to work with homeless and rootless offenders who called at the offices, but as there were no additional resources to cater for offenders new to London, they became 'invisible'.

Summary

A number of interesting themes have emerged in this chapter. First, the idiosyncratic nature of probation practice and the almost complete absence of any control on how main grade probation officers worked with offenders by probation management. This will seem incredible to probation staff recruited since the imposition of National Standards (NS). Officers' caseloads were not controlled either and were allowed to vary according to the work generated by the institutions. Work was a mixture of welfare considerations, traditional casework or whatever else the officer wanted to do. Senior officers led 'from the front' and had responsibility for some institutions, like main grade colleagues. They had managerial responsibility but also worked directly with offenders. The push from senior managers of ACPO (Assistant Chief Probation Officer) grade and above was for seniors to stop having any direct offender contact and to spend all their time 'managing' staff. Their role was to offer leadership (which might be declined) and casework supervision. The ACU represented a further example of trained workers taking over from the old voluntary sector, a phenomenon that had been played out in local offices in the 1930s. What had gone on before was largely disregarded by the new probation and after-care service as it sought to absorb these new tasks. There appeared to be more than a hint of evangelical zeal attached to working with a client group that was not seen to appreciate the new casework methods. However, senior officers had a great deal of sympathy for the clients of the unit and proposed radical new solutions including hostels and day centres, including the Day Training Centre in Inner London. The senior officers in the unit, in the transition to a professionally qualified unit, went on to become very influential in the probation service, becoming chief officers in several different areas, including inner London, and one became the Chief Inspector of Probation. This could be seen as the golden era of the unit, before its stabilization and later decline. The through-care involvement with 'heavy-end' offenders had a significant pay-off on their release as trust and understanding had developed, offenders were prepared for discharge, had discussed their offending in detail and knew that they would be supervised with understanding, some sympathy but with firmness. There was a confidence in the professionalism of the experienced staff group, who were working with difficult and dangerous offenders.

The Community Rehabilitation Team undertook outreach and other community-based activities in 'wet' day centres (centres for people with drink problems that can be used while they are still drinking and therefore do not have their alcohol consumption under control; there are also 'dry' day centres, where people cannot attend if they had been drinking recently), forging links with local prisons and engaging with the hard-to-reach petty persistent recidivist. In cost–benefit terms these offenders highlighted in the Social Exclusion Unit Report *Reducing Reoffending by Ex-Prisoners* (2002) have a personal social cost and a cost to business, but probation services received no money for the work, as the offenders did not qualify for statutory after-care since their sentences were too short. I would add that many of them had enjoyed a career in the armed forces, but could not adjust to civilian life after they had been discharged. Perhaps, one day, probation involvement with these offenders will be reinvented.

8

Through-Care and After-Care of Offenders by the National Offender Management Service

Background

How prisoners are prepared for their re-entry into society is an issue that has exercised both the official sector and benevolent organizations over the centuries. This chapter starts by examining the interplay between the voluntary and statutory sectors, and traces the changes that led to a situation where support for prisoners during their sentence has largely evaporated.

The Probation Service Takes Over Prison Welfare and Working with Prisoners

The move from untrained voluntary organizations to the probation service was replayed when the probation service took over working with ex-prisoners from the Discharged Prisoners' Aid Societies in 1966. The Home Office report *Penal Practice in a Changing Society*, produced in 1959 and repeated in 1966, commented, 'It is a disquieting feature of our society that, in the years since the war, rising standards in material prosperity, education and social welfare have brought no decrease in the high rate of crime reached during the war' (Home Office, 1966b, p. 1). The report acknowledged that since the Gladstone Report of 1895 (Gladstone Committee, 1895) deterrence through fear would not work. However, the report was scathing over the level of overcrowding in the local prisons and the lack of work available in general in prisons. The report noted that many first offenders did not return to prison, but those who did had an increasing number of previous convictions. Like

Rehabilitating and Resettling Offenders in the Community, First Edition. Anthony H. Goodman.

the Home Office (1963) report led by Mr Justice Barry, it wanted to see more trained workers involved with ex-prisoners and it saw the potential value of compulsory after-care.

The first report of the Home Office Research Unit, *Persistent Criminals* (Hammond and Chayen, 1963), focused on what to do with offenders who had repeatedly served prison sentences. These were typically men sentenced to preventative detention under the Prevention of Crime Act 1908 and the 1948 Criminal Justice Act.

This allowed the courts to impose very long terms in prison on offenders aged over 30, who had been convicted of an offence which could receive a sentence of two years or more, who had had three or more previous convictions since the age of 17, as well as at least two experiences of imprisonment. Reconviction figures from the Central After-Care Association, which was absorbed into the ACU, indicated that offenders released with a third of the sentence remitted 'and for whom active attempts at rehabilitation are made appeared to be somewhat less affected by "institutionalization" than those who served five-sixths of their sentence' (Hammond and Chayen, 1963, p. 188). The report was a damning indictment of the system, as it commented:

> 'There is some danger of preventative detention detainees being regarded as the dregs of the criminal population for whom there is little hope save to keep them away from society … Yet only a small proportion of offenders sentenced to preventative detention had ever been given corrective training, many had never received any other treatment than imprisonment and for two thirds, probation had never been tried, the intelligence and abilities of preventative detainees were normal and many had more than average potential.' (Hammond and Chayen, 1963, p. 187)

The Prison Rules from 1948 stated that: '[t]he purposes of training and treatment of convicted prisoners shall be to establish in them the will to lead a good and useful life on discharge and to fit them to do so.' This remains a noble aspiration.

In 1965 a short Home Office paper was published entitled *The Adult Offender* (Home Office, 1965) which started with a quote from Sir Alexander Paterson that 'You cannot train men for freedom in conditions of captivity.' It acknowledged that some offenders were dangerous but many were 'disturbed, unstable and immature' (Home Office, 1965, p. 3). It commented that, 'Long periods in prison may punish, or possibly deter them, but do them no good – certainly do not fit them for re-entry into society. Every additional year of prison progressively unfits them' (Home Office, 1965, p. 3). The report was preparing the ground for the introduction of parole in the 1967 Act. By this stage 28 Discharged Prisoners' Aid Societies out of 36 had passed their after-care responsibilities over to the probation service. The voluntary organizations were meeting together to plan for the future (and in the event became NACRO, the National Association for the Care and Resettlement of Offenders). The use of volunteers was still heavily promoted. In 1966 the Home Office published *Residential Provision for Homeless Discharged Offenders*. This report regarded the provision of discharged prisoner hostels as essential for those with different needs, including alcoholics. Interestingly, it added under the heading 'Education of the public' that 'a real attempt must be made to gain the sympathy of the community as a whole for the special problems and difficulties of the offender' (Home Office, 1966a, p. 23).

In 1967 the Home Office published *The Place of Voluntary Service in After-Care* and declared that 'Discharged offenders need to live in a society which accepts them back into its midst with equal rights' (Home Office, 1967, p. 1). Again a programme of public education was strongly argued for and a case for the extensive use of volunteers was strongly promoted; indeed, it proclaimed that 'after-care begins on the day of sentence' (Home Office, 1967, p. 45). Finally it issued a clarion call to volunteers: 'Could you whole-heartedly subscribe to these views of an early penal reformer written in 1838, but as true today? "The first principle in the management of the guilty seems to me to be to treat them as men and women; which they were before they were guilty, and will be when they are no longer so; and which they are in the midst of it all. Their humanity is the principle thing about them; their guilt is the temporary state"' (Home Office, 1967, p. 47).

Taking all the above together, it can be seen that the probation service was 'pushing against an open door' in its quest to develop work with prisoners and ex-prisoners after 1966. The voluntary sector had been found wanting, both in working within the prisons and post-discharge. The quotations from the Home Office serve to show that humanity, not punishment, was the central ethos at this time.

A Home Office report, *Habitual Drunken Offenders* (1971), discussed a group of offenders which did not receive probation help. The report highlighted the lack of probation orders made on drunken offenders: 303 orders were made in 1968 from 'more than 75 000 cases' (Home Office, 1971, p. 66). The report acknowledged that probation officers had 'heavy caseloads' were reluctant to ask for orders on clients who may not keep to the conditions. The Courts were 'aware of the inadequacy to the habitual drunken offenders' needs of the supervision and support which they would be able to give' (1971, p. 66). The conclusion to the report commented that many offenders had 'a total absence of social ties', also that 'considerable attention would need to be given to building motivation'. These characteristics '[low socioeconomic background, minimum schooling, unskilled, unsettled in employment, unmarried or separated; personality disorder of some kind (taken from list on page)] suggested a background similar to other types of social casualty and one which is generally found with chronic petty recidivists and homeless men generally' (1971, p. 182). For the future it commented that 'The close involvement of professional social work services, the probation and after-care service in particular, will be essential' (1971, p. 183).

A press release on 27 July 1971 to accompany the *Report of the Prison Service* (Home Office, 1971b) commented that the prison population had increased in an 'unprecedented' way the previous year from 35 965 to 40 137. It had doubled in twenty years, and the press release added that: 'structured forms of training' were being strained, as was the potential for informal contact between staff and inmates: 'In overcrowded conditions there is a risk of emphasis turning to the sheer physical and material needs of the population of the prison or borstal and its routine'. Clearly this was an acknowledgement that if this type of work was to be undertaken, it could not be done in a situation of overcrowding.

The Professionalization of Welfare Work with Prisoners and Ex-prisoners

Guy Clutton-Brock founded the London Probation Service in 1935, after four years working as a housemaster in Feltham and Portland Borstals. He told me that he did not recall that at that time 'the officials [inside the borstals] were concerned about their future once they had opened the gates and let the chap out'. Probation at this time, according to him, was either missionaries offering 'five bob and a bible' or the newly qualified workers who wanted to offer more in-depth support. These two groups did not get on very well and his task was to try to integrate them and make links with magistrates. The probation service at this time had no remit to work with prisoners or ex-prisoners.

In an interview with a former member of the Borstal After-Care Association, I was told that he took up his post in 1950. Like many others, he had come from the armed forces and had applied for the job after seeing an advertisement. He had gone straight into the job and had then attended extra-mural courses. An offender coming out of borstal at this time was subject to a formal period on licence. The borstal sentence was indeterminate and many offenders served the full three years inside before the one-year after-care licence. Those coming out earlier would serve longer on licence so that the total time was four years. Caseloads were very high – each officer had approximately 70 offenders out on licence, and they would spend at least six days a month away from home visiting inmates at the borstals.

In 1966 the probation service outside London took over supervision of the licences and my interviewee recalled that officers were paid (and could keep) three pence per offender per month supervision fee and sixpence if the offender was homeless. Probation officers had to submit forms to the Borstal After-Care Association, and these were assidiously followed up. Licencees who did not keep to the conditions were quickly breached. What was most interesting in terms of status was the relationship between the Borstal After-Care Officer and the borstal, and with the police (who carried out arrests for breaches). The Officer was an ex-officio member of the Board of Visitors and enjoyed high status during visits: 'I know one governor, whenever I walked in to his meeting … his chief officer and the house-master, they all got up, stood up for me when I came in'.

He was disparaging about probation contact with prisoners and ex-prisoners, feeling that the service had been less committed to this work than the old voluntary sector. His experience was that POs looked down on resettlement work with the homeless and saw it as being of lower status. However, like Clutton-Brock's experience with the missionaries, voluntary after-care 'mainly, we used to say, it was five bob at the gate and cheerio Charlie!' The same criticism levelled against the quality of the work of the police court missionaries could be stated about contact with ex-prisoners.

The Morison Report (1962) began with a definition of probation from the United Nations (1951): probation is a method of dealing with specially selected offenders consisting of the conditional suspension of punishment while the offender is placed under personal supervision and is given individual guidance or treatment. The report was not an attempt to portray the offender as a victim. It did not like the word 'client'. The caseworker 'needs the fullest possible insight into the individual's personality, capacities, attitudes and feelings and he must also understand the influences in the individual's history, relationships and present environment which have helped to form them' (Morison, 1962, p. 24). It commented that the general view of those that gave evidence to it was that it was valuable for the probationer to accept being placed on probation, however grudgingly, and that this was valuable for the future conduct of the offender. 'Probation extracts from the offender a contribution, within the limits of his capacity, to the well-being of others, whether it be through his useful employment in the community or through his participation in the life of the family or other social group' (1962, p. 4). In this succinct sentence, the report pre-dates the work of writers like Farrall (2002, 2004) and Maruna (1999, 2000, 2001) by highlighting the importance of what is now called *social capital* and the need to get offenders into employment and keep them within a supportive family environment. It summarized the value of probation as follows: 'There is a moral case, in a society founded upon respect for human rights, for a system which allows an offender to continue to live and work in the community' (1962, p. 9).

The Morison Report commented that the demands on the service should increase and this was connected to prison after-care, which had been the remit of the Discharged Prisoners' Aid Societies. At the time of writing, this was under review by the Advisory Council on the Treatment of Offenders (ACTO), discussed next. It saw after-care work as not being 'extraneous to the normal functions of the service' (Morison, 1962, p. 151). Thus it paved the way for its inclusion into the professional task of probation.

The Advisory Council on the Treatment of Offenders was asked to review the arrangements for statutory and voluntary after-care for both adults and juveniles in April 1961 and it produced the Barry Report in October 1963, the year after the Morison Report had indicated that the probation service should take on after-care. The report, led by the Hon. Mr Justice Barry, stated that a system that differentiated between offenders subject to compulsory or voluntary after-care after prison was unfair. It recommended that the Discharged Prisoners' Aid Societies (given statutory recognition by the Act of the same name in 1862) should be taken over by the probation service – to be renamed the probation and after-care service. Prison welfare was also seen as a task to be taken over by the probation service: 'we regard London as pre-eminently an area where a number of local auxiliary after-care committees would be needed. London is the home of many discharged persons and many others are drawn to it by hopes of employment and anonymity. Because of this concentration we are particularly concerned that the organization of after-care in London be given high priority' (Home Office, 1963).

In London, the report noted the New Bridge society had been formed to offer assistance to ex-offenders. Blackfriars Settlement also acted in a voluntary capacity. Barry envisaged the probation service working with ex-prisoners using volunteers, but continued:

> 'The main need of many offenders is for simple encouragement, friendship and human understanding, which could be given by sincere and warm hearted anciliaries.' (para. 121)
>
> 'It will be impossible for the probation and after-care service to undertake this formidable task unaided.' (para. 122)
>
> 'As to training, it is necessary to stress that this is not work for inexperienced amateurs. It requires a warm heart but also a clear head, compassion combined with insight, lack of illusion, and preparedness for disappointment.' (para. 132) (Home Office, 1963)

The National Association of Discharged Prisoners' Aid Societies (NADPAS) saw the solution to 'a flagging voluntary movement' as NAPDAS becoming the central point for after-care, but Barry saw that this would result in two parallel systems, wholly Exchequer-financed, one for compulsory after-care using probation officers as its field agents and one for voluntary after-care, which would also employ social workers in prisons and in the community. The report could see no logic for two separate systems of after-care, especially as offenders could oscillate between compulsory and statutory after-care.

It considered whether the probation service would be linked too strongly with the prison system if it took over the social work role within the prison, and concluded that this was the case with the possible exception of detention centres (for short-sentenced young offenders) as their (locally based) probation officers were likely to be able to visit them. At the time of writing the report, following the earlier Maxwell Report (Home Office, 1963), there was a social worker appointed to every local prison in England and Wales, with more than one in the bigger institutions. Barry recommended that all prisons should have social work support as long-sentenced prisoners were in as much need of this as short-sentenced ones.

Finally the report concluded that there was a strong case for becoming a single service in the community, and recommended that this should be undertaken by an expanded probation service. As the Morison Report had commented, after-care could become the 'Cinderella' of the probation service, and probation officers could regard after-care as secondary to their 'normal functions'. Barry felt that this could be overcome and the organization's new title should be the 'Probation and After-Care Service'. Professor Leon Radzinowicz and two others disagreed with this amalgamation. By 1966 probation had taken over all through-care and after-care functions, and NADPAS became National Association of the Care and Resettlement of Offenders (NACRO).

It was due to the above report that probation staff took over responsibility for the homeless and rootless offenders in London from the voluntary sector and, in particular, the After-Care Unit in London took over responsibility for working with the homeless and rootless, prisoners and ex-prisoners, from the old Discharged Prisoners' Aid Societies in 1965. The formation, growth and closure of the After-Care Unit in London between 1965 and 1990 is discussed in Chapter 7. A senior officer from the Unit, who later became an Assistant Principal there, commented to me that the members of the Discharged Prisoners' Aid Societies were hostile to the takeover, feeling that they knew a lot about prison welfare and the probation service didn't. The informant agreed that there was an element of truth to this.

Home Office Circular 130/1967 (Home Office, 1967b) described the role of the prison probation officer as four-fold: 'As a social caseworker, as a focal point of social work, as the normal channel of communication on social problems with the outside, and as planner of after-care.' The London branch of NAPO produced a report entitled *Social Work in Prison* (NAPO, 1968). This acknowledged that the setting might prevent effective work from taking place. There were issues around the principle of 'less eligibility' linked to the loss of freedom, loss of identity, the enforced impotence of the prisoner, loss of individuality and so on. Work with a probation officer was special treatment or a privilege, an important concept within the prison. The prison probation officer was under pressure to give direct help, rather than to help prisoners to help themselves, a classic casework technique. This was later confirmed by Holborn (1975) in a Home Office report, *Some Male Offenders' Problems*, which described a welfare circle where the offender, cut off from the outside world, requested help from the prison probation officer, who is perceived as the link with the outside world. The prison probation officer (often with pressure from prison officers) complies with the request for help, and this satisfies most prisoners, emphasing the popular conception of the prison probation officer as the 'welfare', reinforcing the prison probation officer as the link with the outside world.

In 1979 Corden, Kuipers and Wilson published *After Prison: A Study of Post-Release Experiences of Discharged Prisoners*. This found that few men interviewed for the study experienced good cooperation between 'the relevant workers throughout their sentence and afterwards' (1979, p. 73). Approximately half the sample of 107 men had not found the prison probation officer to be helpful. Contact with probation officers on discharge was low, with only a third of the men who were not subject to statutory after-care supervision on licence on discharge opting to have voluntary contact with the probation service. They concluded that '[v]ery isolated men may think their problems to be so overwhelming that any attempts on their part to change things seems futile: and they would see little point in making contact with the probation service' (1979, p. 74). The seminal work in prison/probation liaison was Jepson and Elliot *Shared Working Between Prison and Probation Officers* (SWIP) (1985), thus the theme of the more recent prisons–probation review is not new. The concept was that within the prison there should be a division between 'welfare tasks' to be carried out by prison officers and 'social work' tasks by the probation officer, although other research by the prison psychological service had revealed a reluctance by prisoners to reveal personal information to prison officers. The SWIP experiment was encouraging in that many prisoners knew who their personal officer was, and the scheme had the potential to break down some of the barriers between prisoner and prison officer. It would enhance the role of the prison officer, who would be more than just a 'turnkey'.

The problem in prisons is the sheer misery and sense of hopelessness that many prisoners experience. Even if the system works well, the homeless ex-prisoner faces particular difficulties. As Paylor commented, 'The "hidden homeless" is the name given to people who are, from a common-sense viewpoint, homeless, but are not accepted as such under the current legislation. They have no right to, or have little chance of access to, their own secure housing of minimally adequate standard' (Paylor, 1995, p. 23).

The ACU had been able to overcome many of the difficulties faced by the homeless and rootless at the time of its operation, as it had negotiated with the local Department for Health and Social Security (DHSS) for benefits to take such people off the streets and into hostels and bed and breakfast accommodation. This was a powerful incentive for a person literally living in the gutter to be seen and to be given the first step towards regaining their self-respect. However, I wrote an article in 1990 expressing concern that after the social security system had changed to one whereby claimants were paid fortnightly in arrears, it had become virtually impossible to find the money to resettle homeless people without resources (Goodman, 1990). The itinerant was still regarded as different to the rest of the population; in medieval times being seen as a threat, but as the twentieth century entered its final decade the itinerant was no longer a threat to modern society. Instead, they had become invisible, and was regarded as not requiring probation intervention.

Changes Since Probation Became Part of NOMS

The change in the way that probation operates and the end-to-end management of offenders has resulted in offender managers, as they are now known, being able to hold on to cases from the start to the end of the statutory order. Through-care contact is more likely if the offender is deemed to be of high risk. The Criminal Justice Act 2003 brought in a new way of defining offenders. This includes the concepts of phase two and phase three offenders. For phase two offenders, there is the potential for linking in with prison and prison probation staff, whereas this is less likely for Phase Three Indeterminate Public Protection Sentences (IPP). The scandal of IPP was fully described in a joint inspection report by the HM Chief Inspector of Prisons and HM Chief Inspector of Probation (2008). The report highlights the explosion in the number of people being sentenced to indeterminate sentences: nearly 2000 by 2006. These prisoners, because they had to demonstrate that they were no longer dangerous before they could be released, put more strain on to a system already under pressure. The probation service was described in the report as poorly prepared for the extra work that it had to take on as a consequence of IPP. Phase two offenders (those who are high-risk and sentenced to more than 12 months) would be allocated an offender supervisor in the prison, who could be either a prison or a probation officer. Local probation staff liaised with the prison via the offender supervisor, which meant that visits to the prison could take place informally on the wing, perhaps in the television room, the association room or another vacant room, rather than in legal visits.

Trying to ascertain how probation officers liaise and work with prisoners can be tricky, as the service changes so regularly that processes quickly become out of date. Since I interviewed a number of staff to learn about current practice, there has been a change back to generic field teams from specialist units. The analysis is still valid as the contacts with prisoners were demarcated according to the level of perceived risk, and this has endured within the rearranged teams. By the time this book is published, it is possible that specialisms may have been reinvented! During my interviews probation staff worked in a variety of different units, such as public protection units, working with high-risk offenders before and after their release from prison, offender management units that were community-based and included lower-risk offenders, various specialist units relating to addiction and so on. A probation officer who worked in the Public Protection Unit (PPU) estimated that he supervised 12 offenders in the community and 37 in custody. All of these offenders were assessed as being at high risk of serious reoffending. Most of his work with these involved liaison contact with the prisons. Conversely, in Offender Management (OM) teams, there was a high community caseload and less in custody. Work with these was described to me as being 'stagnant'; not a lot of work was done with these offenders apart from liaising with prisons for reports.

In a local area, which were mostly the size of an average London borough, there might be one PPU, four OM teams and a specialist Substance Misuse Unit, which usually has a high community caseload. The level of risk at which the offender has been assessed dictates whether they are allocated to an OM or PPU team. Probation officers and PSOs staffed the OM teams but only POs worked in the PPUs. Probation senior officers might supervise level 2 or 3 cases but never sex offenders or domestic violence offenders.

In the PPU the offender manager could undertake prison visiting when there was a requirement to do so. The service would not prevent this. The most likely reason to go would be for sentence planning, completing parole reports, for the yearly review or post-programme review, and pre-release review six months before a high-risk case is discharged. This latter case was often when a prisoner was sentenced to Indeterminate Public Protection (IPP) and needed to successfully complete a programme before he could be considered for discharge. Some officers told me that they preferred to undertake these tasks face-to-face, but did not do so as it was possible to complete reports via video link. Thus, through-care as a concept has fallen into disuse. Prisoners were visited when reports were needed, or they might be interviewed by video link rather than face-to-face. One PO told me that he only interviewed by video link and never undertook visits.

It was recognized that prisoners appreciated prison visits. The change in prisons that has led to offender supervisors being based in prisons has changed the relationship between prison and probation staff, with less of a silo mentality for each profession. The quality of the information exchanged between prisons and the field has also improved. Prisoners were more comfortable speaking to probation staff on the wing, which was described to me as 'their world'. This is only possible with the active cooperation of the offender supervisors, so the change to NOMS, I was told, was seen as beneficial as it has freed up POs in the community not to undertake visits unless necessary.

The above process resulted in a qualitative difference between the experience of prisoners supervised by PPUs rather than in OM teams. In the latter group, low/medium risk offenders were unlikely to have much contact with offender managers in the community during their time in prison. While a lot of probation staff's time was taken up in preparing the electronic OASys forms that constituted the risk assessment, given the nature of the unit and the fact they had relatively fewer offenders to supervise in the community, there was time to undertake prison trips when necessary. Offender management units had less time to give to offenders in general, and this meant that it was more difficult to pick up cues and changes in the demeanour of the offender.

There is one group of prisoners whose opportunities have not improved since the changes described above. Prisoners sentenced to mandatory life sentences have been 'pushed into the background' in the system. Indeed, one lifer had telephoned his offender manager to say that he had had no contact with prison staff over the past year, and contact with his offender manager had been limited to an exchange of letters. The focus of probation intervention had moved to those on indeterminate sentences. Yet lifers moved slowly through the prison system, eventually ending up in category D open prisons when they had a short time to be prepared for release. Indeed, those on a short tariff might have to backtrack to undertake courses that they were required to complete prior to release.

Within prisons, the changes had resulted in the disappearance of the old lifer units and the contacts between mandatory lifers and prison staff had reduced significantly. There was no procedure whereby (external) OMs were informed about lifer reviews, sentence planning and other activities. In effect, the current concern for prisoners with indeterminate sentences had rendered lifers somewhat invisible to the criminal justice world.

National Standards (NS): PPU and OM Teams

National Standards was not seen as an issue for staff in PPU teams. There was time to see offenders and give them extra attention if necessary. In OM teams there was also more flexibility in how rigidly National Standards were being enforced. It had been accepted that cases were being breached too quickly. Thus NS 2007 planned to change the freedom of offender managers to exercise their professional discretion.

Speaking with a very experienced offender manager based in an OM team confirmed that their priorities were different from PPUs'. He had not undertaken a prison visit for seven or eight years, and always conducted interviews with prisoners by video link. He did not have time to consider undertaking through-care visits, an activity he used to do. He was clear that when an OASys assessment was required on a serving prisoner that this was the responsibility of the prison PO. He was pleased that the role of the PO was now one of punishment rather than 'advise, assist and befriend', believing that prisoner risk levels had not been considered as much as they are today.

He described his philosophy as a simple one: people should take responsibility for themselves, and he had no time for excuses. He felt that the new framework was better and although he was social-work trained, he was not impressed with the old approaches to work with offenders. Half of his caseload was in prison, but he felt under pressure to prepare reports, produce OASys assessments, have video conferences with his prisoners and meet his targets. This meant he had to be in the office most of the time, and he had booked 75 minutes later that day to meet with a young man remanded in Feltham to obtain the information he needed for a court report. The question this raised was whether video conferencing gave the report writer any opportunity to form any sort of relationship/trust/bonding with the young person, or whether it was simply a bureaucratic task to gather information. Has the probation service lost its way as it struggles to reach its performance targets?

Late in 2010, as mentioned, a further reorganization was proposed that would fundamentally change the way that teams were organized, with all staff being merged into generic teams. In order to cut costs, qualified probation staff were to be given the responsibility for overseeing the probation service officers, rather than this being the task of managers. This would impact on the time they had available for lower priority work and consequently would make through-care work with prisoners less likely to happen.

A number of different official reports have commented on prisoner rehabilitation. In March 2010 the National Audit Office (NAO) published *Managing Offenders on Short Custodial Sentences*, which sought to examine how offenders sentenced to less than 12 months' imprisonment were treated. This group makes up around 9 per cent of all prisoners and numbers in excess of 60 000 adults. They are highly likely to reoffend, with an average of 16 previous convictions each, typically for theft and violence. One would imagine therefore that they should attract a great deal of support from the probation arm of NOMS on release, as well as during their time in custody. The report estimates that reoffending by *all* recent ex-prisoners cost the economy between £9.5 billion and £13 billion in the period 2007/08, with short-term prisoners costing around £7–10 billion of this. The NAO report surveyed 91 short-term prisons, interviewing some inmates and analysing prisoner activity in three prisons. Some 1000 prisoners self-harmed in 2008, with the level of need outstripping supplied care. Furthermore, the finding that daytime activity for this group was 'generally inadequate to meet HM Inspectorate of Prison' standard for a healthy prison (National Audit Office, 2010, p. 6) is of great concern, with between a third and a half of short-term prisoners spending almost all day 'banged up' in their cells. The lack of probation involvement can be seen in the worrying comment that 'with the exception of drug services … prisons do not often match individual prisoners with appropriate assistance' (National Audit Office, 2010, p. 7). Similarly, NOMS could not identify whether prisoners' needs in terms of accommodation and employment were being met. Links to services in the community were described as 'limited and inconsistent'. Thus, short-term prison sentencing could be described as warehousing. Finally, the report separated the safety of the incarceration experience from the lack of structured support. While accepting the latter as a problem, it was positive about the former, believing that despite overcrowding, prisoners felt safe. But is this an acceptable and accurate state of affairs?

One aspect of UK prisons that has not received significant analysis is the divide between private and public prisons. According to Bromley Briefings (published by the Prison Reform Trust, 2011), the UK has the most privatized prisons in Europe (holding 11.6 per cent of the prison population) which will rise to 14 per cent when an existing prison is privatized and a new private prison is completed. The USA, meanwhile, has around 9 per cent of its prisons in the private sector. There are significant differences in conditions and performance between public and private prisons in their running costs, staff to prisoner ratio, pay, length of service, staff turnover and so on (Prison Reform Trust, 2011, pp. 60–61). Overcrowding is a problem, with 80 of the 132 prisons in England and Wales overcrowded (p. 5). Again, there are differences between the public and private sectors, with 35.4 per cent of public prisons being overcrowded, but only 22.7 per cent of private prisons, and the HM thematic review stated that 'public prisons were more than five times more likely to perform well for safety than private prisons' (HM Inspectorate of Prisons, 2009). Despite this there has been an ideological drive to move criminal justice services to the private sector by both major political parties, perhaps to limit the power of unions such as the Prison Officer Association, and to 'frighten' staff into being compliant with centralizing directives as budgets are cut.

Coyle (2005), a former prison governor and now a penal academic, added some further concern in *Understanding Prisons*, written in the aftermath of the creation of NOMS. First, he argued that the organization only viewed people through the prism of them being offenders. They then needed to be managed and their 'criminogenic needs' managed in a seamless way. Second, he was concerned with what was happening to probation caseloads and in this respect he cited the annual report of the HM Inspector of Probation (2003). In this the Chief Inspector highlighted what might be described as the inflation creep of the caseload. Offenders who might have previously received a fine were now sentenced to a community penalty, and short custodial sentences had displaced community penalties. The probation service caseload had 'silted up' with lower-risk offenders (Coyle, 2005, p. 58). Third, Coyle described resettlement programmes for prisoners but commented they:

> 'Rarely involve other significant people in the prisoner's life, such as family, friends, a teacher or social worker from outside. Yet when people are sent to prison they leave behind families, friends and many links from their previous life and the "pains of imprisonment" are felt by all of them as much as by the prisoner … With a few notable exceptions, little consideration is given to arranging visits in ways that are likely to reinforce links between partners, children, parents or siblings.' (Coyle, 2005, pp. 162–163)

In 1999 the probation service set up a number of Pathfinder programmes to evaluate new ways of working under the 'what works' initiatives. These were small-scale research programmes to test out ways to reduce offending, working with prisoners sentenced to less than a year in prison. These offenders would have typically received little or no support prior to discharge and on release, but they also have a very high reconviction rate. There was a resettlement Pathfinder (called Focus on Resettlement, or FOR) to test new ways of working with resettling prisoners serving less than 12 months in custody (Clancy *et al.*, 2006). In phase 1, 1081 prisoners participated in the Pathfinder with 114 completing the FOR programme. This was a cognitive behavioural programme of 22 sessions, but not all offenders had the time to complete it. Results were better than relying on voluntary contact, with higher levels of continuity associated with probation-led projects and the FOR programme (p. 5). The research revealed an interesting result in terms of OASys assessment, which is the yardstick by which risk problems are assessed and then calculated. Differences in problem levels, such as drug misuse, financial management, relationships and so on revealed that probation officers were likely to score more highly on cognitive deficits and staff from voluntary agencies similarly on practical issues – Clancy *et al.* wondered if this was a result of their training and culture (p. 12).

Prisoners who completed the programme and maintained contact on their release were more likely to be employed afterwards (p. 64); 72 per cent reported some form of substance misuse prior to starting on the programme and 80 per cent claimed that the FOR programme had had some positive effect on their drug/alcohol use (p. 64), while 82 per cent claimed that the programme had helped them to avoid committing further crime (p. 65).

There is one final result that is very important, and this relates to post-release contact with the helping professions. 'Probation-led projects as a group had better re-conviction outcomes than those led by voluntary agencies' (p. 69) and 'continuity of service "through the gate" is of major importance to the effectiveness of any resettlement programme' (p. 69). This led to the conclusion that 'successful resettlement depends both upon systematic attention to thinking skills and motivation in prison (as practiced by the probation-led projects) and post-release contact with someone with whom the offender has developed a sympathetic relationship while in prison' (p. 75).

Academics such as Ward and Maruna (2007) and Codd (2008) have argued that the most positive approaches to prevent reoffending by ex-prisoners need to focus on desistence. Yet, families are little supported by the helping agencies, including probation, with the current preoccupation on assessment and the individual offender.

> 'Whilst in the UK there are many books offering critical perspectives on prisons, many such books barely mention families. Yet family relationships and their erosion or destruction is a fundamental preoccupation of many prisoners. It is easy in our current risk-obsessed culture to denigrate prisoners' families for being poor, or behaving in ways that are socially unacceptable, for forming part of an undesirable underclass, this contributing to the ongoing risk of criminality.' (Codd, 2008, p. 169)

In conjunction with the findings of the Pathfinder programme, the skills needed to encourage and promote desistence are those enjoyed by probation staff, both inside and outside the prison, working in partnership. Prison POs can work with other professionals inside, including in mental health, substance misuse education (Counselling, Assessment, Referral, Advice and Through-Care (CARATs), and so on.

Finally, no consideration of prison resettlement can ignore issues of difference. This is particularly acutely felt by the author, who spent three years working in Holloway Prison and saw first-hand how badly many women cope within the criminal justice system, including their time in prison. The prison system for women is small, and many women are incarcerated far from home, rendering desistence highly problematic. The Chief Inspector of Prisons David Ramsbotham (2005) gave his view of prisons in his book, titled *Prisongate. The Shocking State of Britain's Prisons and the Need for Visionary Change*. He described the impression of his unannounced visit to Holloway Prison in 1995 as follows:

> 'What I had seen in Holloway was an affront to human decency that was wholly unworthy of a civilized society. If my experienced professional inspectors were as shocked as I, a complete outsider to prisons, who had seen a number of appalling sights in my military career, what did this say about the standards of those who were responsible for the institution? I had never before encountered so many deeply unhappy or emotionally damaged people for whom so little was being done. Heaven knows what their lives outside Holloway were like if they did not find its conditions a deterrent.' (Ramsbotham, 2005, pp. 24-25)

The important report by Lady Corston (2007) made a number of cogent points starting from the basis that equal outcomes for men and women required different approaches. This was because women were frequently primary carers for children, self-harm was a bigger problem for women, women were often victims (including, often, of serious violence) as well as offenders, many women lose their accommodation while in prison, there is a higher prevalence of mental health problems in women and so on. The report made many recommendations which are, sadly, still to be implemented, and probation has a major role to play in this.

Lord Bradley (2009) reviewed people with mental health problems or learning difficulties in the criminal justice system, which highlighted the growing number of people with mental health problems in prison. Although diversion (removing the person from the criminal justice system and instead helping him with his mental health problems) has been supported by governments over many years, it has never been applied consistently. His report highlighted that different approaches were needed for adults and young people, and specialists needed further training to understand how to recognize and intervene, preferably from early on. Professional organizations needed to work to a joint protocol, with suitable facilities outside police stations. Defendants with mental health problems had to be treated as vulnerable, like vulnerable witnesses; probation staff needed to have mental health and disability awareness training; and all organizations in the criminal justice system needed to agree on a local service agreement for psychiatric reports. In terms of the theme of this chapter, prison resettlement, further research was needed on mental health treatment requirements. This was also true for imprisonment for public protection sentences and mental health or learning disability issues.

Disability issues in general have not been handled sensitively in criminal justice. In terms of race, and the duty not to discriminate, the over-representation of black people has been an issue over many years. The Criminal Justice Act 1991 includes the following in section 95:

1. The Secretary of State shall in each year publish such information as he considers expedient for the purpose of:
   (a) enabling persons engaged in the administration of justice to become aware of the financial implications of their decisions; or
   (b) facilitating the performance of such persons of their duty to avoid discriminating against any persons on the ground of race or sex or any other improper ground.
2. Publication under subsection (1) above shall be effected in such a manner as the Secretary of State considers appropriate for the purpose of bringing the information to the attention of the persons concerned.

Despite this attempt to publicize the statistics on race and gender, black people are more likely to be arrested (see Hood, 2002, and Equality and Human Rights Commission, 2008), and are over-represented in prisons. In June 2007, members of black and minority ethnic (BME) groups accounted for 26 per cent of the total prison population of 79 734 (including foreign nationals). For British nationals only, this figure is 19 per cent. The proportion of black British prisoners relative to the general population was 7.4 per 1000 compared to 1.4 per 1,000 for white people. In contrast, people from 'Chinese or other' ethnic backgrounds were least likely to be in prison, with a rate of 0.5 per 1000. The rate for people from Asian groups was higher than for white people, but lower than that for the mixed or black groups, that is, 1.7 per 1000. Females accounted for less than 5 per cent of the British national prison population. Edgar (2007) catalogues a sorry history of discrimination within prisons and an adversarial response to complaints by the prison authorities.

Summary

Petersilia (2003), describing the worrying growth of incarceration in the USA, highlighted the problems of developing a prison works approach. Furthermore, she questioned 'the impact [that] constant churning of large segments of the resident population' had on those that remain out of prison (Petersilia, 2003, p. v). She believed that pre- and post-release programmes could make the system more humane and just. I would argue that this country often turns to the USA for advice, for example, the 'broken windows' approach to crime management. 'Broken windows' refers to the approach whereby all crimes and acts of vandalism are dealt with immediately to stop them getting out of hand. The reality is that police approaches cannot hope to catch all incivilities, so there will always have to be an element of discretion. Tough approaches to law and order tend to be directed at particular sections of the community, who may become alienated and oppressed.

This chapter has emphasized that resettlement needs to begin during the prison experience and to continue post-release. Despite an infatuation with bringing in the private and voluntary sector to help with public-sector jobs (which is done because the private sector is often cheaper, as people are not so well trained and they can draw on short-term employed staff. This can lead to a crisis in morale and insecurity, not to be recommended when the public may be put at risk), there is convincing evidence that probation has much to offer in this work. The reasons why POs started resettlement work were related to efficiency and professionalism, and this is still relevant today. The criminal justice system must not discriminate, and is mandated not to do so. It requires high-level knowledge and skills to recognize mental health, substance misuse and other problems, and it would be worrying if ideological rhetoric to privatize and break up public services instead led to offenders failing and reoffending.

9

Issues Around Rehabilitation

Using History as an Indicator of Future Social Problems

As early chapters in the book made clear, understanding how the criminal justice system grew reveals the changing nature of justice and how offenders have been both punished and reformed. Merely giving punishment, public humiliation and banishment does not enable the problem of deviance to disappear. As interventions with offenders became more measured, the criminal justice system began to view offenders as individuals with particular problems, but penal populism has meant that exemplary punishment has been invoked right up until the present day. More benevolent forms of intervention have been tried, typically called welfare, casework, etc. This was the time when professionals had great freedom and limited accountability for their work, and later chapters highlighted how the probation service was constrained and forced into being correctional and restrictive. Of interest is that the ideology of the practitioners has not changed but their sense of limited freedom to operate has. More recently, the 'control-freakery' of New Labour has been relaxed, but is the purpose of this to encourage professional judgement and discretion, or to enable parts of the work with offenders to be hived off to the private, for-profit sector (possibly in conjunction with voluntary organizations, as has occurred in the prisons)?

The After-Care Unit (ACU) is a good example of how vulnerable and dangerous offenders were given support to change without recourse to coercive measures, and where initiatives were encouraged from the bottom up in response to meeting the needs of vulnerable people, the exact opposite to the top-down controls of recent years. Charles Preece (2000) worked at the ACU after 12 years

Rehabilitating and Resettling Offenders in the Community, First Edition. Anthony H. Goodman.

working in London prisons, and he said: 'Here, the probation service was hammering out its own experience of after-care on the anvil of trying to meet the needs of the most difficult men and women it had known' (Preece, 2000, p. 86). He described how the POs would adopt unorthodox practices to meet the needs of the clients; one interviewed a paranoid offender under his table where this person felt safe. Another, a former army officer with a medical qualification, kept a skeleton in the corner and somehow his eccentricity made a number of the clients feel secure and safe. These officers were part of the folklore of the ACU and I heard about them years later when I worked there. Preece confirmed that they were true! There was something special about the work there that Preece captured in his book:

> 'There was one thing which I thought endeared us to a wondering authority and that was our ability to contain some 800 or more of those just discharged from custodial sentences. This was the normal complement of a prison such as Brixton, and with a mere handful of staff, possibly about 40 people including the admin and clerical officers instead of ten times that amount of prison staff. Most of our callers would have been in prison again had they not had the Borough and its band to which to turn.' (Preece, 2000, p. 86)

The special essence of the ACU was its creativity and willingness to think out of the box. This is precisely the conclusion a group of probation academics and former practitioners drew at the end of their edited book:

> 'Creative and constructive practice is concerned to challenge the 'otherness' and 'exclusion' of those who may be both in need and presenting potential risks. How this is done requires a local, relational, and dynamic context that supports an inclusive, accountable (but not risk-averse or risk driven) and reflexive practice context.' (Brayford, Cowe, and Deering, 2010, p. 266)

What does it Mean to be a Professional?

The 'denigration of professionals by Thatcher' was the time when the public sector was seen as expensively trained, precious and not accountable (Senior, Crowther-Dowey and Long, 2007, p. 70). This led to the growth of assistants to complement and later deputize for the fully trained personnel, this process taking place in education, policing, probation and other organizations. The end of voluntary after-care and outreach work, to be replaced by community enforcement, spelled the end of the ACU. Individualism was not acceptable; rather, conformity to national standards was required. Richard Sennett in his book *The Craftsman* captures the essence of having skills to undertake quality work that can be applied to a number of professions, including work with offenders. It is the antithesis of the assembly line mentality:

> 'Craftsmen take pride in skills that mature. That is why simple imitation is not a sustaining satisfaction; the skill has to evolve. The slowness of craft time serves as a source of satisfaction; practice beds in, making the skill one's own. Slow craft time also enables the work of reflection and imagination – which the push for quick results cannot.' (Sennett, 2008, p. 295)

A snapshot of recent changes to probation personnel reveal that professionally qualified staff rose by 12 per cent, staff training to be POs fell by 34 per cent, PSO's (less well trained and qualified) rose by 53 per cent, and the ratio of offenders to qualified POs rose from 41.2 to 46.5, an increase of 13 per cent (Oldfield and Grimshaw, 2010). This would indicate that, increasingly, work with offenders would be undertaken by staff who had not had the time to hone their skills. This is reflected in some of the critical responses to the growth of the cognitive behavioural approach to work with offenders. Farrall (2002), reflecting on his study of how probationers positively changed, found probation intervention irrelevant. Instead, motivation increased from changes in the social contexts in which they lived. Good motivation, gaining employment, mending damaged relationships, starting new relationships, moving home and so on…' (Farrall, 2002, pp. 213–214).

This led Farrall to promote a change in work with offenders from offending-related to desistance-focused. 'Desistance-focused' means that instead of focusing on the faulty thinking processes in the offenders, such as a cognitive-behavioural approach to encourage offenders to think in a socially positive way, the emphasis should instead be placed on the problems that needed to be resolved, such as accommodation, employment and other more practical needs that the offender was immediately concerned about. This marks a return to more traditional ways of working with offenders (one might say, with a little irony, that the professional practice that was the 'state of the art' before the 'what works' revolution was useful after all)! Indeed, the need to form a relationship with the offender and understand what they were concerned about was a fundamental aspect of desistance-focused interventions, as it was essential to know and understand what was important to the offender if they were to successfully integrate into law-abiding society.

Certainly, the evidence for strict adherence to the 'what works' agenda is mixed (Goodman, 2008). It works as Pawson and Tilley (1997) aptly said, for some people in some circumstances. Those who completed programmes often changed their behaviour, but those who did not, often fared worse.

Life in the Community

Ward (2010), investigating the rave scene, found this in her interviews:

> 'It was without doubt that the drugs culture and drug-using lives of the people on whom my study focused were based on leisure pleasure experiences, … but it is important to add, the drug-using lifestyles I observed were not solely quick-fix hedonism located in "time out" lives, but incorporated a range of functions such as providing

> incomes, jobs, status, and a sense of identity derived from being a member of this unique leisure culture. Alongside nights out in clubs, the people I observed were entrepreneurial economic actors who used their involvement in drug-selling as a form of alternate work, and to some extent paralleled the worth elicited through conventional work roles.' (Ward, 2010, p. 151)

That offending can be equated to work fits in with Merton's taxonomy of how people try to live the American dream through either legitimate or illegitimate means. People might enjoy using drugs, but it didn't mean that they rejected the idea of living and participating in society, albeit with an enjoyment of illicit substances and the rewards, physical and financial, this offered. For others, there was little on offer, legal or illicit, to break the monotony of poverty, lack of opportunity and distrust of services like the police.

Jock Young prophetically detailed the state of anxiety and tension that prefaced the unrest in London and other major cities in the United Kingdom in 2011, following the police killing of a person suspected by them of being about to fire a gun. The suspect was black, and his family felt that they had not been given a proper explanation by the police of their response. Young accurately predicted how the media and the judiciary would react to the riots:

> 'Vertigo is the malaise of late modernity: a sense of insecurity of insubstantiality, and of uncertainty, a whiff of chaos and a fear of falling… The obsession with rules, an insistence on clear uncompromising lines of demarcation between correct and incorrect behaviour … an easy resort to punitiveness and a point at which simple punishment begins to verge on the vindictive.' (Young, 2007, p. 12)

The aftermath of the riots in the summer of 2011 prompted a great deal of soul-searching by politicians and the media. This focused on whether the young people involved could and should be described as 'feral' but also in the fitness for purpose of community and custodial sentences. The Prime Minister had regularly used the phrase 'broken Britain' to describe what he saw as the breakdown of the family and its values. Kenneth Clarke, the justice secretary, stated that 75 per cent of those aged 18 and over involved in the riots already had previous convictions (Clarke, 5 Sept. 2011). He described the penal system as 'broken', where the unrest and '…riots can be seen in part as an outburst of outrageous behaviour by the criminal classes – individuals and families familiar with the justice system, who haven't been changed by their past punishments' (Clarke, 5 Sept. 2011). Clarke warned against criticism of the judiciary, which he described as independent.

He was robust in his views on the causes of crime and how it could be tackled. For the former he started from a societal overview: '[R]eform can't stop at our penal system alone. The general recipe for a productive member of society is no secret. It has not changed since I was inner cities minister 25 years ago. It's about having a job, a strong family, a decent education and, beneath it all, an attitude that shares in the values of mainstream society' (Clarke, 5 Sept. 2011).

Second, Clarke had a solution to dealing with these problems, which was:

> '[I]ntroducing radical changes to focus our penal system relentlessly on proper, robust, punishment and the reduction of reoffending. This means making our jails places of productive hard work, addressing the scandal of drugs being readily available in many of our prisons and toughening community sentences so that they command public respect. And, underpinning it all, the most radical step of all: paying those who rehabilitate offenders, including the private and voluntary sectors, by the results they achieve, not (as too often in the past) for processes and box-ticking.' (Clarke, 5 Sept. 2011)

This 'common sense' response may superficially seem very attractive but it begs a number of questions. Will the public, in whose name these reforms are being promulgated, welcome tougher community sentences? Will these be given for more serious crimes or will there be an inflation creep, with tougher community sentences being given out to those who would have been given a community sanction anyway? There is a history of this within criminal justice and the consequence is a rise in 'technical' breaches of community sanctions.

The problem of the inner city is picked up by Byrne (2005), drawing on the work of Harrison (1982) in Hackney, who considered the 'Brazilianization of advanced capitalism'; by which he meant that there were neighbourhoods only a few miles away from very affluent areas of London, like Hampstead, which were more akin to developing-world slums, leading to social exclusion (Byrne, 2005, p. 49). So within the inner city are the homeless and rootless, often part of the revolving door of the short-sentenced prison population and without probation support; and the adults and young people with little prospect of making their lives more fulfilling and for whom modern-style probation has little meaning unless it is freed from the pressure of spending so much time on administrative tasks.

Operating in the Criminal Justice System

Informed views on the problems facing the criminal justice system are not hard to find. In 2004 Lord Coulsfield produced *Crime, Courts & Confidence: Report of an Independent Inquiry into Alternatives to Prison*. This commented on the lack of public confidence in the criminal justice system, which was ill-informed on whether crime was increasing, when the opposite was the case; that prison overcrowding was increasing, and that numbers of black and female offenders in prison were rising steeply. It commented that:

> 'The probation service is overstretched because the volume of community penalties has also increased, and its morale is low following two major changes in structure since the millennium. Many of those subject to community penalties, and some of those who are in prison, present a low risk of reoffending and an even lower risk of causing significant harm.' (Coulsfield, 2004, p. 4)

This problem of low morale was evident from the comments of my informants which were presented in Chapter 6, and Ken Clarke was aware of the 'tick box mentality' that pervaded the organization. The centralizing nature of National Standards over many years had compounded this. Coulsfield commented that the solution could not be simple or dramatic. He proposed that the public should be better informed about sentencing, where time in custody should reflect the sentence given, that there needed to be more honesty on what can be achieved in prison and in the community and, as Clarke commented, there needed 'to be more sophisticated ways of measuring the effectiveness of sentences than two-year reoffending rates. Reduction in frequency and seriousness of offending are also relevant, as is the acquisition of skills which will enable offenders to obtain employment – which is associated with reduction in offending' (Coulsfield, 2004, p. 6).

In this respect, the complexity of 'effectiveness' as a construct begins to be unpacked. The danger is that Clarke's proposal is a recipe for the continuation of the tick box mentality he claims to want to get away from. The government's own Green Paper proposal, *Breaking the Cycle: Effective Punishment, Rehabilitation and Sentencing of Offenders* (Ministry of Justice, 2010a) was published in December 2010. This laid the blame for the parlous state of the criminal justice system on a 'Whitehall knows best' approach, which was seen as 'stifling innovation'. A top-down approach by both prison and probation services was blamed for a concentration on the process of justice rather than on results, leading to an increase in re-conviction rates for those serving sentences of under a year from 58 per cent to 61 per cent between 2000 and 2008 (Coulsfield, 2004, p. 6).

The rhetoric of the proposed reforms included making prisons places of 'hard work and industry', ensuring that community sentences are about punishing offenders with tougher curfew orders, tougher use of electronic tagging, more intensive community payback schemes, more financial reparation to victims, increased use of restorative justice approaches, integrated offender management approaches with local partnerships, tackling offenders' substance misuse, managing offenders with mental health problems, diversifying service providers to include public, private, voluntary and community sectors, and using payment by results. This latter process could be via local incentive schemes using local partnerships.

It was recognized that 'cherry picking' offenders who were more likely to be successful would be perverse, but this would not stop the process and management of offenders from changing, hence the weakening of National Standards requirements. The consequences of this for prison and probation work was spelled out. NOMS is to be significantly slimmed down. It is worth citing proposals in detail:

> 'We will fundamentally reshape prison and probation services to reduce unnecessary bureaucracy, empower frontline professionals and make them more accountable by:
>
> - Reforming the way in which Probation Trusts and prisons are managed;
> - Reviewing targets and standards to ensure greater flexibility and professional discretion;

- Considering the scope and value of different business models such as public sector workers forming employee owned cooperatives; and
- Reforming the National Offender Management Service to reduce costs and enable local commissioning in the longer term.' (Ministry of Justice, 2010a, p. 46)

The Green Paper represents something of a return to sanity for probation staff in that it recommends that they should regain the ability to exercise professional judgement to decide 'the number and scheduling of appointments; when to undertake full risk assessments and when offenders should start courses or programmes' (2010a, p. 59).

After publication, there were over 1200 public responses over a 12-week period and the government published its response to the consultation. This produced a re-statement of purpose but also some inconsistencies. Offenders were still to be punished and 'have no choice but to confront the consequences of their crimes' (Ministry of Justice, 2010b, p. 3) and there was an ambition to make the working week in prison last for a full 40 hours. It might be considered somewhat disingenuous to blame the previous government for leaving a 'big failure ... – the national scandal of reoffending' (2010b, p. 1). The paper concedes that punishment does not stop reoffending, but this does not stop the tenor of the report being steeped in the rhetoric of credible punishments, tougher punishments, more control, tougher curfews and such restrictions. While complaining about excessive bureaucracy from the past, it did not advocate the end of NOMS but a 'world first' payment *only* for results when working with offenders. While this was not for all offenders, it was thought (somewhat optimistically) that it *could* (my italics) 'lead to a reduction in crime of more than 500 000 offences per annum from 2016–2017 and generate economic benefits of over £0.6 billion per annum' (Ministry of Justice, 2011b, p. 8). All rehabilitation services were to be tested to ascertain whether the most effective and efficient provider resided in the private, voluntary or community sector.

This latter requirement would seem to indicate a 'hands-off' approach to what is done to and with offenders as long as it works. So it is difficult to square this with the mandate within the government response that insisted that non-custodial sentences 'need to be tough and demanding' (2011b, p. 4). It complained that 10 per cent of community orders 'contain only a "supervision" requirement' (in other words, meetings with a probation officer). Community orders were to be 'transformed' to be more 'credible punishments'.

One might suspect that this proposal was more than slightly tinged by being viewed through rose-tinted ideological spectacles. This is not just the opinion of this author. In July 2011, the Parliamentary Justice Committee published its report on the role of the probation service and the chairman, Sir Alan Beith MP, commented: 'We see a lot of scope for new organizations to come into the provision of probation services. Nevertheless there is an important duty for accountability to the courts and for offender management strategy which needs to rest with a public body' (House of Commons Justice Committee, 2011).

The report was a damning indictment of how probation had been used as a political football, and MPs stated that they were concerned that probation staff spent three-quarters of their time undertaking administrative tasks rather than working directly with offenders. Yet our knowledge of how much need is out there is constantly being updated and analysed. As well as working with offenders, their families' needs should also be considered. The recent report from the Howard League for Penal Reform (September 2011), *Voice of a Child*, disclosed that:

- At least 17 000 children are separated from their mother every year, with half of the 4500 women having children under 16.
- 65 per cent of children with a convicted parent will go on to offend and have at least double the risk of mental health problems compared to their peers. (Howard League for Penal Reform, 2011)

Codd (2008) details the impact this has on children, which she refers to as 'disenfranchized grieving', as their loss (of parental contact) is not recognized by society, with the consequences mentioned above. Smith *et al.* (2007) investigated 41 families and found that imprisonment had exacerbated financial problems, with family and relatives losing an average of £175 per month. In previous times probation would have offered support to the families of prisoners but as it became more of an enforcement agency this has ceased (Codd, 2008, p. 15). Given the potential for future offending, this would appear to be a very short-sighted use of resources when time on computers generating assessments is seen as more important than direct help to prisoners and their families. Through- and after-care need to be resurrected as appropriate work for probation with the task of helping to keep families together and to facilitate the prisoner changing into a citizen with a stake in society.

Toughening up the System and Alternative Approaches

As has been made clear in numerous examples in earlier chapters, finances for criminal justice have been directed into measures that look tough and have a good soundbite. A major source for this is the increased use of electronic tagging, which has been critically commented upon for many years by Nellis (2004). Electronic monitoring (EM) has not been linked to 'what works' but to compliance with orders. It has not been demonstrated that EM reduces offending, but it is expensive. According to Travis (2011) the use of EM is to be massively expanded, with the latest government contract up for renewal worth £1 billion. This is to increase public confidence in community sentences. There will be a lengthening of curfews from 12 hours per day to 16 and it is proposed that curfew orders may last for 12 months instead of 6. It does not take a genius to realize that if this happens, the level of violations will rise and this will lead to an increase in custody. The inflation creep of community sanctions and other restrictive measures such as dispersal zones (brought in with the Anti-Social Behaviour Act 2003) are therefore set to continue.

The 2003 Act also creates the power for the police to remove any young person under 16 who is out on the streets not accompanied by an adult in a dispersal zone between 9 p.m. and 6 a.m., and to take them home. This would accord with the American experience of curfews, which are used to keep minors off the streets, in ghettos and poor areas, so that police and punishment are used 'in those very areas where it is retracting its safety net' (Wacquant, 2009, p. 67).

The growth figures for EM are astonishing; from 3500 in 1999 to 70 000 in 2010. Nellis (2007) commented that New Labour had also been infatuated with this technology so it was as well that some chief probation officers were happy to engage with it. As probation and EM were located on the public and private sectors they had led a parallel rather than an integrated existence, but under the Conservative–Liberal Democrat coalition this is likely to change, as the private sector buys in ex-public officials as advisors and the public sector employs leaders from the private sector so that they can remain acceptable to ministers. Thus public policy drives probation into partnership with private companies, and the line between private and public grows increasingly fuzzy.

There are other ways that criminal justice could progress, particularly in the concept of restorative justice (RJ), where the offender has the obligation to repair the harm he has caused to the victim. This is not the case in a punitive criminal justice system, where retribution is one of the aims of the court disposal, or welfare where rehabilitation of the offender is paramount. Ruggiero (2011) has linked RJ with an abolitionist perspective, which criticizes the current process of RJ: 'RJ may be essentially defined as a process bringing the actors and communities affected by a problematic situation back into the condition in which the problem arose' (Ruggiero, 2011, p. 2).

According to Ruggiero, for abolitionists, two processes are in play; first, there needs to be the discovery of the resources needed to ameliorate the events and situations that caused the problem. Second, abolitionists need to critique the notion that all those situations that are currently called criminal have something in common. The concept of the victim is also problematic as 'they can become the victims of the stereotypes imposed upon them' (Ruggiero, 2011, p. 5). Crime in this context is, in Hulsman's terms, seen as a natural disaster and the resolution is to embrace solidarity for all affected to take action to prevent reoccurrence in the future. This is a concept that could be a positive development for community justice as it is dynamic and encourages the community to be actively involved in changing the conditions that encourage problematic behaviour. It can be applied to the conditions that exploded into the riots in the summer of 2011, which I would contend was caused by a lack of hope in many young people, and which was then allowed to spiral out of control.

I know from my discussions with many community workers and activists that from being marginalized and ignored by statutory authorities, their advice was suddenly sought, on how the local youth could be brought back under control. Probation used to be in a strong position to assist here but it has become marginalized to the community, with the exception of a few specialist post-holders, as it has become part of the mechanism that '[k]eeps the lid on problems through pragmatic risk assessment and management policies and practices geared to individuals, and to social collectivities and problem areas' (Stenson, 2001, p. 25).

The infatuation with risk assessments faced a further complication in how it was enacted, namely that the programmes that were being implemented were designed overseas for a different client group than in this country, described as 'taking a large gamble … with no guarantee of success in the English and Welsh context'. In addition, Ellis and Winstone commented that a further problem was the lack of finance so that in one area there was an inability to deliver 'short basic skills programmes' so they were replaced by one long cognitive-behavioural programme (Ellis and Winstone, 2002, p. 352).

McNeill and Whyte, (2007, p. 177) examine community justice in the Scottish context, which has retained its social work base. They start from a more positive stance than in England and Wales with its high degree of prescription, adopting a pro-social philosophy in terms of both human capital and social capital. In their model social integration is essential and social capital is encouraged by a commitment to maximize 'social networks, relationships within families and wider communities that can create and support opportunities for change'. Their model is therefore more based on desistance, or stopping offending, and it allows for the potential to explore the changes envisaged by Ruggiero above. An important facet of engagement with the community is partnership between probation and voluntary organizations. This has always been a feature of probation; however, this has changed with the centralization agenda becoming more of a financial transaction than real partnership. In this respect there is no evidence that this will improve effectiveness (Nellis, 2002, p. 371).

Supervision, NOMS and (in)Flexibility?

For now the management of probation is located within the National Offender Management Service (NOMS) and this organization has set down guidelines on how supervision will be operated. It has already been suggested that NOMS might be slimmed down. Offenders subject to supervision are divided into four levels of risk and the language makes explicit what each tier will offer: punishment, punishment and help, punishment, help and change; the fourth tier adds control. Many readers will be incredulous at this type of categorization and as Maguire (2007) questions: what will be the extent of the help offered? What about those with long-term problems? What about those who are indicating that their level of risk might increase? Sadly this typology bears all the hallmarks of being dreamed up by bureaucrats who have never actually been face-to-face with an offender and yet again places probation officers in the absurd position of having to carry out instructions that they know to be nonsensical. It is overly connected to actuarial risk management and relies overmuch on OASys assessments. 'OASys' stands for Offender Asessment System, and is a computerized clinical evaluation of the risk of an offender reoffending based on data input on their personal characteristics, offending behaviour, responses to supervision and so on.

Risk and its Assessment

Risk has supplanted many other aspects of work with offenders, and this book has examined some of the results that have arisen from this. As mentioned, Fitzgibbon (2011) highlighted the cost to practitioners of being blamed when cases go tragically wrong and, as a result of this, there is a danger of overly predicting and categorizing risk to protect the worker. Fitzgibbon has described this as pre-emptive criminalization. There is a danger that individual differences in people can get lost in the process. 'Risk assessment characteristically treats race, class and gender as controllable variables' (Denney, 2005, p. 131).

The language of risk is complicated. As Kemshall (2008) points out, high risk and dangerousness are often used interchangeably, and the terms 'serious risk' and 'serious harm' are also used. OASys and OGRS, two of the main prediction tools used by probation officers, operate with an accuracy of around 70–75 per cent, but this still leaves plenty of scope for error. It is a helpful tool for practitioners but cannot be used as an alternative to professional knowledge, judgement and experience. It is a support to clinical expertise, not an alternative. Staff need time to work with high-risk offenders and the opportunity to discuss cases between themselves. This has been evident on the Master's programme I run on public protection.

Kemshall highlights the complexity of how data is aggregated to form statistical judgements. Forming a judgement can introduce bias, stereotyping and the dangers of false positive and false negatives. This is not meant to criticize meta-analysis and risk assessment tools, but to warn that interpretation of results has to be treated with some caution. False positives can lead to a prisoner remaining in custody when he is no longer dangerous. False negatives can lead to a dangerous person being released and going on to kill, as in the Sonnex case in 2008, discussed earlier. The tragedy was further compounded by the case being allocated to an inexperienced worker with a huge caseload and little supervision.

Nash and Williams (2008, p. 83) cite research carried out by Harris *et al.* which found that clinical judgement had never been found to be superior to actuarial judgement in predicting recidivism, but the opposite had been found to be the case. In their book they analyse four serious case enquiries that led to death in each case. They found that the inquiries and reviews examined whether a '*defensible position* could be taken' (Nash and Williams, 2008, p. 234, their italics). They found that there had been numerous breaches of licence conditions during supervision, including curfews (p. 240). Mistakes had been made at different levels, including by the supervisor, his line manager and at a procedural level. Nash (2006) commented that the work of probation officers in supervising cases subject to multi-agency public protection arrangements and child protection is very difficult. Furthermore, 'professional judgement and skills are regarded as essential attributes to successful public protection systems' (Nash, 2006, p. 149).

The author has had the privilege of working with two cohorts of experienced probation officers on a post-graduate programme in public protection. The commitment to the professional task, and concern to balance the protection of the public with the right to be fair to the offender, was exemplary. Not having worked in probation when the level of required administrative tasks was so high, it was a learning experience for me too. The probation officers put a huge amount of energy and thought into their assignments and appreciated time out from being on the front-line. They took their responsibilities seriously and gained from having space to reflect on their cases and to look critically at how public protection was working. As long as staff could continue in this way, I felt optimistic for the future but would the structure of the system encourage this?

The Government, Probation and the Future

The government responded to the Justice Committee's Report, *The Role of the Probation Service*, on 14 October 2011 (Ministry of Justice, 2011a). It is worth recalling the concern of the Justice Committee over the work of NOMS and what was happening to probation services. Areas of concern will be highlighted – there are many. Universally negative comments were received about the drivers for the performance framework, which were concerned, for example, in the West Yorkshire Trust 'about timeliness, volumes or other tick boxes' (2011a, para. 81). Furthermore, 'Even the domain heading public protection is a misnomer, as the targets within that domain only have a loose connection with protecting the public from serious offenders' (2011a, para. 81). The final comment from this section alone should seriously concern the government 'This therefore is an example [in] which the collection of data has become an end in itself, which is only tenuously connected with what the public or government might reasonably expect from the probation service' (2011a, para. 81). Indeed, the ethos was described as a 'tick-box, bean-counting culture' which they hoped new national standards should curb (2011a, para. 83). What a shameful admission by a centralized management out of touch with what probation services should be doing to protect the public and rehabilitate offenders!

One might have hoped that if NOMS was about the joint management of prisons and probation then prison resettlement would be an area of some success (although, as was discussed at length, through-care is no longer practiced). In a section entitled 'end-to-end management' it was evident that while this was happening in the community it had failed in the prisons, with probation officers failing to direct the management of prisoners. In the community there were insufficient resources to provide group work programmes, community payback and other elements of probation work (Ministry of Justice, 2011a, para. 131). This was described as unacceptable. '*The absence from the [government] Green Paper, and from the government's response, of a clear statement about the role of probation in any commissioning model has fuelled concerns, expressed by our witnesses, about the future direction of probation trusts*' (Ministry of Justice, 2011a, para.131, italics in original).

The government response recognized some of the inflexibilities within the system and wanted to see relaxations in national standards and the use of accredited programmes. The tick-box culture that had prospered under New Labour was specifically criticized. The point about programmes has alarmed the probation officers' union, NAPO, in case it heralds the growth of cheaper and untested programmes delivered by the private sector.

So yet again probation and work with offenders stands at a crossroads. Will the drive to develop an outcome-based payment model (that is, payment for results gained) result in lucrative contracts going to the private sector, leaving a core of protection work for the statutory sector? This is important because the government has based much of its future probation strategy on this new concept of payment by results. This means that private services will be paid if they are able to demonstrate that, thanks to what they offer, offenders reoffend less. This sounds fine in principle, but it is untested and unproven. The danger is that the private sector will 'cherry-pick' offenders, only taking on those to believe to be less risky to work with, thus distorting the results. It is an experiment: should policy be decided in this way? It is symptomatic of a desire to engage with the private sector on ideological grounds as it is seen as progressive, ignoring knowledge that has been gained over time by professionals who are experienced and skilled in this slow and difficult work. This may sound elitist, but it is not meant to be. Working with offenders, empowering them, gaining their trust and helping them to change, cannot be achieved as a quick fix.

It is to be hoped that ideology will not drive through measures that deliver work with offenders to organizations that have profit motives as part of their *raison d'être*. Interviews with probation staff reveal that moral is fragile, and this cannot be helpful for the protection of the public and the rehabilitation of offenders.

References

Advisory Council on the Treatment of Offenders (Barry Report) (1963) *The Organisation of After-Care*, HMSO, London.

Aldridge, M. and Eadie, T. (1997) Manufacturing an issue: the core of probation officer training. *Critical Social Policy*, 5017 (1), 111–124.

Annison, J., Eadie, T. and Knight, C. (2008) People first: probation officer perspectives on probation work. *Probation Journal*, 55 (3), 259–272.

Appleyard, G. (1971) Prison welfare? *Howard Journal of Penology, XIII* (2), 106–113.

Ash, L. (2000) Criminals go home. *The Times*, Times2 Analysis 5, 7 December.

Audit Commission (1989) *The Probation Service: Promoting Value for Money*, HMSO, London.

Audit Commission (1991) *Going Straight: Developing Good Practice in the Probation Service*, Occasional Paper No. 16, HMSO, London.

Barnes, M. and Warren, L. (1999) *Paths to Empowerment*, Policy Press, Bristol.

Bartrip, P. (1981) Public opinion and law enforcement: the ticket of leave scares in mid-Victorian Britain, in *Policing and Punishment in Nineteenth Century Britain* (ed. V. Bailey), Croom Helm, London, pp. 150–181.

Bauman, Z. (1994) *Alone Again: Ethics After Certainty*, Demos, London.

Bauman, Z. (1998) *Work, Consumerism and the New Poor*, Open University Press, Buckingham.

Beattie, J.M. (1986) *Crime and the Courts in England 1660–1800*, Clarendon Press, Oxford.

Beccaria, C. (1986) *On Crimes and Punishments*, Hackett, Indianapolis.

Beck, U., Giddens, A. & Lash, S. (1994) *Reflexive Modernization: Politics, Tradition and Aesthetics in the Modern Social Order*, Polity Press, Cambridge.

Benson, G. (1937) *Flogging: The Law and Practice in England*, 2nd rev. edn, Howard League for Penal Reform, London.

Biestek, F. (1961) *The Casework Relationship*, George Allen and Unwin, London.

Bindoff, S. (1978) *Tudor England*, Pelican Books, Harmondsworth, Middlesex.

Blagg, H. and Smith, D. (1989) *Crime, Penal Policy and Social Work*, Longman, Harlow.

Rehabilitating and Resettling Offenders in the Community, First Edition. Anthony H. Goodman.

Boateng, P. (1999) *Speech to Chief Probation Officers and Chiefs of Probation Committees*, HMSO, London.

Bochel, B. (1976) *Probation and After-Care: Its Development in England and Wales*, Scottish Academic Press, Edinburgh.

Bonger, W. (1916) *Criminality and Economic Conditions*, Political Economy Club, Vancouver.

Bottoms, A. and McWilliams, W. (1979) A non-treatment paradigm for probation practice. *British Journal of Social Work*, 9 (2), 159–202.

Bradley, Right Hon. Lord (2009) *Review of People with Mental Health Problems or Learning Disabilities in the Criminal Justice System*, DH Publications, London.

Brayford, J., Cowe, F. and Deering, J. (2010) What else works – back to the future?, in *What Else Works? Creative Work with Offenders* (eds J. Brayford, F. Cowe and J. Deering), Willan Publishing, Cullompton, pp. 254–268.

Brownlee, I. (1998a) *Community Punishment: A Critical Introduction*, Longman, London.

Brownlee, L. (1998b) New Labour – new penology? Punitive rhetoric and the limits of managerialism in criminal justice policy. *Journal of Law and Society*, 25 (3), 313–335.

Burke, L., Crowley, T. and Girvin, A. (eds) (2000) *The Routledge Language and Cultural Theory Reader*, Routledge, London.

Byrne, D. (2005) *Social Exclusion*, 2nd edn, Open University Press, Maidenhead.

Cameron, J. (1983) *Prisons and Punishment in Scotland: From the Middle Ages to the Present*, Canongate, Edinburgh.

Carlisle Committee (1988) *The Parole System of England and Wales: Report of the Review Committee*. Cm 532, HMSO, London.

Carter, P. (2003) *Managing Offenders, Reducing Crime*, Home Office, London.

Chapman, T. and Hough, M. (1998) *Evidence-based Practice: A Guide to Effective Practice*, HM Inspectorate of Probation, London.

Clancy, A., Hudson, K., Maguire, M., Peake, R. *et al.* (2006) *Getting Out and Staying Out*, Policy Press, Bristol.

Clarke, K. (2011) Punish the feral rioters but address our social deficit too. *Clarke*, 5 September.

Codd, H. (2008) *In the Shadow of Prison. Families, Imprisonmentand Criminal Justice*, Willan Publishing, Cullompton.

Cohen, S. (1979a) How can we balance justice, guilt and tolerance? *New Society*, 1 March, 475– 477.

Coker, J. (1988) *Probation Objectives: A Management View*, University of East Anglia Probation Monograph, Norwich.

Coleman, D. (1989) *Home Office Review of Probation Training: Final Report*, Home Office, London.

Collins English Dictionary (1991) Glasgow, HarperCollins.

Cook, T. (1975) *Vagrant Alcoholics*, Routledge and Kegan Paul, London.

Corden, J., Kuipers, J. and Wilson, K. (1979) *After Prison*, Department of Social Administration and Social Work, University of York, York.

Cornish, W., Hart, J., Manchester, A. and Stevenson, J. (1978) *Crime and Law in Nineteenth Century Britain*, Irish University Press, Dublin.

Corston, Lady J. (2007) *The Corston Report. A Report on Women with Particular Vulnerabilities in the Criminal Justice System*, Home Office, London.

Coulsfield, Lord (2004) *Crime, Courts and Confidence. Report of an Independent Inquiry into Alternatives to Prison*, Esmeé Fairbairn Foundation, London.

Coyle, A. (2005) *Understanding Prisons*, Open University Press, Maidenhead.

Craissati, J. and Sindall, O. (2009) Serious further offences: an exploration of risk and typologies. *Probation Journal*, 56 (3), 219–223.

Davies, M. and Wright, A. (1989) *Probation Training: A Consumer Perspective*, University of East Anglia, Norwich.

Denney, D. (1992) *Racism and Anti-Racism in Probation*, Routledge, London.

Denney, D. (1998) *Social Policy and Social Work*, Clarendon Press, Oxford.

Denney, D. (2005) *Risk and Society*, Sage, London.

Deering, J. (2010) Attitudes and beliefs of trainee probation officers: a 'new breed'? *Probation Journal*, 57 (1), 9–26.

Dews, V. and Watts, J. (1994) *Review of Probation Officer Recruitment and Qualifying Training*, Home Office, London.

Dicey, A.V. (1905) *Law and Opinion in England*, Macmillan, Basingstoke.

Dobash, R., Dobash, R. and Gutteridge, S. (1986) *The Imprisonment of Women*, Basil Blackwell, Oxford.

Dobson, G. (2004) Get Carter. *Probation Journal*, 57 (3), 144–154.

Dominey, J. and Hill, A. (2010) The higher education contribution to police and probation training: essential, desirable or an indulgence? *British Journal of Community Justice*, 8 (2), 5–16.

Doward, J. and McVeigh, T. (2011) 'Brain drain' warning for British prisons, *The Observer*, London, 9 October.

Drakeford, M, and Vanstone, M. (eds) (1996) *Beyond Offending Behaviour*, Ashgate, Aldershot.

Dunbar, I. and Langdon, A. (1998) *Tough Justice: Sentencing and Penal Policies in the 1990s*, Blackstone Press, London.

Edgar, K. (2007) Black and minority ethnic prisoners, in *Handbook on Prisons* (ed. Y. Jewkes), Willan Publishing, Cullompton.

Ellis, T. and Winstone, J. (2002) The policy impact of a survey of programme evaluations in England and Wales, in *Offender Rehabilitation and Treatment* (ed. J. McGuire), John Wiley & Sons, Ltd, Chichester, pp. 353–358.

Elton, G. (1985) *Policing and Police: The Enforcement of the Reformation in the Age of Thomas Cromwell*, Cambridge University Press, Cambridge.

Emsley, C. (2005) The changes in policing and penal policy in nineteenth-century Europe, in *Crime and Empire 1840–1940* (eds B. Godfrey and G. Dunstall), Willan Publishing, Cullompton, pp. 8–24.

Equality and Human Rights Commission (2008) *How Fair is Britain?* Equality and Government Equalities Office, London.

Fairclough, N. (1989) *Language and Power*, Longman, Harlow.

Fairclough, N. (1992) *Discourse on Social Change*, Polity Press, Cambridge.

Farrall, S. (2002) *Rethinking What Works with Offenders: Probation Context and Desistence from Crime*, Willan Publishing, Cullompton.

Farrall, S. (2004) Social capital and offender reintegration: making probation desistence focused, in *After Crime and Punishment* (eds S. Maruna and R. Immarigeon), Willan Publishing, Cullompton, pp. 57–84.

Farrow, K. (2004) Still committed after all these years? Morale in the modern-day probation service. *Probation Journal*, 51 (3), 206–220.

Faulkner, D. (1995) The Criminal Justice Act 1991: policy, legislation and practice, in *Probation, Working for Justice* (eds D. Ward and M. Lacey), Whiting and Birch, London, pp. 51–72.

Feeley, M. and Simon, J. (1992) The new penology: notes on the emerging strategy of corrections and its implications. *Criminology*, 30 (4), 449–474.

Feeley, M. and Simon, J. (1994) Actuarial justice: the emerging new criminal law, in *The Futures of Criminology* (ed. D. Nelken), Sage, London, pp. 173–201.

Fielding, N. (1984) *Probation Practice: Client Support Under Social Control*, Gower, Aldershot.

Finer, C.J. (1998) The new social policy in Britain, in *Crime and Social Exclusion* (eds C. J. Finer and M. Nellis), Blackwell, Oxford.

Fitzgibbon, W. (2011) *Probation and Social Work on Trial*, Palgrave Macmillan, Basingstoke.

Fletcher, H. (2011) Sentencing bill, standards diluted and prison numbers will rise. *NAPO NEWS*, 3 (233), October.

Folkard, M., Smith, D. and Smith, D. (1974) *Intensive Matched Probation and After-Care Treatment (IMPACT)* Volume 1 Home Office Research Study 24, HMSO, London.

Ford, P., Pritchard, C. and Cox, M. (1997) Consumer Opinions of the Probation Service: Advice, Assistance, Befriending and the Reduction of Crime. *Howard Journal of Criminal Justice*, 36 (1), 42–61.

Foren, R. and Bailey, R. (1968) *Authority in Social Casework*, Pergamon Press, Oxford.

Foucault, M. (1977) *Discipline and Punish*, Penguin Books Limited, Middlesex.

Fowler, R. (1988) Notes on critical linguistics, in *Language Topics*, vol. 2 (eds R. Steele and T. Threadgold), Benjamins, Amsterdam, pp. 481–492.

Gallo, E. and Ruggiero, V. (1991) The immaterial prison. *International Journal of the Sociology of Law*, August, 273–291.

Garland, D. (1985) *Punishment and Welfare: A History of Penal Strategies*, Gower, Aldershot.

Garland, D. (1990) *Punishment and Modern Society*, Clarendon Press, Oxford.

Garland, D. (1996) The limits of the sovereign state: strategies of crime control in contemporary society. *British Journal of Criminology*, 36, 445–471.

Garland, D. (2000) The culture of high crime societies: some preconditions of recent 'law and order' policies. *British Journal of Criminology*, 40 (3), 347–375.

Garland, D. (2001) *The Culture of Control: Crime and Social Order in Contemporary Society*, Oxford University Press, Oxford.

Gatrell, V. (1994) *The Hanging Tree: Execution and the English People 1770–1868*, Oxford University Press, Oxford.

Giddens, A. (1994) Living in a post-traditional society, in *Reflexive Modernization: Politics, Tradition and Asthetics in the Modern Social Order* (eds G. Beck, A. Giddens and S. Lash), Polity Press, Cambridge, pp. 56–109.

Gladstone Committee (1895) *Report from the Departmental Committee on Prisons*, PP1895 (C.7702), Gladstone Committee, London.

Godfrey, B. and Lawrence, P. (2005) *Crime and Justice 1750–1950*, Willan Publishing, Cullompton.

Godfrey, B., Lawrence, P. and Williams, C. (2008) *History and Crime*, Sage, London.

Goldblatt, P. and Lewis, C. (1998) *Reducing Offending: An Assessment of Research Evidence on Ways of Dealing with Offending Behaviour*, Home Office Research Study 187, Home Office, London.

Goodman, A. (1990) State care or contempt. *Social Work Today*, 4 January, 20–21.

Goodman, A. (2008) The evidence base, in *Addressing Offending Behaviour: Context, Practice and Values* (eds S. Green, E. Lancaster and S. Feasey), Willan Publishing, Cullompton, pp. 39–57.

Greimas, A. (1987) *On Meaning: Selected Writings in Semiotic Theory*, Frances Pinter Publishers Ltd, London.

Guardian (21 August 2000) *Postcode Sentencing: Computers Cannot Deliver Justice*. Editorial.

Halliday, J. (2001) *Making Punishments Work*, Home Office, London.

Halliday, M.A.K. (1973) *Explorations in the Functions of Language*, Edward Arnold, London.

Hammond, W. and Chayen, E. (1963) *Persistent Criminals: A Study of All Offenders Liable to Preventative Detention in 1956*, Home Office Research Unit Report, HMSO, London.

Hardiker, P. (1977) Social work ideologies in the probation service. *British Journal of Social Work*, 7 (2), 131–154.

Harding, J. (2000a) The probation service in the 21st century. *Criminal Justice Matters*, 38, 27–28.

Harding, J. (2000b) A community justice dimension to effective probation practice. *Howard Journal of Criminal Justice*, 39 (2), 132–149.

Harper, G. and Chitty, C. (2005) *The Impact of Corrections on Reoffending: A Review of What Works*, Home Office Research Study 291, Home Office, London.

Harris, G., Rice, M. and Quinsey, V. (1993) 'Violent Recidivism of Mentally Disordered offenders: The Development of a Statistical Prediction Instrument, *Criminal Justice and behaviour* 20, 315–335.

Harris, R. (1989) Social work in society or punishment in the community? in *The Criminal Justice System: A Central Role for the Probation Service* (eds R. Shaw and K. Haines), Institute of Criminology, University of Cambridge, Cambridge, pp. 22–35.

Harris, R. (1996) Telling tales: probation in the contemporary formation, in *Social Theory, Social Change and Social Work* (ed. N. Parton), Routledge, London, pp. 115–134.

Harrison, P. (1982) *Inside the Inner City: Life Under the Cutting Edge*, Penguin, London.

Hawkes, T. (1977) *Structuralism and Semiotics*, Methuen and Company Ltd, London.

Haxby, D. (1978) *Probation: A Changing Service*, Constable, London.

Hay, D. (1975) Property, authority, and the criminal law, in *Albion's Fatal Tree: Crime and Society in Eighteenth-Century England* (eds D. Hay, P. Linebaugh, J. Rule, E. Thompson and C. Winslow), Allen Lane, London, pp. 17–63.

Hearnden, I. and Millie, A. (2003) *Investigating Links between Probation Enforcement and Effective Supervision*, Home Office On-line Report 41/03, Home Office, London.

Hedderman, C. and Hearnden, I (2001) *Setting New Standards for Enforcement: The Third ACOP Audit*, ACOP, London.

Hedderman, C. and Hough, M. (2000) Tightening up probation: a step too far? *Criminal Justice Matters*, 39, 5.

Hinde, R.S.E. (1951) *The British Penal System 1773–1950*, Duckworth and Co. Ltd, London.

HM Chief Inspector of Prisons and HM Chief Inspector of Probation (2008) *The Indeterminate Sentence for Public Protection. A Thematic Review*, Home Office, London.

HM Inspectorate of Prisons (2009) *The prison characteristics that predict prisons being assessed as performing 'well': A thematic review by HM Chief Inspector of Prisons*, London.

HM Inspectorate of Probation (1993a) *The Criminal Justice Act 1991 Inspection*, Home Office, London.

HM Inspectorate of Probation (1993b) *Annual Report: 1992–93*, Home Office, London.

HM Inspectorate of Probation (1996a) *Probation Services Working in Partnership: Increasing Impact and Value for Money. Report Of a Thematic Inspection*, Home Office, London.

HM Inspectorate of Probation (1996b) *The Work of Prison Probation Departments. Report of a Thematic Inspection*, Home Office, London.

HM Inspectorate of Probation (1998b) *Exercising Constant Vigilance: The Role of the Probation Service in Protecting the Public from Sex Offenders. Report of a Thematic Inspection*, Home Office, London.

HM Inspectorate of Probation (1999) *Offender Assessment and Supervision Planning: Helping to Achieve Effective Intervention With Offenders. Report of a Developmental Thematic Inspection Undertaken in Collaboration with 46 Probation Services*, Home Office, London.

HM Inspectorate of Probation (2000a) *Towards Race Equality*, Home Office, London.
HM Inspectorate of Probation (2000b) *The Use of Information by the Probation Service. A Thematic Inspection in 4 Parts. A Study by HMIP of Enforcement Practice in Community Penalties*, Home Office, London.
HM Inspector of Probation (2003) *Annual Report*, Home Office, London.
HM Prison Service (1995) *Corporate Plan 1995–98*, Home Office, London.
Hobhouse, S. and Brockway, A. (1922) *English Prisons Today*, Longman, London.
Holborn, J. (1975) Casework with short-term prisoners, in *Some Male Offender's Problems*, Home Office Research Unit Report 28, HMSO, London.
Holmes, T. (1900) *Pictures and Problems from London Police Courts*, Thomas Nelson & Sons, London.
Home Affairs Committee (HAC) (1998) *Alternatives to Prison Sentences*, Third Report, Volumes I and II, 28 July, The Stationery Office, London.
Home Department (1936) *Report of the Departmental Committee on the Social Services in Courts of Summary Jurisdiction*, Cmnd 5122, HMSO, London.
Home Department (1959) *Penal Practice in a Changing Society: Aspects of Future Development (England and Wales)*, Cmnd 645, HMSO, London.
Home Office (1953) *Report of the Committee on Discharged Prisoners' Aid Societies* (the Maxwell Report), HMSO, London.
Home Office (1962) *Report of the Departmental Committee on the Probation Service*, Cmnd 1650, HMSO, London.
Home Office (1963) *The Organisation of After-Care. Report of the Advisory Council on the Treatment of Offenders* (Barry Report), HMSO, London.
Home Office (1965) *The Adult Offender*, Cmnd 2852, HMSO, London.
Home Office (1966a) *Residential Provision for Homeless Discharged Offenders: Report of the Working Party on the Place of Voluntary Service in After-Care*, HMSO, London.
Home Office (1966b) *Penal Practice in a Changing Society*, Home Office, London.
Home Office (1967a) *The Place of Voluntary Service in After-Care: Second Report of the Working Party*, HMSO, London.
Home Office (1967b) *Circular 130/1967, The Role of the Prison Welfare Officer*, Home Office, London.
Home Office (1971a) *Habitual Drunken Offenders: Report of the Working Party*, HMSO, London.
Home Office (1971b) *Report of the Prison Service*, Home Office, London.
Home Office (1984) *Probation Service in England and Wales. Statement of National Objectives and Priorities (SNOP)*, HMSO, London.
Home Office (1990a) *Crime, Justice and Protecting the Public. The Government's Proposals for Legislation*, Cm 965, HMSO, London.
Home Office (1990b) *Supervision and Punishment in the Community. A Framework for Action*, Cm 966, HMSO, London.
Home Office (1990c) *Partnership in Dealing with Offenders in the Community*, a discussion paper issued by the Home Office to complement the White Paper, *Crime, Justice and Protecting the Public* (Cm 965) and the Green Paper *Supervision and Punishment in the Community: A Framework for Action* (Cm 966), HMSO, London.
Home Office (1991 – although undated) *Organising Supervision and Punishment in the Community: A Decision Document*, Home Office, London.
Home Office (1992a) *A Quick Reference Guide to the Criminal Justice Act 1991*, Home Office Probation Service Division, London.
Home Office (1992b) *National Standards for the Supervision of Offenders in the Community*, Home Office, London.

Home Office (1995a) *National Standards for the Supervision of Offenders in the Community*, Home Office, London.

Home Office (1998) *Joining Forces to Protect the Public. Prisons-Probation: A Consultation Document*, Home Office, London.

Home Office (1999a) *What Works: Reducing Reoffending: Evidence-Based Practice*, HMSO, London.

Home Office (1999b) *Diploma in Probation Studies*, HMSO, London.

Home Office (2000) *National Standards for the Supervision of Offenders in the Community*, Home Office, London.

Home Office (2001) *Criminal Justice: The Way Ahead*, Cm 5074, Home Office, London.

Home Office (2002) *National Standards for the Supervision of Offenders in the Community*, Home Office, London.

Home Office (2004) *Reducing Crime – Changing Lives*, Home Office, London.

Home Office (2005a) *The NOMS Offender Management Model, Version 1*, Home Office, London.

Home Office (2005b) *National Standards for the Supervision of Offenders in the Community*, Home Office, London.

Home Office (2005c) *Restructuring Probation to Reduce Reoffending*, Home Office, London.

Home Office (2005d) *National Standards 2005*, Probation Circular 15/2005, Home Office, London.

Home Office (2007) *National Standards for the Supervision of Offenders in the Community*, Home Office, London.

Home Office Research Unit (1971) *Explorations in After-Care*. Report 9, Home Office, London.

Hood, R. (2002) *Race and Sentencing*, Oxford University Press, Oxford.

House of Commons Justice Committee (2011) *The role of the Probation Service: Eighth Report of Session 2010–12*, House of Commons, London.

House of Commons Official Report: Parliamentary Debates (Wednesday 6 December 1995) *(Probation) (Amendment) Rules 1995 (S.I.1995, No 2622)* First Standing committee on Delegated Legislation, HMSO, London.

House of Lords (1995) *Select Committee Report. Probation Officers: Qualifications* 923-949 476 LD12 – PAG1/22-489 LD12-PAG1/35, HMSO, London.

Howard, D.L. (1960) *The English Prisons: Their Past and Future*, Methuen, London.

Howard, J. (1929) *The State of the Prisons*, J.M. Dent & Sons Ltd, London.

Howard, M. (1996) *Speech to the Annual Conference of the Chief Officers of Probation*, Home Office, London.

Howard League for Penal Reform (2011) *Voice of a Child*, Howard League for Penal Reform, London.

Hughes, R. (1987) *The Fatal Shore*, Collins Harvill, London.

Ignatieff, M. (1978) *A Just Measure of Pain: The Penitentiary in the Industrial Revolution 1750–1850*, Macmillan, London.

ILPS (1985) *Statement of Local Objectives and Priorities. Response to the SNOP Document*, ILPS, London.

ILPS (1986) *Assignment and Reassignment of Probation Officers*, ILPS, London.

James, A. (1995) Probation values for the 1990s – and beyond? *Howard Journal of Criminal Justice*, 34 (4), 326–343.

James, A. & Raine, J. (1998) *The New Politics of Criminal Justice*, Longman, London.

Janetta, J. and Halberstadt, R. (2011) *Kiosk Supervision for the District of Columbia*, Urban Institute Justice Policy Center, Washington DC.

Jarvis, F.V. (1972) *Advise, Assist and Befriend. A History of the Probation and After-Care Service*, National Association of Probation Officers, London.

Jepson, N. and Elliot, K. (1985) *Shared Working Between Prison and Probation Officers*, Home Office, London.

Johnston, H. (2008) Moral guardians? Prison officers, prison practice and ambiguity in the nineteenth century, in *Punishment and Control in Historical Perspective* (ed. H. Johnston), Palgrave Macmillan, Basingstoke, pp. 77–94.

Johnston, H. (2009) Histories of prison and imprisonment 1770–1952, in *Criminal Justice* (eds A. Hucklesby and A. Wahidin), Oxford University Press, Oxford, pp. 125–144.

Kamenka, E. (1979) What is justice? in *Justice: Ideas and Ideologies* (eds E. Kamenka and A. Tay), Edward Arnold, London, pp. 1–24.

Kemshall, H. (1997) Offender risk and probation practice, in *Good Practice in Risk Assessment and Risk Management* (eds H. Kemshall and J. Pritchard), Jessica Kingsley Publishers, London, pp. 133–145.

Kemshall, H. (1998) *Risk In Probation Practice*, Ashgate, Aldershot.

Kemshall, H. (2008) *Understanding the Community Management of High Risk Offenders*, Open University Press, Maidenhead.

King, J. (1964) *The Probation Service*, 2nd edn, Butterworth, London.

King, J. (1969) *The Probation and After-Care Service*, Butterworth, London.

Lacey, N. (1998) *Image and Representation: Key Concepts in Media Studies*, Macmillan, Basingstoke.

Lea, J. (1999) Social crime revisited. *Theoretical Criminology*, 3 (3), 307–325.

Lea, J. (2002) *Crime and Modernity*, Sage, London.

Leach, T. (2000) Effective practice: some possible pitfalls. *Vista*, 5 (2), 141–149.

Leach, T. (2003) Oh my country, how I leave my country: some reflections on a changing probation service. *Probation Journal*, 50 (1), 20–29.

Ledger, J. (2010) Rehabilitation revolution: will probation pay the price? *Probation Journal*, 57 (4), 415–422.

Lloyd, C. (1986) *Response to SNOP*, Institute of Criminology, University of Cambridge, Cambridge.

Lyon, J., Dennison, C. and Wilson, A. (2000) *Tell Them So They Listen: Messages From Young People in Custody*, Home Office Research Study 201, HMSO, London.

Maguire, M. (2007) The resettlement of ex-prisoners, in *Handbook of Probation* (eds L. Gelsthorpe and R. Morgan), Willan Publishing, Cullompton, pp. 398–424.

Mair, G. (1997a) Community penalties and the probation service, in *The Oxford Handbook of Criminology*, 2nd edn (eds M. Maguire, R. Morgan and R. Reiner), Clarendon Press, Oxford, pp. 1195–1232.

Mair, G. (2011) The community order in England and Wales: policy and practice. *Probation Journal*, 58 (3), 215–232.

Martin, B. (1995) *The Search for Gold*, Philomel Productions Ltd, Dublin.

Martin, B. and Ringham, F. (2000) *Dictionary of Semiotics*, Cassell, London.

Martin, B. and Ringham, F. (2006) *Key Terms in Semiotics*, Continuum, York.

Martinson, R. (1974) What works? Questions and answers about prison reform. *The Public Interest*, 35, 22–54.

Martinson, R. (1979) New findings, new views: a note of caution regarding sentencing reform. *Hofstra Law Review*, 7 (2), 243–258.

Maruna, S. (1999) Desistence and development: the psychosocial process of going straight, in *British Society of Criminology Conference Selected Proceedings* (ed. M. Brogden), 2, 1–35.

Maruna, S. (2000) Desistence from crime and offender rehabilitation: a tale of two research literatures. *Offender Programs Report*, 4, 1–13.

Maruna, S. (2001) *Making Good*, American Psychological Association, Washington DC.

Matthews, R. (1999) *Doing Time: An Introduction to the Sociology of Imprisonment*, Macmillan, Basingstoke.

Matthews, J. (2009) People first: probation officer perspectives on probation work – a practitioner's response. *Probation Journal*, 56 (1), 61–67.

May, C. (1990) *The National Probation Survey*, Research and Planning Paper 72, Home Office, London.

May, T. (1991) *Probation: Politics, Policy and Practice*, Open University Press, Milton Keynes.

May, T. (1995) Probation and community sanctions, in *The Oxford Handbook of Criminology* (eds M. Maguire, R. Morgan and R. Reiner), Clarendon Press, Oxford, pp. 861–887.

May, C. and Wadwell, J. (2001) *Enforcing Community Penalties: The Relationship between Enforcement and Reconviction*, Home Office Findings No. 155, Home Office, London.

Mayhew, H. and Binny, J. (1971) *The Criminal Prisons of London and Scenes of Prison Life*, Frank Cass & Co. Ltd, London.

McClelland, M. (2000) Who knows where the time goes? *NAPO News*, 122 (4), August.

McConville, S. (1981) *A History of English Prison Administration 1750–1877*, Routledge and Kegan Paul, London.

McGowan, R. (2000) Revisiting the hanging tree: Gatrell on emotion and history. *British Journal of Criminology*, 40 (1), 1–13.

McGuire, J (ed.) (1995) *What Works: Reducing Reoffending*. John Wiley & Sons, Ltd, Chichester.

McLaren, V. and Spencer, J. (1992) Rehabilitation and the CJA 1991: a world still to win. *Probation Journal*, 39 (2), 70–73.

McNay, L. (1994) *Foucault: A Critical Introduction*, Polity, Cambridge.

McNeill, F. (2002) *Beyond 'What Works': How and Why Do Some People Stop Offending?* (CJSW Briefing Paper 5, August), Criminal Justice Social Work Development Centre, Edinburgh.

McNeill, F. and Whyte, B. (2007) *Reducing Reoffending: Social Work and Community Justice in Scotland*, Willan Publishing, Cullompton.

McWilliams, B. (1983) The mission to the English police courts 1876–1936. *Howard Journal of Criminal Justice*, 22, 129–147.

McWilliams, B. (1985) The mission transformed: professionalization of probation between the wars. *Howard Journal of Criminal Justice*, 24 (4), 257–274.

McWilliams, B. (1986) The English probation system and the diagnostic ideal. *Howard Journal of Criminal Justice*, 25 (4), 241–260.

McWilliams, B. (1987) Probation, pragmatism and policy. *Howard Journal of Criminal Justice*, 26 (2), 97–121.

McWilliams, B. (1992) The rise and development of management thought in the English probation system, in *Managing the Probation Service: Issues for the 1990s* (eds R. Statham and P. Whitehead), Longman, Harlow.

Melossi, D. (2008) *Controlling Crime, Controlling Society*, Polity Press, Cambridge.

Melossi, D. and Pavarini, M. (1981) *The Prison and the Factory: Origins of the Penitentiary System*, Macmillan, London.

Ministry of Justice (2010a) *Breaking the Cycle: Effective Punishment, Rehabilitation and Sentencing of Offenders*, Cm 7972, Home Office, London.

Ministry of Justice (2010b) *Breaking the Cycle: Government Response*, Cm 8070, Home Office, London.

Ministry of Justice (2011a) *Government Response to the Justice Committee's Report: The Role of the Probation Service*, Cm 8176, Home Office, London.

Ministry of Justice (2011b) *Breaking the Cycle – Government Response Impact Assessment*, Home Office, London.

Monger, M. (1972) *Casework in Probation*, Butterworths, London.

Mooney, J. (2000) *Gender, Violence and the Social Order*, Macmillan, Basingstoke.

Morison, R. Sir (1962) *Report of the Home Office Departmental Committee on the Probation Service*, Cmnd 1650, Home Office, London.

Morris, T. (1999) What's all this about punishment? *Howard League Magazine*, 17 (1), 6–8.

Morris, A., Giller, H., Szwed, E. and Geach, H. (1980) *Justice for Children?* Macmillan, London.

Morrison, B. (2008) Controlling the 'hopeless': revisioning the history of female inebriate institutions *c.* 1870–1920, in *Punishment and Control in Historical Perspective* (ed. H. Johnstone), Palgrave Macmillan, Basingstoke.

NAPO (1968) *Social Work in Prison*, NAPO, London branch.

NAPO (1989), New facts and figures on imprisonment, *Napo News*, February (7), 2, NAPO, London.

NAPO (undated but pre-1994) *CJA 1991 and National Standards: Limiting the Damage*.

Nash, M. (1999) *Police, Probation and Protecting the Public*, Blackstone Press, London.

Nash, M. (2006) *Public Protection and the Criminal Justice Process*, Oxford University Press, Oxford.

Nash, M. and Williams, A. (2008) *The Anatomy of Serious Further Offending*, Oxford University Press, Oxford.

National Audit Office (1989) *Home Office: Control and Management of Probation Services in England and Wales*, Report by the Comptroller and Auditor General, HMSO, London.

National Audit Office (2010) *Managing Offenders on Short Custodial Sentences*, Report by the Comptroller and Auditor General, HMSO, London.

National Probation Service (2008) *Probation Circular: Distinctive Clothing for Offenders Undertaking Community Payback (Revised)*, National Offender Management Service, London.

Nellis, M. (1995) Probation values for the 1990s. *Howard Journal of Criminal Justice*, 34 (1), 19–44.

Nellis, M. (2002) Probation, partnership and civil society, in *Probation: Working for Justice* (eds D. Ward, J. Scott. and M. Lacey), Oxford University Press, Oxford.

Nellis, M. (2004) Electronic monitoring and the community supervision of offenders, in *Alternatives to Prison* (eds A. Bottoms, S. Rex and G. Robinson), Willan Publishing, Cullompton.

Nellis, M. (2007) Humanising justice: the English probation service up to 1972, in *Handbook of Probation* (eds L. Gelsthorpe and R. Morgan), Willan Publishing, Cullompton.

Nellis, M. and Goodman, A. (2009) Probation and offender management, in *Criminal Justice* (eds A. Hucklesby and A. Wahidin), Oxford University Press, Oxford.

Oldfield, M. and Grimshaw, R. (2010) *Probation Resources, Staffing and Workloads 2001–2008*, rev. edn, with R. Garsdie and F. Silberhorn-Armantrading, Centre for Crime and Justice Studies, London.

Oldfield, M. and Grimshaw R. (2008) *Probation Resources, Staffing and Workloads 2001–2008*, Centre for Crime and Justice Studies, London.

Omand, D. (1998) At the helm in the Home Office. *Probation* 6–7, ILPS, London.

Page, M. (1992) *Crime Fighters of London*, ILPS Benevolent and Educational Trust, London.

Page, R. (1973) *Down Among the Dossers*, Davis Poynter, London.

Parry-Khan, L. (1988) *Management by Objectives in Probation*. Social Work Monographs, University of East Anglia, Norwich.

Parton, N. (2000) Some thoughts on the relationship between theory and practice in and for social work. *British Journal of Social Work*, 30 (4), 449–464.

Paterson, Sir A. (1951) *Paterson on Prisons*. Frederick Muller, London.

Pawson, R. and Tilley, N. (1997) *Realistic Evaluation*, Sage Publications, London.

Paylor, I. (1995) *Housing Needs for Ex-Offenders*, Avebury, Aldershot.

Petersilia, J. (2003) *When Prisoners Come Home*, Oxford University Press, Oxford.

Pinder, R. (1982) On what grounds negotiating justice with black clients, *Probation Journal*, 29 (1), 19.

Pinder, R. (1984) *Probation and Ethnic Diversity, monograph*, University of Leeds, Leeds.

Pitts, J. (1988) *The Politics of Juvenile Crime*, Sage, London.

Potter, H. (1993) *Hanging in Judgement*, SCM Press, London.

Pound, J. (1986) *Poverty and Vagrancy in Tudor Britain*, Longman, Harlow.

Pratt, J. (2003) The decline and renaissance of shame in modern penal systems, in *Comparative Histories of Crime* (eds B. Godfrey, C. Emsley and G. Dunstall), Willan Publishing, Cullompton.

Preece, C. (2000) *Travels with Alice*, A.McLay & Co Ltd, Cardiff.

Priestley, P. (1985) *Victorian Prison Lives. English Prison Biography 1830–1914*, Methuen, London.

Prison Reform Trust (2011) *Bromley Briefings Factfile*, Prison Reform Trust, London.

Probation Circular (2000) 24/00 *Guidance on Enforcement of Orders Under National Standards 2000*, Home Office, London.

Pugh, R. (1968) *Imprisonment in Medieval England*, Cambridge University Press, Cambridge.

Quinn, J. (1997) *Letter to ACOP, 29 July*, Home Office, London.

Radzinowicz, L. (ed.) (1958) *The Results of Probation: A Report of the Cambridge Department of Criminal Science*, Macmillan, London.

Raine, J. and Willson, M. (1993) *Managing Criminal Justice*, Harvester Wheatsheaf, London.

Ramsbotham, D. (2005) *Prisongate: The Shocking State of Britain's Prisons and the Need for Visionary Change*, Simon & Schuster, London.

Rawlings, P. (1999) *Crime and Power: A History of Criminal Justice 1688–1998*, Longman, Harlow.

Raynor, P. and Vanstone, M. (2001) Straight thinking on probation: evidence-based practice and the culture of curiosity, in *Offender Rehabilitation in Practice* (eds G. Bernfield, D. Farringdon and A. Leschied), John Wiley & Sons, Ltd, Chichester.

Raynor, P., Smith, D. and Vanstone, M. (1994) *Effective Probation Practice*, Macmillan, London.

Rex, S. (1999) Desistance from offending: experiences of probation. *Howard Journal of Criminal Justice*, 38 (4), 366–383.

Rex, S. (2001) Beyond cognitive-behaviourism? Reflections on the effectiveness literature, in *Community Penalties: Challenges and Changes* (eds A. Bottoms, L. Gelsthorpe and S. Rex), Willan Publishing, Cullompton.

Robinson, A. (2011) *Foundations of Offender Management: Theory, Law and Policy for Contemporary Practice*, The Policy Press, Bristol.

Ross, R., Fabiano, E. and Ewles, C. (1988) Reasoning and rehabilitation. *International Journal of Offender Therapy and Comparative Criminology*, 32, 29–35.

Ruggiero, V. (2010) *Penal Abolitionism*, Oxford University Press, Oxford.

Ruggiero, V. (2011) An abolitionist view of restorative justice. *International Journal of Law, Crime and Justice*, 1–11, doi:10.1016/j/ijlcj.2011.03.001.

Ruggles-Brise, E. (1924) *Prison Reform at Home and Abroad*, Macmillan, London.

Rusche, G. and Kirchheimer, O. (1968) *Punishment and Social Structure*, Russell & Russell, New York.

Rutherford, A. (1993) *Criminal Justice and the Pursuit of Decency*, Oxford University Press, Oxford.

Ryan, M. (1999) Criminology re-engages the public voice. *Criminal Justice Matters*, 34, 11–12.

Ryan, M. and Sim, J. (1998) Power, punishment and prisons in England and Wales 1975–1996, in *Comparing Prison Systems* (eds R. Weiss and N. South), Gordon and Brench Publishers, Amsterdam.

Ryan, M. and Ward, T. (1989) *Privatisation and the Penal System*, Open University Press, Milton Keynes.

Schön, D. (1991) *The Reflective Practitioner: How Professionals Think in Action*, Ashgate, Aldershot.

Scott, D. (2009) 'who's protecting who?' *Probation Journal*, 57 (3), 291–295.

Scull, A. (1977) *Decarceration: Community Treatment and the Deviant – A Radical View*, Polity, Cambridge.

Senior, P. (2000) Fact and fiction: another perspective on probation training. *Criminal Justice Matters*, 40, 17–18.

Senior, P. (2010) Editorial. *British Journal of Community Justice*, 8 (2), 1–4.

Senior, P. (2011) The voluntary and community sector: the paradox of becoming centre-stage in the big society. *British Journal of Community Justice*, 9 (1/2), 37–54.

Senior, P., Crowther-Dowey, C. and Long, M. (2007) *Understanding Modernisation in Criminal Justice*, Open University Press, Maidenhead.

Sennett, R. (2008) *The Craftsman*, Penguin Books, London.

Sharpe, J. (1990) *Judicial Punishment in England*, Faber & Faber, London.

Shaw, A. (1998) *Convicts and the Colonies: A Study of Penal Transportation from Great Britain & Ireland to Australia & Other Parts of the British Empire*, The Irish Historical Press Ltd, Dublin.

Shaw, H. (2008) Punishment, reformation, or welfare: responses to 'the problem' of juvenile crime in Victorian and Edwardian Britain, in *Punishment and Control in Historical Perspective* (ed. H. Johnston), Palgrave Macmillan, Basingstoke.

Shaw, H. (2011) Reforming the juvenile in nineteenth and early twentieth century England. *Prison Service Journal*, 197, 4–9.

Simon, J. (1993) *Poor Discipline: Parole and the Social Control of the Underclass 1890–1990*, University of Chicago Press, Chicago.

Sleightholm, D. (1998) Optimistic view of the future by new deputy chief. *Probation*, ILPS 12.

Smith, D. (2000a) The logic of practice in the probation service today. *Vista*, 5 (3), 210– 218.

Smith, D. (2000b) *What Works as Evidence for Practice? The Methodological Repertoire in an Applied Discipline*. Paper presented to the ESRC-funded Seminar Series Theorising Social Work Research, University of Wales, Cardiff, 27 April.

Smith, D. and Stewart, J. (1998) Probation and social exclusion, in *Crime and Social Exclusion* (eds C. Finer and M. Nellis), Blackwell Publishers Ltd, Oxford.

Smith, R., Grimshaw, R., Romeo, R. and Knapp, M. (2007) *Poverty and Disadvantage Among Prisoners' Families*, Joseph Rowntree Foundation, York.

Social Exclusion Unit (2002) *Reducing Reoffending by Ex-Prisoners*, Office of the Deputy Prime Minister, London.

Spencer, J. (1995) A response to Mike Nellis: probation values for the 1990s. *Howard Journal of Criminal Justice*, 34 (4), 344–349.

Stafford, G. (1968) After-care in the penal system. *Case Conference*, 14 (11), 429–434.

Stanton, W. (1935) *Sidelights on Police Court Mission Work*, Ebenezer Baylis & Son Ltd, Worcester.

Stenson, K. (2001) The new politics of crime control, in *Crime, Risk and Justice* (eds K. Stenson and R. Sullivan), Willan Publishing, Cullompton.

Stewart-Ong, G., Harsent, L., Roberts, C., *et al.*; Burnett, R. & Al-Attar, Z.(2004) *What Works: Think First Prospective Research Study: Effectiveness and Reducing Attrition*, Home Office, London.

Straw, J. (May 1999) Speech to Chief Probation Officer. *NAPO News*, NAPO, London.

Swaaningen, R. van (1997) *Critical Criminology: Visions from Europe*, Sage, London.

Tomlinson, M.H. (1981) Penal servitude 1846–1865: a system in evolution, in *Policing and Punishment in Nineteenth Century Britain* (ed. V. Bailey), Croom Helm, London.

Travis, A. (2008) Revolt grows over 'community payback' jackets, *The Guardian*, 30 Dec.

Travis, A. (2011) Ministers plan big rise in use of electronic tags. *The Guardian*, 30 Sept.

Turley, C., Ludford, H., Callanan, M. and Barnard, M. (2011) *Delivering the NOMS Offender Management Model*, Ministry of Justice Research Series, July.

Underdown, A. (1998) *Report of the HMIP What Works Project: Strategies for Effective Offender Supervision*, Home Office, London.

United Nations (1951) *Probation and Related Measures*, Department of Social Affairs, Chapter 1, para. 3, United Nations, New York.

Vanstone, M. (1995) Ethics in social work. *Vista*, 1 (1), 49–58.

Vanstone, M. (2004) *Supervising Offenders in the Community: A History of Probation Theory and Practice*, Ashgate, Aldershot.

Vass, A. (1984) *Sentenced to Labour*, Venus Academica, St Ives.

Vass, A. (1996) Community penalties: the politics of punishment, in *Working with Offenders: Issues, Contexts and Outcomes* (eds T. May and A. Vass), Sage, London.

Wacquant, L. (2009) *Punishing the Poor*, Duke University Press, Durham, NC.

Ward, D. (1995) Finding the balance, in *Probation: Working for Justice* (eds D. Ward and M. Lacey), Whiting and Birch, London.

Ward, J.R. (2010) *Flashback: Drugs and Dealing in the Golden Age of the London Rave Scene*, Willan Publishing, Cullompton.

Ward, T. and Maruna, S. (2007) *Rehabilitation*, Routledge, London.

Webb, S. and Webb, B. 1963. (1922) *English Prisons Under Local Government*, English Local Government, Vol. 6, Frank Cass & Co. Ltd, London.

Weber, M. (1948) *From Max Weber: Essays in Sociology* (translated, edited and with an introduction by H. Garth and C. Wright Mills), Routledge & Kegan Paul, London.

Whitehead, P. (2010) *Exploring Modern Probation: Social Theory and Organisational Complexity*, The Policy Press, Bristol.

Whitehouse, P. (1982) Race bias and social enquiry reports. *Probation Journal*, 30 (2), 43–49.

Wiener, M. (1990) *Reconstructing the Criminal: Culture, Law and Policy in England, 1830–1914*, Cambridge University Press, Cambridge.

Williams, B. (ed.) (1995) *Probation Values*, Venture Press, Birmingham.

Williams, B. (1996) *Freedom on Probation: A Case Study of the Home Office Enforced Changes to the University Education and Training of Probation Officers*, Association of University Teachers, London.

Williams, Z. (2009) Straw's vest is full of holes. *The Guardian*, London, 1 Jan.

Wood, N. (1999) *The Politics of Competence: A Core Study of Developments Within Professional Training for Qualification as a Probation Officer*, M.Ed. thesis, University of Sheffield.

Worrall, A. (1997) *Punishment in the Community: The Future of Criminal Justice*, Longman, London.

Young, J. (1998) Breaking windows: situating the new criminology, in *The New Criminology Revisited* (eds P. Walton and J. Young), Macmillan, Basingstoke.

Young, J. (2007) *The Vertigo of Late Modernity*, Sage, London.

Further Reading

Allen, R. (1991) Out of jail: the reduction in the use of penal custody for male juveniles 1981–1988. *Howard Journal of Criminal Justice*, 30 (1), 30–52.

Archard, P. (1979) *Vagrancy, Alcoholism and Social Control*, Macmillan, London.

Barker, M. (1993) *Community Service and Women Offenders*, ACOP, London.

Beck, U. (1992) *Risk Society – Towards a New Modernity*, Sage, London.

Boswell, G., Davies, M. and Wright, A. (1993) *Contemporary Probation Practice*, Avebury, Aldershot.

Broad, B. (1991) *Punishment Under Pressure: The Probation Service in the Inner City*, Jessica Kingsley, London.

Broad, B. and Denney, D. (1996) Users' rights and the probation service: some opportunities and obstacles. *Howard Journal of Criminal Justice*, 35 (1), 61–77.

Butterworth, J. (1962) *Report of the Inquiry into the Work and Pay of Probation Officers and Social Workers*. Cmnd 5076, HMSO, London.

Camp, J. (1974) *Holloway Prison: The Place and the People*, David & Charles, Newton Abbot.

Clark, J. and Newman, J. (1997) *The Managerial State*, Sage, London.

Cohen, S. (1979) Some modest and unrealistic proposals. *New Society*, 29 March, 731–734.

Cohen, S. (1979) The punitive city: notes on the dispersal of social control. *Contemporary Crises*, 3, 339–363.

Cohen, S. (1979b) Community control: a new Utopia. *New Society*, 15 March, 609–611.

Cohen, S. (1985) *Visions of Social Control*, Polity Press, Cambridge.

Cook, T. (ed.) (1979) *Vagrancy: Some New Perspectives*, Academic Press, London.

Cullen, F.T. and Gilbert, K.E. (1982) *Reaffirming Rehabilitation*, Anderson Publishing Co., Cincinnati.

Currie, E. (1996) *Is America Really Winning the War on Crime and Should Britain Follow Its Example?* NACRO 30th anniversary lecture, NARCO, London.

Cutler, T. and Waine, B. (1994) *Managing the Welfare State*, Berg, Oxford.

Rehabilitating and Resettling Offenders in the Community, First Edition. Anthony H. Goodman.

Criminal Justice Act 1948, Fifth Schedule administrative provisions as to probation, section 3, subsection (5).

Cresswell, J. (1994) *Research Design Qualitative and Quantitative Approaches*, Sage, London.

de Lacy, M. (1986) *Prison Reform in Lancashire 1700–1850: A Study in Local Administration*, Manchester University Press, Manchester.

de Vaus, D.A. (1987) *Surveys in Social Research*, George Allen and Unwin, London.

Dominelli, L. (1997) *Anti-Racist Social Work*, 2nd edn, Macmillan, London.

Emsley, C. (1996) *Crime and Society in England 1750–1900*, 2nd edn, Longman, London.

Fletcher, H. (1989) Carlisle Report. An Opportunity Lost. NAPO, 7 (1).

Ford, J., Foley, J. and Petri, M. (1995) *Research on a Human Scale*. School of Social Policy: Middlesex University.

Forsythe, W.J. (1987) *The Reform of Prisoners 1830–1900*, Croom Helm, London.

Gibbs, A. (2000) Probation service users: to empower or to exclude. *Criminal Justice Matters*, 39, 16–17.

Godfrey, B. and Dunstall, G. (eds.) (2005) *Crime and Empire 1840–1940*, Willan Publishing, Cullompton.

Godfrey, B., Emsley, C. and Dunstall, G. (2003) *Comparitive Histories of Crime*, Willan Publishing, Cullompton.

Goode, E. and Ben-Yehuda, N. (1994) *Moral Panics: The Social Construction of Deviance*, Blackwell, Oxford.

Goodman, A. (1987) *Probation Intervention with Prisoners During and After Their Sentence (Through-Care and After-Care). An Analysis of Service Delivery to Prisoners and Ex-Prisoners from Both Field Units and the Specialist Liaison Schemes with ILPS*, ILPS Benevolent and Educational Trust, London.

Goodman, A. (1998) The future of probation. *Criminal Justice Matters*, 34, Winter, 28–29.

Goodman, A. (1995) The Criminal Justice and Public Order Act 1994. *Capital and Class*, 56, 9–13.

Goodman, A. (2007) 289 Borough High Street, The After-Care and Resettlement Unit, in the Inner London Probation Service 1965–1990. *Special centenary edition, British Journal of Community Justice*, 5, 9–28.

Gordon, D. (1994) *The Return of the Dangerous Classes: Drug Prohibition and Policy Politics*, W. W. Norton, London.

Grundy, S. (1996) Towards empowering leadership: the importance of imagining, in *New Directions in Action Research* (ed. O. Zuber-Skerritt), Falmer Press, London, pp. 106–120.

Harris, R. (1992) *Crime, Criminal Justice and the Probation Service*, Routledge, London.

HM Inspectorate of Probation (1993c) *Offenders Who Misuse Drugs: The Probation Service Response. Report of a Thematic Inspection*, Home Office, London.

HM Inspectorate of Probation (1994) *Automatic Conditional Release: The Probation Service Response: Report of a Thematic Inspection*, Home Office, London.

HM Inspectorate of Probation (1994) *The Quality and Provision of Expedited Pre-sentence Reports Prepared for the Crown Court by the Probation Service: Summary Report*, Home Office, London.

HM Inspectorate of Probation (1994) *Young Offenders And the Probation Service: Report of a Thematic Inspection*, London: Home Office.

HM Inspectorate of Probation (1995) *Probation Orders with Additional Requirements: Report of a Thematic Inspection*, London: Home Office.

HM Inspectorate of Probation (1997) *Community Service: A Report of an Inspection of Probation Services' Compliance with the National Standards*, Home Office, London.

HM Inspectorate of Probation (1997) *Tackling Drugs Together: Report of a Thematic Inspection on the work of the Probation Service with Drug Misusers*, Home Office, London.

HM Inspectorate of Probation (1997) *The Work of the Probation Service in the Crown and Magistrates' Courts: Report of a Thematic Inspection*, Home Office, London.

HM Inspectorate of Probation (1997) *Annual Report*, Home Office, London.

HM Inspectorate of Probation (1998) *Inner London Probation Service: Follow-up to the Quality and Effectiveness Inspection No. 14*, Home Office, London.

HM Inspectorate of Probation (1998a) *Delivering an Enhanced Level of Community Supervision: Report of a Thematic Inspection on the Work of Approved Probation and Bail Hostels*, Home Office, London.

Home Office (1953) *Report of the Committee on Discharged Prisoners' Aid Societies*, Cmnd 8879, HMSO, London.

Home Office (1968) *The Rehabilitation of Drug Addicts: Report of the Advisory Committee on Drug Dependence*, HMSO, London.

Home Office (1968) *The Regime for Long-Term Prisoners in Conditions of Maximum Security: Report of the Advisory Council on the Penal System*, HMSO, London.

Home Office (1970) *Non-Custodial and Semi-Custodial Penalties: Report of the Advisory Council on the Penal System*, HMSO, London.

Home Office (1978) *Youth Custody and Supervision: A New Sentence*, Green Paper, HMSO, London.

Home Office (1990) *Supervision and Punishment in the Community: A Framework for Action*, HMSO, London.

Home Office (1995b) *Strengthening Punishment in the Community. A Consultation Document*, Cm 2780, HMSO, London.

Home Office Research Study (1998) *Reducing Offending: An Assessment of Research Evidence on Ways of Dealing With Offending Behaviour*, 187, Home Office, London.

Home Office Research Unit Report (1966) *Probation Research: A Preliminary Report, no. 7*, HMSO, London.

House of Commons Employment Committee (Session 1991/92) *Employment in Prisons and for Ex-Offenders*, HMSO, London.

Folkard, M.S., Smith, D.E. and Smith D.D. (1976) *IMPACT: The Results of the Experiment*, Volume 2 Home Office Research Study 36, Home Office, London.

Inglebury Report (1960) *Report of the Committee on Children and Young Persons*, Cmnd 1191, HMSO, London.

Jarvis, F.V. (1967) The prison welfare service. *NAPO Journal*, 13 (1), 6–13.

Justice Committee (2011) *Justice Committee – Eighth Report. The Role of the Probation Service*, House of Commons, London, at www.publications.parliament.uk/pa/cm201012/cmselect/cmjust/519/51902.htm, accessed 8 January 2012.

Kelling, G. and Coles, C. (1996) *Fixing Broken Windows*, The Free Press, New York.

Kemshall, H. and Pritchard, J. (1997) *Good Practice in Risk Assessment and Risk Management 2: Protection, Rights and Responsibilities*, Jessica Kingsley Publishers, London.

Lewis, P. (2000) Evidence-based management: the challenge of effective practice. *Vista*, 5 (1), 23–36.

Maguire, M., Raynor, P., Vanstone, M. and Kynch, J. (2000) Voluntary after-care and the probation service: a case of diminishing responsibilities. *Howard Journal of Criminal Justice*, 39 (3), 234–248.

Mair, G. (1991) *What Works – Nothing or Everything?* Home Office Research Bulletin 30, 3–8, HMSO, London.

Mair, G. (ed.) (1997b) *Evaluating the Effectiveness of Community Penalties*, Avebury, Aldershot.

Marshall, T. and Merry, S. (1990) *Crime and Accountability*, HMSO, London.

May, T. and Vass, A. (eds) (1996) *Working with Offenders*, Sage, London.

McAllister, D., Bottomley, K and Leibling, A. (1992) *From Custody to Community: Through-Care for Young Offenders*, Avebury, Aldershot.

Monger, M. (1967) *Casework in After-Care*, Butterworths, London.

Murphy, M. (1977) *Attitudes to Prison Welfare Work: Islington Survey of Probation Officers*, ILPS, London.

NAPO (1984) *Probation, Direction, Innovation and Change in the 1980s*, National Association of Probation Officers, London.

NAPO (1986) *Community Based Through-Care, the Case for Withdrawal of Seconded Officers from Prison,* National Association of Probation Officers, London.

NAPO News (2000) Peers oppose benefits suspension, 120, June, 1.

NAPO News (2000) Legislation – Lords victory! 121, July, 1–4.

Nelken, D. (ed.) (1994) *The Future of Criminology*, Sage, London.

Nuttall, P. and Lewis, C. (1998) *Reducing Offending: An Assessment of Research Evidence on Ways of Dealing with Offending Behaviour*, Home Office Research Study 187, Home Office, London.

Parton, N. (ed.) (1996) *Social Theory, Social Change and Social Work*, Routledge, London.

Probation Circular (1999) *PC 22/99: Key Performance Indicators (KPIs) and Targets for 1999–2000*, Home Office, London.

Riley, J. (1996) *Getting the Most From Your Data*, Technical and Educational Services Ltd, Bristol.

Roberts, J. and Domurad, F. (1995) Re-engineering probation: lessons from New York City. *Vista*, 1 (1), 59–68.

Roberts, C., Burnett, R., Kirby, A. and Hamill, H. (1996) *A System for Evaluating Probation Practice*. PSU Report No. 1, University of Oxford Probation Studies Unit, Centre for Criminological Research, Oxford.

Rough Sleepers Unit (December 1999) *Coming in from the Cold: The Government's Strategy on Rough Sleeping*, RSU Department of the Environment, Transport and the Regions, London.

Sharpe, J. (1984) *Crime in Early Modern England 1550–1750*, Longman, London.

Silberman, M. and Chapman, B. (1971) After-care units in London, Liverpool and Manchester, in *Explorations in After-Care*. Home Office Research Unit Report 9, Home Office, London.

Simon, J. (2007) *Governing Through Crime*, Oxford University Press, Oxford.

Statham, R. (1992) Towards managing the probation service, in *Managing the Probation Service: Issues for the 1990s* (eds R. Statham and P. Whitehead), Longman, Harlow.

Stedman Jones, G. (1971) *Outcast London: A Study in the Relationships Between Classes in Victorian Society*, Penguin Books, Harmondsworth.

Stewart, J. (1975) *Of No Fixed Abode: Vagrancy and the Welfare State*, Manchester University Press, Manchester.

Stewart, J., Smith, D., Stewart, G. and Fullwood, C. (1994) *Understanding Offending Behaviour*, Longman, Harlow.

Vass, A. (1990) *Alternatives to Prison: Punishment, Custody and the Community*, Sage, London.

Wacquant, L. (1999) *Prisons of Poverty*, University of Minnesota Press, Minneapolis.
Wade, S. (2000) The probation service and managerialism. *Criminal Justice Matters*, 40, 15–16.
Walker, H. and Beaumont, B. (1981) *Probation Work: Critical Theory and Socialist Practice*, Basil Blackwell, Oxford.
Walker, H. and Beaumont, B. (1985) *Working with Offenders*, Macmillan, London.
Webb, S. and Webb, B. (1910) *English Poor Law Policy*, Longman, Harlow.
Weinberger, B. (1981) The police and the public in mid nineteenth century Warwickshire, in *Policing and Punishment in 19th Century Britain* (ed. V. Bailey), Croom Helm, London.
Wengraf, T. (1994) *Semi-Structured Depth Interviewing: A Conceptual and Practical Guide*, vols 1 and 2, Middlesex University, London.
Williams, B. (1991) *Work with Prisoners*, Venture Press, Birmingham.
Young, J. (1999) *The Exclusive Society*, Sage, London.

List of Inner London Probation Service (ILPS) Reports Consulted

ILPS (1976) *A Report to Commemorate the Centenary of Probation in London.*
ILPS (1974) *Developments in Prison Welfare in the Islington Region.*
ILPS (1974) *Report of the Working Party on the Role of Probation and After-Care Service in the London Prisons.*
ILPS (1977) *Attitudes to Prison Welfare Work, Survey of Islington Probation Officers.*
ILPS (1978) *The Professional Task of the Service: Report of the Working Party.*
ILPS (1982) *N.E. Division Report on Divisional Review into Through- and After-Care.*
ILPS (1983) *Supervision of Parole: Report of the Southwark Parole Project.*
ILPS (1983) *Survey of Social Enquiry Reports.*
ILPS (1984) *Report of Review on Voluntary Through- and After-Care, SE Division.*
ILPS (1984) *Statement of Aims and Objectives.*
ILPS (1986) *Implementation of ILPS Statement of Aims and Objectives in South of Thames Field Services Division.*
ILPS (1986) *The Professional Task of the Prison Probation Officer.*
ILPS (1987) *Review of Civil Work.*
ILPS (1987) *Statement of Aims and Objectives including the Corporate Strategy.*
ILPS (1987) *The Sherborne House Day Centre Activity Programme for Young Offenders.*
ILPS (1988) *Review of Through-Care.*
ILPS (1989) *Tackling Offending: An Action Plan.*
ILPS (1989) *Inspection of Probation Supervision.*

Index

Rehabilitating and Resettling Offenders in the Community, First Edition. Anthony H. Goodman.